WIDER PROFESSIONAL PRACTICE
in **EDUCATION** and **TRAINING**

SAGE was founded in 1965 by Sara Miller McCune to support the dissemination of usable knowledge by publishing innovative and high-quality research and teaching content. Today, we publish over 900 journals, including those of more than 400 learned societies, more than 800 new books per year, and a growing range of library products including archives, data, case studies, reports, and video. SAGE remains majority-owned by our founder, and after Sara's lifetime will become owned by a charitable trust that secures our continued independence.

Los Angeles | London | New Delhi | Singapore | Washington DC | Melbourne

WIDER PROFESSIONAL PRACTICE
in **EDUCATION** and **TRAINING**

Sasha Pleasance

Los Angeles | London | New Delhi
Singapore | Washington DC | Melbourne

Los Angeles | London | New Delhi
Singapore | Washington DC | Melbourne

SAGE Publications Ltd
1 Oliver's Yard
55 City Road
London EC1Y 1SP

SAGE Publications Inc.
2455 Teller Road
Thousand Oaks, California 91320

SAGE Publications India Pvt Ltd
B 1/I 1 Mohan Cooperative Industrial Area
Mathura Road
New Delhi 110 044

SAGE Publications Asia-Pacific Pte Ltd
3 Church Street
#10-04 Samsung Hub
Singapore 049483

Editor: James Clark
Assistant editor: Robert Patterson
Production editor: Nicola Marshall
Proofreader: Sarah Cooke
Indexer: Martin Hargreaves
Marketing manager: Dilhara Attygalle
Cover design: Naomi Robinson
Typeset by: C&M Digitals (P) Ltd, Chennai, India
Printed and bound by CPI Group (UK) Ltd,
Croydon, CR0 4YY

Library of Congress Control Number: 2015954666

British Library Cataloguing in Publication data

A catalogue record for this book is available from
the British Library

ISBN 978-1-4739-1617-3
ISBN 978-1-4739-1618-0 (pbk)

At SAGE we take sustainability seriously. Most of our products are printed in the UK using FSC papers and boards.
When we print overseas we ensure sustainable papers are used as measured by the PREPS grading system.
We undertake an annual audit to monitor our sustainability.

TABLE OF CONTENTS

LIST OF FIGURES AND TABLES

Figures

Tables

LIST OF ABBREVIATIONS

AoC	Association of Colleges
ALI	Adult Learning Inspectorate
ATL	Association of Teachers and Lecturers
BAME	Black, Asian or Minority Ethnic
BERA	British Educational Research Association
BIS	Department for Business, Innovation and Skills
BTEC	Business and Technology Education Council
CBI	Confederation of British Industry
CIF	Common Inspection Framework
CPD	Continuing Professional Development
DCSF	Department for Children, Schools and Families
DfE	Department for Education
DfES	Department for Education and Skills
ESD	Education for Sustainable Development
ESOL	English for Speakers of Other Languages
ETF	Education and Training Foundation
FE	Further Education
FEFC	Further Education Funding Council
FELTAG	Further Education Learning Technology Action Group

FSM   Free school meals
GCSE   General Certificate of Secondary Education
HE   Higher Education
IfL   Institute for Learning
IPPR   Institute for Public Policy Research
ITE   Initial Teacher Education
LEAs   Local Education Authorities
LSC   Learning and Skills Council
LSIS   Learning and Skills Improvement Service
NCFE   National Council of Further Education
NEET   Not in Education, Employment or Training
NFER   National Foundation for Educational Research
NIACE   National Institute of Adult Continuing Education
OECD   Organisation for Economic Co-operation and Development
Ofsted   Office for Standards in Education, Children's Services and Skills
ONS   Office for National Statistics
QTLS   Qualified Teaching and Learning Status
QCA   Qualification and Curriculum Authority
SFA   Skills Funding Agency
UTCs   University Technical Colleges

FOREWORD

Professional practice in the further education (FE) sector operates within a constantly changing landscape of shifting sands, as acknowledged by many writers and researchers, including James Avis, Ann-Marie Bathmaker, Norman Lucas and Kevin Orr. This book represents an oasis in those shifting sands by providing a strong foundation of research, debates and discussions around key themes in professional practice, and uses this foundation to pose practical questions and include activities and case studies for the readers that can be used in both initial teacher education and continuing professional development (CPD). These combine well to provide an engaging platform which should make a major contribution to helping teaching practitioners understand and develop their own practice.

The selected focus on wider professional practice, rather than on the broad range of teaching and learning themes which tend to feature in other textbooks, has made it possible to go deeper into the field, and this is most welcome. Room is found for debates and competing discourses from an impressive range of sources and the reader is challenged to engage in these debates and to think critically about their own practice.

The overriding philosophy of the book represents teachers as the humane contributors to social justice, which most of us have always believed that we are rather than the over-managed and restrictive professionals which various forces inside and outside of the sector have sought to produce. It also seeks to offer strategies and solutions for actively working towards a more democratic professional future.

As would be hoped for in a book for teachers, there is an important focus on the centrality of learners and the learner voice. There is a very interesting review of research and debates on teachers' expectations, and how factors such as ethnicity, social class, assessment practices and cultural capital can all contribute towards establishing a 'self-fulfilling prophecy' about some learners which can seriously affect their own capacity to achieve and can also affect teacher approaches to them in a number of negative ways. This underlines the importance of fostering high expectations as a crucial part of the contribution that teachers can make to equality and social justice.

It is still relatively unusual to find the inclusion of Education for Sustainable Development as a theme in course books for initial teacher education (ITE) programmes, but the author provides a strong engagement with the 'transformative' dimensions of education as represented in the Education for Sustainable Development (ESD) principles of working to build 'a strong, healthy and just society'. This is reinforced by a series of useful case studies which bring the ideas to life.

The approach which runs throughout this extremely well-researched, scholarly and well-written book is an emphasis on the socially constructed aspects of teaching and learning related to the life cycle in a refreshingly human way.

The reader is left in no doubt about the challenges that teachers face to establish a more positive and democratic environment where positive professional practice can flourish, but the book provides a very positive framework to move in that direction.

Dr Jim Crawley
Bath Spa University

ABOUT THE AUTHOR

Sasha Pleasance has worked in further education for almost twenty years. She first taught English, and then moved into teaching Adult Literacy and English to Speakers of Other Languages (ESOL). This led to an opportunity to work in prisons as part of a pilot project called 'Storybook Dads', now a national scheme.

She has also undertaken teaching projects involving family learning, refugee centres and community projects for people with learning difficulties and disabilities. She has latterly taught a range of social science subjects on Access pathways and Foundation degrees, and modules for the BA Hons in Childcare in Education, and continues to supervise dissertations for degree programmes.

For the past 10 years she has been a teacher educator in further education. She is passionately committed to the transformative power of education through dialogic teaching and sees the exposure of education to market forces, within further education and throughout the UK school system, as a serious threat both to this fundamental principle and to the values of social justice which guide her own practice and which lie at the heart of further education.

ACKNOWLEDGEMENTS

First, I wish to thank all my family and friends who between them support me in every way that is possible to be supported, however there a few who deserve a special mention. My boys, who are proud of their mum and encourage me; my granny who believed in me when I didn't; my parents, who between them opened my eyes to the world and instilled in me a keen sense of justice.

Second, to all the extraordinary teachers that I have had the privilege to work with over the years, whose dedication and inner spirit is a constant source of inspiration, and sustain my belief that what we do in FE matters. I would like to offer an individual thank you to Stephen Ball and Susan Wallace who generously endorsed this book and to Jim Crawley for his support, and agreeing to write the foreword.

I would also like to acknowledge the contribution that my doctoral studies on the EdD programme at Plymouth University have made to some of the content in this book.

And finally, a big thank you to the publishing team at SAGE who have supported and encouraged me in my authorial debut, but in particular James Clark without whom this book would not have got off the ground.

INTRODUCTION

This book has been written with the intention that it will be a valuable and practical textbook to support initial teacher education qualifications in further education (FE). When I first secured a post as a teacher educator, Wider Professional Practice was one of the first modules I was given responsibility for planning, teaching and assessing. It quickly became apparent that there was no key text to support this particular module. My research in preparation to teach this module over the years has taken me to several key texts, research papers, think tanks, policy documents and theorists and it has always been an idea of mine to try to collate this into a book. I have amalgamated the source material which I draw upon when teaching this module into one cohesive textbook to support both trainee teachers and teacher educators in the hope that it may be helpful to have a 'go to' source to support your own initial teacher education studies or teaching of this module, respectively.

The timing of the book itself is quite significant because the UK is going through key political changes with a new government in 2015, and extensive austerity measures which are having, and will continue to have, a substantial impact on the wider socioeconomic situation, and ultimately the most vulnerable in society. The proposed funding cuts to the further education budget threaten the core of FE, with predictions that adult learning as we know it will be non-existent by 2020, if not sooner in some regions across the country. These cuts also jeopardise the provision of the mainstay of FE, 16–19 programmes, as cuts means job losses ultimately, and with a sector already cut to its bones, it is difficult to see how further job losses and increased workloads for those left working in the sector can have anything but a severely detrimental effect on the sector, its workforce, learners and future provision. The challenge is to work towards a democratic professional future in these austere conditions.

The education sector in the UK has gone through perhaps its most significant changes since the ascendancy of neoliberalism in the 1980s. The two key characteristics of neoliberalism are performativity and managerialism, which have created a market-orientated education system. The consequence of this has been fundamental changes to how we conceptualise learning and therefore teaching and assessment, and the work of teachers has become increasingly reductive and bureaucratic, with intensified scrutiny by managers and external agencies in terms of auditable output measures. This, in turn, has resulted in a relentless churn of standards-driven educational reform promoted as quality initiatives. So, we now have an education system where decisions about what to teach, and increasingly how to teach, are being imposed on teachers from external agencies and monitored through high-stakes performance management regimes such as observation and key performance indicators where accountability can be monitored – accountability of individual institutions as well as of individual teachers.

This book discusses these themes in relation to further education, the wider sociopolitical context and the impact on professionalism, learners and the future of the further education sector. Having worked in further education for most of my own teaching career, I am passionate about what we do, about the teachers who dedicate so much to the learners they work with and the diversity of learners who seek out opportunities within the sector. To this end, I offer a critical eye on some key issues within the sector, as well as exploring some aspects of education as a whole, in terms of how we conceptualise learning, but also what it means to be an educated person in the twenty-first century. Where possible, thematic issues are supported by case studies which have been kindly contributed by a range of teachers who work within the sector with the intention that this helps not only to contextualise some of the issues under discussion, but also generates discussion within your own teacher education experience and with your colleagues.

Opportunities for professional discussion is one of the aspects of initial teacher education that all the trainee teachers whom I have had the privilege to work with over the years repeatedly feedback as being one of the most valued aspects of their teacher education experience, so I hope that this book helps to enrich this aspect of your own experience of initial teacher education (ITE).

CHAPTER 1

UNDERSTANDING LEARNERS IN THE FURTHER EDUCATION SECTOR

The focus of this chapter is the diverse demography of learners in the Further Education and Training Sector, henceforth referred to as FE, including vocational learners, those on courses such as A level and Higher Education (HE) programmes, post-16 programmes for young people with learning difficulties and/or disabilities, as well as those on 16–19 study programmes; their needs, aspirations and motivation. The chapter will explore issues which are often inherited from the schools sector, including disengagement, demotivation and problems regarding English and maths within the context of the raised participation age. The effects of the lack of parity of esteem, or equality in status, between vocational and academic education will also be discussed in light of these topics.

This chapter will cover the following:

- An overview of vocational education, past and present
- A profile of learners in further education
- A summary of adult education in further education

(Continued)

(Continued)

- Offender learning provision
- English and maths
- Issues around engagement in education and training
- Motivation of learners in further education

The History of Vocational Education and Training

The FE sector has gone through several name changes over the years, from the technical and vocational education sector to the post-compulsory sector to the learning and skills sector, to the lifelong learning sector, before reverting back to the further education sector more recently.

In the UK, social structure has historically been influenced by social class and there is a longstanding history of hierarchical ranking of educational provision according to social class. The campaign for mass education in the late 1800s sought an education system which provided for all. However, this was not a popular movement, and many were opposed to the idea of different classes being educated together, arguing that the education system should be divided according to social class. This opposition was founded on the traditional view that the purpose of education was to maintain social position, and that an education that could be more readily converted into money would lower social standing. The traditional view of education, often described as a liberal education, is associated with intellectual activity and personal development versus a vocational education, which in turn is associated with practical activity and employment. The Taunton Report, published in 1868, although linking technical education with general education for the first time, proposed that secondary education curricula should be based on social class, and should be provided in separate schools. This perpetuated the hierarchical view of education, and its purpose, along class lines. The higher status given to traditional academic education pathways often results in a derisory view of vocational education and skilled trades, and this perpetuates the notion that a vocational pathway is a second-tier option and ensures that FE remains 'ghettoised as working-class institutions with all the attendant sense of inferiority which that brings' (Morrison, 2010: 68).

The Edge Foundation (2014) released research that revealed that many young people are being actively discouraged from opting for vocational pathways, with 22 per cent being told that they are 'too clever' for vocational education by schools and just a quarter of parents considering vocational education to be worthwhile.

In his book, Richard Pring challenges the divisions between vocational and academic education, suggesting that education should encompass both, rather than having a two-tiered education system, and argues for the:

> abandonment of those dualisms of education and training, between thinking and doing, between theory and practice, between the intrinsically worthwhile and the useful which bedevils our deliberations on education. Surely if we focus on what it means to fully become a person ... then there seems no reason why the liberal should not be conceived as something vocationally useful and why the vocationally useful should not be taught in an educational and liberating way. (1999: 183)

Unless the association between vocational education, lower socioeconomic status and lower ability are challenged, and messages about social mobility defined as university education and professional employment are challenged, then parity of esteem cannot be achieved.

Activity 1.1

* How is the status of further education, its learners and its qualifications viewed today?

Incorporation of further education

Historically, further education in the UK has been influenced by external factors, namely wider socioeconomic priorities. The Education Act 1944 introduced the tripartite system of state-funded secondary education and made all schooling, including secondary education, free. The tripartite system organised secondary education into a structure containing three types of school: grammar school, secondary technical school, sometimes described as technical grammar schools, and secondary modern school. Following this Act, the school-leaving age was raised to 15, although the stated intention of raising it to 16 was not achieved until 1972. The Act required local authorities to support and manage education for their population, which up until 1992 included provision for further education. This meant that compulsory schooling and post-16 education were brought under the public sector. Much of what we would associate with further education now was provided in secondary technical schools, which taught mechanical, scientific and engineering skills to serve industry and science. The diversification of FE as multipurpose providers has had a chequered history, but the 1960s saw the rapid growth of the sector, offering a wide range of vocational as well as non-vocational learning at different points, becoming a post-16 alternative to school for resits and A level study whilst maintaining its employment-related tradition. The economic downturn in the 1970s saw the expansion of adult learning in FE, and a focus on training, upskilling and retraining for unemployed young people and adults. In this way, FE superceded secondary technical schools and secured its position in post-compulsory education.

Prior to 1992, further education colleges were owned and controlled by Local Education Authorities (LEAs), which were locally responsible for educational provision. The Further and Higher Education Act of 1992 released colleges from LEA control. This phase in 1993, which is referred to as 'Incorporation', created the further education sector with independent institutions that were funded directly by government. However, although freed from local authority involvement, this transition was subject to external control in three principal ways. First, detailed and prescriptive government regulation. Second, complex and frequently changing financial and funding mechanisms from ever-changing sector organisations – namely, the Further Education Funding Council (FEFC), the Learning and Skills Council (LSC) and its more recent successor the Skills Funding Agency (SFA) – which still directly links almost all college funding to the recruitment, retention, achievement and, more recently, destinations of learners. Third, an external inspection system which was established by the FEFC, followed by the Adult Learning Inspectorate (ALI), which in 2007 then became part of the Office for Standards in Education, Children's Services and Skills (Ofsted). Some of the thematic issues introduced with this restructuring of the further education sector will be explored in more detail in Chapter 2.

Learners in Further Education

According to the Department for Education (DfE, 2013a) there are approximately 400 general further education colleges in the UK which are state-funded. These institutions provide a wide range of full-time and part-time courses, covering a range of levels, for over 4 million learners aged between 14 and 90 years, although a significant proportion of learners who attend are aged between 16 and 25 years. Further education colleges provide the majority of state-supported adult learning provision and, together with sixth form colleges, are the majority provider of young people's learning from ages 16 to 19.

Since the announcement of the raising of the participation age, which from 2015 requires young people to remain in some form of education or training until their eighteenth birthday, there has been a loss of teaching staff within the FE sector as competition between schools and colleges to retain learners has increased, with schools and sixth form colleges providing more vocational options alongside the traditional academic subjects. Further education colleges are the main provider of vocational education and training in the UK, but also offer many academic courses such as A levels, and increasingly higher education courses. The diversity of contexts is also significant, as this includes general further education colleges, apprenticeships, work-based learning, adult and community learning and offender learning. It is a reasonable assertion that the majority of learners in further education are seizing a second chance with education and learning, and that they have left school feeling demotivated and disenfranchised. Further education is seen by many learners as an alternative route back into education and learning to support their social and economic aspirations:

> It is further education which has invariably given second chances to those who were forced by necessity to make unfulfilling choices. It said 'try again' to those who were labelled as failures and who had decided education was not for the likes of them. (Kennedy, 1997: 2)

According to Buddery et al. (2010: 25), FE in the UK offers learning opportunities to some of the most disadvantaged members of our society:

* 56 per cent of 17-year-olds on full-time courses are from lower socio-economic backgrounds, compared to only 22 per cent in maintained school sixth forms
* 29 per cent of learners in general further education colleges are from disadvantaged postcodes, compared to 25 per cent of the population as a whole
* The achievement gap between the poorest learners at 19 and their better-off peers has narrowed at Level 2 and Level 3
* Ethnic minority learners are nearly twice as likely to be enrolled in further education institutions as their peers in the general population
* Further education is the main provider of post-16 provision for learners with learning difficulties and/or disabilities

In general, minority groups and women both have higher than average rates of participation in further education provision in the UK. Over-representation of women and minority learners is particularly noticeable amongst adult learners, with approximately 57 per cent female adult learners, and nearly 20 per cent from a Black, Asian or Minority Ethnic (BAME) background (SFA, 2012). As women and minority adult learners are over-represented in further education, this means that they have been disproportionately affected by the overall cut of 25 per cent in adult provision over the past few years, and will continue to be affected due to the recent announcement of £460 million being cut from the adult skills budget (BIS, 2014). Changes to the funding system for adult provision resulted in the introduction of FE loans that have had a detrimental impact on the number of adults participating in government-funded FE courses: figures show that there was a 10.7 per cent decrease in adult learners in the academic year 2013/14 (SFA, 2014a).

Data from the Department for Business, Innovation and Skills (BIS) (2011a) shows that 34 per cent of adult learners enrolled on further education courses were studying for their first full Level 2 qualification, and 54 per cent for their first full Level 3 qualification – GCSE and A level equivalents, respectively.

Data shows that women outnumber men in pursuing degree-level qualifications in further education, as well as higher education institutions. Overall, one in twelve HE learners attends an FE college, thereby playing an important role in widening participation in HE for people from disadvantaged backgrounds.

Adult Education and Basic Skills in FE

Further education has gone through several redefinitions in recent years, from post-compulsory, to lifelong learning, vocational and technical and further education and skills. These rebrands have been influenced by broader economic, political and cultural climates over time. Adult education in the UK is not new and has been long established, but the most significant growth has occurred since the 1970s in adult basic education provision, which was principally literacy, but also numeracy. Funding was allocated for prison education and English for Speakers of Other Languages (ESOL) for immigrants, as well as family learning. The Further and Higher Education Act of 1992 made adult basic education part of the system of further education but with a distinctive shift from a political commitment to addressing social inequality towards policy based on economic efficiency. Government funding for adult education hereafter has been targeted in assisting adults to improve their qualifications, update their skills, and progress in their present career or into a new career.

In 1999, the Moser Report, *A Fresh Start: Improving Literacy and Numeracy*, concluded that 7 million adults, about 20 per cent of the adult population, lacked the basic literacy skills required to function at work and in society and estimated that 30–50 per cent of adults had problems with numeracy. The report attributed this situation to home circumstances but mostly to poor schooling in the past. It expressed concern about how low levels of basic skills disadvantage both the individual and the productivity of the UK as well as being linked to other social problems such as crime. Government policy in addressing poor basic skills in adults is founded on the underlying belief that these are essential if more people are to realise their full potential and the UK is to remain competitive in an increasingly global economy.

Following the publication of Moser Report, the Skills for Life national strategy for adult basic skills was launched in 2001, offering nationally recognised literacy and numeracy qualifications, provided largely by further education colleges. In 2010, Skills for Life and its component Key Skills, were replaced by the Functional Skills suite of qualifications and the terms 'literacy' and 'numeracy' were supplanted with English and maths. Despite the widespread distribution of the national Skills for Life strategy, in FE and elsewhere, issues with literacy and numeracy persist among the adult population in the UK, as well as among school leavers and young people. The term 'functionally' illiterate or 'functionally' innumerate is used to describe people who would not pass an English or maths GCSE and have literacy or numeracy levels at or below those expected of an 11-year-old. According to the National Literacy Trust (2014), 16 per cent of the adult population, or 5.2 million adults, in the UK are functionally illiterate, and around four in five adults have a low level of numeracy (National Numeracy, 2012).

English and Maths GCSE Provision in FE

In 2013/14, the percentage of 16-year-olds achieving 5 or more GCSEs, or equivalent, at grade A* to C (including English and maths), was 52.6 per cent (DfE, 2014a). In addition, 61 per cent of 16-years-olds gained at least a C in English and 62 per cent gained at least a C in maths (ibid.). This means that approximately 40 per cent of 16-year-olds do not get an English and maths GCSE grade C, or the gold standard of five GCSEs grade A* to C. Research carried out by Sheffield University (2010) revealed that 22 per cent of 16–19-year-olds are functionally innumerate, and 17 per cent are functionally illiterate.

Since the raising of the participation age was introduced (2015), the funding condition for learners aged 16–19 who have no prior attainment of a C in English and/or maths is that they must continue to study GCSE English and maths, rather than the lower-level functional skills, until they leave education or training at 18.

This government initiative stemmed from Alison Wolf, a professor at King's College London, who proposed the change in her 2011 review of vocational education. At the time, she said that it was 'scandalous' that half of 16-year-olds were leaving school without good GCSEs in English and maths (*The Guardian*, 2013). The Wolf Report heavily criticised the plethora of vocational qualifications which were not recognised by employers, asserting that most further education colleges offer a staple 'diet of low-level vocational qualifications, most of which have little to no labour market value' (Wolf, 2011: 7). This review recommended that GCSEs were the gold standard qualification and since then, GCSE A*–C English and maths has become the benchmark and grade C is now the minimum entry requirement for many occupations, for example early years education, social work and nursing. Employees with no qualifications on average earn 20 per cent less than those who leave school with the gold standard of five GCSEs grades A*–C (ONS, 2011). This benchmark is also set for adults in further education:

> Our ambition is that, by 2020, adults aged 19 and over and apprentices of all ages studying English and maths will be working towards achievement of the reformed GCSEs, taking stepping stone qualifications if necessary. Functional skills will continue to be part of apprenticeship completion requirements but we will work with apprenticeship providers to enable them to offer GCSEs to their apprentices. (DfE, 2014b)

Activity 1.2

- How has your institution responded to the provision of GCSE English and maths?
- What (potential) issues arise from this provision for you, your colleagues and/or learners?

Offender Learning Provision

Since 2011, the Ministry of Justice planned to place greater emphasis on developing the vocational and employability skills that offenders need to find sustainable employment on release from prison which benefits them as individuals, but which also benefits wider society. This provision for offenders is seen as the first step towards economic, social and community re-engagement and critical to reducing reoffending. Reoffending is estimated to cost the UK economy somewhere between £9.5 billion and £13 billion a year (BIS, 2011b). The broad aim of educational provision is to provide opportunities for offenders to gain nationally recognised qualifications up to Level 2 (equivalent to a C grade GCSE). All prisons have to provide a core curriculum that covers social and life skills, information technology and preparation for work, in addition to English and maths. There should also be opportunities for prisoners to gain employability skills through a range of activities. However, the main focus is on English and maths for offenders, because '80 per cent have the writing skills, 65 per cent the numeracy skills and 50 per cent the reading skills at or below the level of an 11-year-old' (Social Exclusion Unit, 2002: 6). Despite the critical importance of providing educational opportunities for offenders, the prison service is not immune to the financial pressures and profit-driven marketisation policies to which education is subjected. The danger is that prison education is no longer a priority in a competitive retendering system where cost-cutting for profit overrides the rehabilitation of offenders.

Disengagement and Re-engagement

Young people who are not in education, employment or training are described as NEET, and growing youth unemployment figures since the global financial crisis in 2008 mean that the number of young people falling into this category has increased. Youth unemployment has long been above the overall rate of unemployment of people of working age in the UK, but this gap has grown sharply since 2008. Disengagement from learning and education in the UK has been a persistent problem.

In the first quarter of 2015, according to the Institute for Public Policy Research (IPPR), 5.5 million unemployed young people aged 15–24 in the European Union (EU) were looking for work but were unable to find it (Thompson, 2013). Despite a fall in the youth unemployment rate between 2013 and 2014 in the UK, there are still close to 1 million unemployed young people aged between 16 and 24 (ibid). Of these young people, 60 per cent are still NEET, while the remaining 40 per cent are in education or training (ONS, 2014).

The IPPR suggests that there is a mismatch between what young people are training for and the types of jobs available and show that youth unemployment is lower in countries such as Germany and the Netherlands, where the vocational route into employment through formal education and training is as clear as the academic route – which gives both routes a parity of esteem (Thompson, 2013: 3). This is not the case in the UK, and as a result, vocational education and training is seen as a lower-status pathway than the general academic route by employers. This compromises the labour-market value of vocational qualifications, many of which do not translate into employment. This was first highlighted in the Wolf Report (2011), and further described by the National Careers Council (2013), which reported that the supply and demand mismatch between the vocational education and training acquired by young people, and actual labour market vacancies, still persists, with skills shortages impeding recruitment by employers and ultimately resulting in high youth unemployment in the UK.

Young people described as NEET have a diverse range of characteristics, needs, attributes and ambitions. The reasons that learners become NEET are so varied that it is impossible to generalise, but it is fair to say that some young people face multiple and complex difficulties in their lives which often then become a barrier to engagement in education and training. NEETs can be categorised into three groups: sustained; open to learning; and undecided

(Spielhofer et al., 2009). The majority of NEETs fall into the 'open to learning' or 'undecided' categories, which means that with the appropriate intervention these young people can be re-engaged (NfER, 2012).

The introduction of 16–19 study programmes and traineeships from 2013/14 is central to the reform of 16–19 education and the raising of compulsory participation in education or training to 18 in 2015. The key features of these programmes are based on many of the recommendations in the Wolf Report (2011). Participation can be any one of the following:

- Full-time education including A levels (known as a 'Study Programme')
- An apprenticeship
- Full-time work involving at least 280 hours of education
- A traineeship
- Home education (NCFE, 2013)

Study Programmes for 16–19 are aimed at supporting progression to further education and/or employment. These programmes include qualifications such as functional skills or GCSE in English and maths and non-accredited provision such as personal and social development and vocational skills in work placements. These programmes were introduced to allow more opportunity for a personalised curriculum according to learners' individual needs, and as colleges are funded per learner rather than per qualification, there is more freedom and flexibility to tailor programmes more individually. One key feature is the non-qualification activity that creates opportunities for learners to develop personal, employability and study skills.

Differences in Motivation

As outlined in this chapter, FE provision caters for a broad range of learners who are diverse in age, personal circumstances and previous educational experience. Therefore, their reasons for enrolling onto courses are equally disparate. Historically, FE provision has had two main strands: the personal development of learners, and more focused work-related training. These two principal strands remain the key motivating factors for most learners in FE, with some provision being targeted more towards the development of the learner as an individual, while other courses have a more work-focused approach. In reality, both aspects need to be considered and provision that takes both motivations into account is likely to be the most effective. Intrinsic motivation such as personal development, a passion for a subject, and extrinsic motivation, such as getting a certificate or a job promotion, are often pitted against each other as polar opposites, but in reality they coexist in most of us. However, intrinsically motivated learners are more likely to sustain interest and engagement, and be more committed than those who are more extrinsically motivated. Intrinsic motivation 'seems to be central to high-quality involvement in a task and be self-maintaining and self-terminating' (Curzon and Tummons, 2013: 256)

One of the many strengths of the further education sector is the commitment to learners that teachers bring to their teaching role. This creates an ethos of support, encouragement, choice and challenge in FE, where learners are involved in their own learning through a range of teaching and learning approaches that foster active engagement in the learning process, which in turn create the conditions to help learners become self-motivated. Teachers in FE mostly have a holistic view of the learners they work with, and the work they do, and as a result attach importance to forming and maintaining positive working relationships with their learners. Younger learners frequently feedback that they get treated with respect in FE colleges, and they respond positively to this.

By encouraging learners to reflect on how they learn, defined as 'metacognition', we can begin to engage them in discussions about their learning.

Activity 1.3

- Make a list of questions about learning that you could ask learners as part of an induction activity to start the dialogue about the learning process.

Frank Coffield, a leading educationalist, in his report *Just Suppose Teaching and Learning became the First Priority …* (2008: 64), offers a set of questions which he has found useful in getting the discussion on learning going (see Appendix 1).

A key challenge in FE is motivating learners to continue studying English and maths. Although these subjects have been embedded in vocational subjects since the Skills for Life strategy was introduced in 2001, it was quite an informal practice. One area of concern amongst FE teachers has been around the wholesale introduction of English and maths teaching, alongside teaching their curriculum subject, which became a significant part of their role following the launch of the Functional Skills qualifications in 2010. Part of the concern relates to many teachers' own confidence in being able to teach English and maths, with anecdotes being made such as: 'I'm a plumber teaching plumbing, not an English teacher.' However, the main issue currently being experienced by FE teachers is the difficulty in motivating learners who have spent 11 school years learning English and maths, and failed to achieve the all-important GCSE grade C, and being given only an academic year (36 weeks) to meet this considerable challenge. This sentiment has been repeated since the raising of the participation age and the requirement for learners without that all-important grade C, to continue to study GCSE English and maths alongside their chosen course, although English and maths teachers rather than vocational subject teachers now have this principal responsibility. The challenge to motivate learners who have struggled with these subjects throughout their schooling remains a substantial one.

Conclusion

While it is not possible to do justice to the diversity of the further education sector in so few words, this chapter has sought to highlight how wide-ranging the provision is, and how this is designed to meet a very diverse range of learners. FE has long suffered a low status within the education system in the UK, and some of the history behind the perceived inferiority of vocational education compared to academic education has been discussed, but unfortunately the evidence shows that this perception still persists today. This is reflected in successive government spending reviews which have hit core college budgets which are not ring-fenced like the schools budget for 5-16 year olds. This means that recent austerity measures to cut public spending have fallen mainly on the funding of education for 16-19 years olds and adults. Further evidence is demonstrated in the government policy to deregulate mandatory initial teacher education in further education which strikes at the heart of FE professionalism. The inextricable link between further education and economic imperatives has also been outlined, and this highlights some of the complex challenges which the sector has met, and continues to meet. It also demonstrates the undervalued expertise of its teachers who work with very diverse learners with a very diverse range of needs and aspirations – an expertise that comprises the knowledge, skills and commitment to engage, and re-engage, young people and adults in learning.

Suggested Further Reading

Coffield, F. (2008) *Just Suppose Teaching and Learning became the First Priority* ... London: Learning and Skills Network.
Wolf, A. (2011) *Review of Vocational Education: The Wolf Report*. London: DfE.

CHAPTER 2

PROFESSIONALISM AND PROFESSIONAL PRACTICE IN FURTHER EDUCATION

This chapter will use the deregulation of Initial Teacher Education (ITE) in FE following the Lingfield Report into Professionalism (2012) to frame debates, both historical and current, around professionalism in FE. Professionalism and its significance to teachers working in FE will be discussed amidst the longstanding stigmatisation of vocational education and the concurrent struggle for FE teachers to raise their professional status and gain professional recognition within the education sector.

The place and value of FE teachers as professionals will be examined within the competing discourses of competent practitioner (Moore, 2004; Weber, 2007) and reflective practitioner set within a discussion on the marketisation of FE. Internal and external factors which potentially influence professional values, and therefore professional practice, will be critically examined.

This chapter will cover the following:

- Professionalism in FE – from past to present
- Globalisation and the knowledge economy

(Continued)

(Continued)

- Deregulation of initial teacher education in FE
- Being a professional in FE; two different notions of professionalism
- Professional values and identities; influences and constraints

Activity 2.1

- What are the key characteristics of being a 'professional'?

There are varying interpretations of what being a professional means, but when we describe a professional we usually combine elements of behaviour, attitude and personal characteristics alongside features such as qualifications and ethics. Millerson (1964) identified the core characteristics of a profession based on the long-established professions of law and medicine.

Dedication by practitioners to interests of clients	Practice is based on a body of (scientific) knowledge	Practitioners go through initial training or education

Occupational code of ethics is in place	Self-organisation by occupation to control entry and to discipline members who do not meet professional standards

Figure 2.1   A model of a profession

Source: Adapted from Millerson (1964) and the six core traits of a profession

Activity 2.2

- Does being a teacher in the FE sector meet Millerson's characteristics of a profession?

Professionalism in Further Education

To be better able to understand where we are now as a profession, it is important to understand what has happened in the past that has brought us to this point. Until the late 1990s, FE was unregulated by government and whilst most teachers held qualifications in their subject specialism, in 1997 only 40 per cent of FE teachers had recognised teacher qualifications (Lucas, 2004). The FE workforce was employed largely on casual part-time contracts, either fixed-term or hourly paid, and professional identities were closely linked to teachers' subject specialisms or vocational expertise which led to a 'fragmented and impoverished professional culture in FE' (Lucas and Nasta, 2010: 446). However, as the role of FE became more important to the economic future of the UK, government intervention increased significantly. State regulation of FE teachers began in 2001, when the requirement for teachers to be qualified was first introduced. Subsequently, a highly critical report by Ofsted (2003) concluded that the system of training FE teachers was unsatisfactory and ill-prepared them for their teaching role, leading to the *Equipping our Teachers for the Future* review (DfES, 2004) and the subsequent Foster Review of FE (2005), '*Realising the Potential: A review of the future role of further education colleges*'.

Since 2001, extensive reforms of the FE workforce, in pursuit of quality, have been implemented. This drive to improve quality included the need to raise the status of FE professionals and to professionalise the workforce. Following the Foster Review of FE (ibid.), and the subsequent White Paper *Raising Skills, Improving Life Chances* (DfE, 2006), the sector was subject to a state-regulated strategy to professionalise the workforce. Regulation enforcement was managed by the state-funded Institute for Learning (IfL), which became the professional body for FE teachers. It was declared that: 'regulations will ensure consistency and compliance, and drive forward teachers' qualification reform to meet the target for a fully qualified work-force by 2010' (House of Commons, 2007: 8). The Foster Review resulted in significant policy changes – which included a set of professional standards, a new suite of Initial Teacher Education qualifications, compulsory member-ship of the IfL, a period of professional formation in order to gain Qualified Teaching and Learning Status (QTLS) as well as a Continuing Professional Development (CPD) requirement to maintain QTLS, all of which came into force on 1 September 2007 for all new FE teachers:

> The overall aim of government policy was to create a national system for fur-ther education ITT qualifications comparable to that operating in the schools sector that would raise the professional status of teachers in post-compulsory education. (Lucas et al., 2011: 679)

However, state-funding for the IfL ceased in 2009 amidst criticisms concerning value for money, which instigated a further review into FE, undertaken by Lord Lingfield (2012). This review is responsible for the deregulation of qualified teachers in the FE Sector. So, in effect, we have gone full circle with government policy regarding the professional status of teachers within FE as we are now back to a patchy and inconsistent system of initial teacher education within the sector; the arbitrariness of the system was poignantly criticised by Lingfield himself in his review.

Vocational education and its workforce have long lacked parity with academic education and its respective workforce. FE is often metaphorically referred to as the Cinderella of the education sector (Brooks, 1991), or the neglected middle child (Foster, 2005). Disparity between vocational and academic education is deeply rooted in the class-stratified education system in the UK, and in part accounts for the low professional status of FE teachers. This differs greatly from other countries, such as Germany and the Netherlands, which have more 'unified educational systems' as opposed to the 'tradition of separatism' found in the UK (Lucas and Nasta, 2010: 442).

Globalisation and the Knowledge Economy

The Foster Review of FE in 2005 was carried out at a time of large-scale youth unemployment, increasing globalisation and a subsequent emphasis on a knowledge economy in government policy. The term 'knowledge economy' is fuzzy at best, but it came about due to the competitive challenge posed to developed countries such as the UK from the rapid emergence of a global labour market with an abundance of highly skilled, low-cost knowledge workers in developing countries. Whilst there are several definitions of a knowledge economy, we can summarise this to mean that investment in knowledge, or human capital, is overtaking investment in physical capital such as low-skilled labour and natural resources. This is because, over the last decades, industrial economies based on manufacturing have shifted to a more service economy driven by information, knowledge and innovation:

> The growth of the knowledge economy is seen as part of the strategic response to the threat to UK jobs of imports from low wage economies and, rather confusingly, also as a necessary response to low wage economies such as China and India investing heavily in knowledge. (Brinkley, 2006: 9)

So, the knowledge being prioritised in a knowledge economy is that which is seen as an economic good; that which will give countries a competitive edge in an increasingly globally competitive world:

> Economic success is increasingly based upon the effective utilisation of intangible assets such as knowledge, skills and innovative potential as the key resource for competitive advantage. The term "knowledge economy" is used to describe this emerging economic structure. (ESRC, 2005, cited in Brinkley, 2006: 4)

It has been argued that this is not a new phenomenon, that the economy has always been driven by knowledge and innovation, but this focus on a knowledge economy highlighted the skills shortages in the UK, and other Western countries, and brought about the realisation that creating a highly skilled workforce required twenty-first-century skills (this will be discussed in more detail in Chapters 9 and 10). Globalisation and the emphasis on a knowledge economy coupled FE with economic prosperity in its primary function to provide skills-based curricula to secure global competitive advantage.

Activity 2.3

- Do you agree or disagree with the statement below? Why/why not?

  o   'The first task of teachers is to serve the economy.'

- What constitutes an educated young person in the twenty-first century? What skills and knowledge does an educated young person in the twenty-first century need?

The knowledge economy quickly repositioned FE into a pivotal role providing education and skills for 14–19-year-olds, and was the focus of government policy which aimed to achieve the dual purposes of social inclusion and global competitive advantage. The need to create a highly skilled workforce increased the involvement of business and employers within the FE sector.

The crucial role of FE in the UK economy spearheaded standards-led reforms and led to the advancement of managerialism within FE, and education systems across all sectors, and resulted in what Ball refers to as the 'commodification of education' (2004). Managerialism arises when the government decentralises the powers of efficiency and accountability to individual public sector institutions. The managerial approach has restructured how FE institutions self-manage performance, resulting in an audit-driven culture and the marketisation of the FE sector. This approach to management has introduced a new culture of standards and measures of performance in quantitative terms. With ambiguous notions of quality and efficiency dominating policy-making, continuous improvement increasingly becomes synonymous with value for money. Thereby, institutions and their practices become subject to economic criteria, which Lyotard (1997) calls the 'principle of performativity'. It would seem that, despite extensive reforms of the sector, performance-management regimes of accountability and control will continue to prevail. As Gleeson and James (2007) argue, the FE sector sustains the narrowest form of professionalism, in its traditional sense of professional autonomy.

Activity 2.4

- In what ways is your professional autonomy restricted, and what freedoms do you have t?

Managerialist working conditions create a culture of individualism where competition, rather than collegiality, reigns. This discourages the flourishing of a democratic professionalism where teachers can work collaboratively with others invested in teaching for a just society, and hinders progress towards the equity agenda. Equity issues in education refer principally to equality of opportunity, which is seen as a key feature of social development in terms of social cohesion and quality of life (Whitty, 2006).

Lingfield and Deregulation

In 2010, Ofsted reported confusion in the FE sector over the interpretation of the 2007 Regulations. Moreover, Lucas et al. (2011) reported that, rather than bringing coherence, the regulations had fragmented the sector even further, indicating that the implementation of the professionalisation strategy had been problematic. The introduction of qualifications in an attempt to raise the professional status of the workforce was largely welcomed by institutions and FE teachers alike. However, issues of compliance, namely contractual obligations, coupled with the complexity of the regulations themselves, began to threaten their continuation.

Confusion over the segmented teaching roles, associate teacher and full teacher, led to divisive and often extended periods of ITE, as roles within FE rapidly change. In addition, the poor take-up of QTLS, and difficulties enforcing the five-year time frame within which FE teachers should become qualified, all contributed to questions regarding the validity of the 2007 Regulations. However, the most significant circumstance which led to the Lingfield review of FE in 2012 was provoked by the end of state funding to the IfL. The IfL, consequently, compelled the workforce to pay membership fees to maintain their license to practice in compliance with the 2007 Regulations, which not only alienated the workforce and unions, but also managers. This rift occurred because executing the regulations would have meant the whole-scale dismissal of those teachers who refused to pay the IfL registration fee. Ultimately, this contributed to Lingfield's conclusion that the regulations were unenforceable (2012).

Key recommendations from the Lingfield Review (ibid.) included the revocation of the 2007 Regulations from 1 September 2012, and included: the statutory obligations in respect of the IfL; the IfL to become a voluntary body for FE staff; a new professional body to be established; and a review of the ITE qualifications and professional standards. This led to the Draft Deregulation Bill (House of Commons, 2013), which, in Schedule 13 of the Bill (Section 32), removed regulations in the Education Act (2002) that required FE teachers to be qualified. However, Lingfield equated the qualification of FE teachers with the poor take-up of QTLS, when in fact, 'approximately 80 per cent of all teaching staff within FE colleges (regardless of their start date in the sector) are estimated to have or be working towards a recognised qualification' (BIS, 2012: 7). In addition, an IfL survey found that 87 per cent of teachers agreed that teaching qualifications should be mandatory and 89 per cent agreed that nationally recognised minimum teaching qualifications add to the status and standing of the profession (2012: 6).

The major focus of education on economic imperatives has exposed tensions with policies that aim to promote social justice and economic growth. Where education becomes marketised, profit motives replace ethical notions of equality and care. As Peters argues: 'enterprise culture does not adopt the narrative of equality of opportunity, or attempt to redress the power imbalances or socioeconomic inequalities' (2001: 66). Moreover, the rhetoric of social inclusion in government policy is exposed when economics becomes the primary driver, and learners and their needs become secondary, where the lower status of vocational education is retained, and disadvantage is reproduced in a stratified society and education system.

Two Discourses of Professionalism

The notion of professionalism is fraught with tensions because of its different meanings to those teaching within the education system and those who make education policies. Tensions exist in how we define ourselves as professionals, and how we are defined as professionals by external agencies. Professionalism is imbued with ideas about what knowledge should be prioritised which impacts on our teaching roles and influences how we see ourselves as professionals and what it means to be a professional in FE.

For a period from the 1980s onwards, there was a surge in interest in the knowledge stemming from reflection. Key influences from this era were Schön (1983, 1987) and his work on 'reflective practice' and the 'action research' movement which was advanced by Carr and Kemmis (1986) – see Chapter 11 for more on action research. Reflective practice resulted in the growth of the reflective practitioner discourse, which promotes development through reflection in order to better understand and improve professional practice. This encourages professional autonomy, autonomy to make decisions about our own practice on the basis of the expertise we develop from reflecting on our practice. The popularity of reflective practice, and more significantly professional autonomy, came about in response to the growth in professional accountability emerging in the education system in the 1980s. Reflective practice as a result became formalised in ITE curricula and in this way appropriated by policy-makers and managers. With the growth of managerialism and an audit culture in the 1990s and its emphasis on professional accountability, the reflective practitioner discourse became superseded, but not replaced, by the competent practitioner discourse, which remains the dominant discourse of professionalism. Moore (2004) refers to this as the 'competent craftsperson', where the focus in teaching is on discrete skills, or competences, which can be measured and assessed. Formalising reflective practice in ITE offsets the theoretical content in favour of prescriptive competences and standards. This has defined the parameters of effective teaching and enabled mechanisms by which professional accountability can be measured and monitored.

There has been much opposition to this development, centred on the impact this has had on professional identities and the increasing bureaucratic pressures to meet targets and performance-management regimes. According to Zeichner (2010), who writes about the education situation in the USA, ITE is in danger of preparing teachers for their roles as administrators. Weber (2007) argues that the discourse of the competent practitioner destabilises and reconstitutes teachers' identities within new performance cultures which claim moral authority and rework teachers into compliant technicians. Ball has been highly critical of performativity and its cost to the profession where there is a 'potential "splitting" between teachers' own judgements about "good practice" and students "needs" and the rigours of performance' (2003: 221). Ball argues that the 'hard logic of a performance culture' (ibid.: 223), manifested through marketisation and managerialism, reconstructs what it means to be a teacher and increasingly creates inner conflicts for teachers between their own beliefs and the values of performativity, and causes feelings of inauthenticity stemming from the pressure to perform and continuously improve in a performative environment.

Moore (2004) summarises some of the positive aspects that the competent practitioner discourse offers. He primarily attributes transparency in the ITE assessment process with clearly defined criteria and also cites the introduction of continuing professional development, especially with regard to subject knowledge, and the planning of lessons being joined up with outcomes, target-setting and evaluation. However, one of the key concerns is that the competent practitioner discourse defines the parameters of what is seen as good practice, and effective teaching, and in so doing constrains teachers from being creative and innovative, thus limiting the extent to which they can take risks and try out new ideas – both being processes which underpin reflective practice and action research. As Ruddock writes: 'good teaching is essentially experimental, and habit, if it is permitted to encroach too far on practice, will erode curiosity and prevent the possibility of experiment' (1988: 284).

Activity 2.5

- Reflect on your own experience of initial teacher education:

  o What competences were/are you assessed against?
  o How much of your course involves/involved developing reflective practice?
  o Which discourse of professionalism do you think your ITE qualification prepared you for?
  o In your opinion, what are the advantages and disadvantages of both the reflective and the competent practitioner discourses of professionalism?

Professional Values

Professional identities can be defined as how we see ourselves as professionals, and are largely based on our beliefs, values, attitudes, motives and experiences. Our professional values influence the decisions we make in our teaching practice, and those we make within our teaching role in FE. The professional values we bring with us to our teaching, and which we then develop, can be influenced by a variety of factors such as:

- Society
- Attitudes to education and learners
- Morals and ethics
- Colleagues/institutions

These factors are discussed in more detail on the next page.

Society

The society, and culture, we are raised in and live in has a profound effect on our value system. The institutions and people we interact with also shape our values. We are bombarded by images in the media and how different groups in society are represented, which will also have an influence on our values. As teachers, our professional values will be largely shaped by our own experiences of schooling, our family's attitude to education and their educational experiences. Most important, however, is the way in which society constructs teachers, their status and perception within society, how they are portrayed in society. The purpose of education, and therefore the role of teachers in relation to this, are also important factors.

Attitudes to education and learners

Our own educational experiences will also play a key part in our attitude to education and learners. I think it is a reasonable assumption that teachers would not become teachers if they did not have a vested interest in education and what it offers to individuals. Attitudes to learners may be more variable, again depending on our own experiences and preconceptions. An ethic of altruism is central to the concept of professionalism. Research shows that amongst FE professionals, there is a 'strong commitment to teaching, to fostering student learning and development, to attending to learners' needs and to self-development or learning as a professional' (James and Biesta, 2007: 130).

Morals and ethics

Our parents, or primary caregivers, provide our moral foundation, with most psychologists agreeing that by the age of seven these moral principles of right and wrong behaviour are established. As teachers, we are role models of integrity and morality. One of the guiding values of teachers is a commitment to our learners, which requires a morality of equality and an emotional investment in what we do. Ethics are the shared principles we have as teachers in FE which guide our professional practice, for example staff codes of conduct and professional standards are based on ethics. As teachers, our principal shared ethical responsibility is to understand our position of trust and influence by acting with professionalism and integrity.

This ethical responsibility has been incorporated into the Professional Values and Attributes section in the revised Professional Standards (Education and Training Foundation, 2014) as follows:

• Reflect on what works best in your teaching and learning to meet the diverse needs of learners

- Evaluate and challenge your practice, values and beliefs
- Inspire, motivate and raise aspirations of learners through your enthusiasm and knowledge
- Be creative and innovative in selecting and adapting strategies to help learners to learn
- Value and promote social and cultural diversity, equality of opportunity and inclusion
- Build positive and collaborative relationships with colleagues and learners

(Education and Training Foundation, 2014: 2)

Colleagues and institutions

Who we work with and where we work have a significant influence on shaping our personal professional values. We come into teaching with our own pre-existing set of values, attitudes and beliefs, and these can be either in harmony, or in tension, with those we work with or those manifest in our place of work. The culture of our institution will have an influence on the professional values we hold. The values of management will affect the way we behave and go about our teaching role. A strong supportive institutional culture builds morale and a culture of openness, whereas a culture that does not offer support will more likely create cliques and an atmosphere of fear.

Activity 2.6

- Make a list of your personal professional values and consider their influences.
- Then complete the grid with your top five personal professional values, listing them in order of importance to you and reflecting on their impact on your teaching practice.
- You could ask some of your colleagues to do the same and see how they compare to your own.

My professional values are:	The impact on teaching and learning is:
1.	
2.	
3.	
4.	
5.	

Professional Identity

The concept of professional identity has attracted much research which has primarily focused on what affects teachers' professional identity and its development. Whilst there are varying definitions of professional identity, it is generally seen as how teachers see themselves as teachers. Day and Kington (2008) suggest teacher professional identity has three dimensions (Figure 2.2).

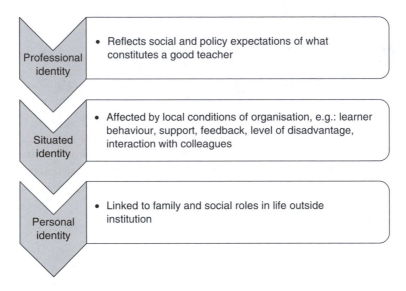

Figure 2.2   The dimensions of identity

Source: Adapted from Day and Kington (2008)

The personal and contextual factors of these three dimensions interact and form different identities which affect our perceptions of ourselves as teachers and influence our professional behaviours. Professional identities manifest themselves in job satisfaction, commitment, motivation and self-efficacy, which in turn affect every aspect of our practice. Our professional identities are not fixed or static, rather they are in a state of flux and subject to change. Repositioning our identities is par for the course as we adapt to educational reform which affects the realities of our practice on a daily basis. Our relationship to policies and their implementation is affected by our sense of professional identity, but can equally impact this sense of identity. More recently, the marketisation of education has resulted in policy initiatives and performance management regimes that have intensified the bureaucratic workload for teachers. The nature of this educational reform mandates what we should teach but also increasingly how to teach, which constrains our practice and reduces our autonomy as professionals. Although it is often said that teachers working in FE have a 'fragile sense of identity' (Gleeson et al., 2007), the one universal and unifying part of this fragile identity is our shared commitment to the learners we work with. In their research, Jephcote and Salisbury (2009) reported that in FE, the teachers' sense of professional identity consists of a belief that the sector compensates for previous educational disadvantage, and that as a result they have a primary sense of responsibility to the social well-being of their learners, rather than just teaching a curriculum subject.

Activity 2.7

- In your opinion, what is the principal purpose of education?
- Now examine the underlying beliefs and assumptions which informed your answer and how they relate to your professional values and your sense of identity as a teacher.

Conclusion

Issues of social inclusion and quality, which were prevalent in the Foster Review, have furthered tensions in the professional identities of FE teachers. Professional values in relation to teaching and commitment to learners, which are rooted in broader ethical issues of social inclusion, are being brought into conflict with the constraints of performance management regimes. 'In such circumstances teaching becomes a constant struggle against rather than with students' (Gleeson et al., 2007: 453), which further threatens an already fragile, and restricted, sense of professionalism in FE. Teachers' identification with principles of equity and social justice become increasingly difficult within the confines of managerialism which constructs professional identities shaped by accountability, to meet the imperatives of performativity: economy, efficiency and effectiveness. This is increasingly evident with the encroachment of 'business-speak', which is now a feature of the everyday parlance of teachers and managers. Professionalism has gone through a process of reculturation by developing '"designer teachers" who demonstrate compliance to policy imperatives and perform at high levels of efficiency and effectiveness' (Sachs, 2001: 156).

The marketisation of FE has done nothing to address the workforce concerns Foster reported on regarding retention, casualisation and lack of comparative parity in pay and conditions, which he claimed impoverished the professionalism of the sector in 2005, as these still persist today. The pendulum swing back to deregulation fragments the profession and threatens to further destabilise the professional identities of those who teach within the sector. ITE qualifications, and their funding, will now be at the discretion of individual institutions; this disparate approach to ITE will undoubtedly make the reality of a collective sense of professional identity impossible. This clearly goes against the drive for quality at a time when the high-stakes quality measures are at their zenith. Some argue that the revocation of ITE requirements is part of an ongoing strategy to deskill and deprofessionalise the workforce (Avis, 2002; Beck and Young, 2005). Deregulation in FE runs parallel to policy regarding unqualified teachers in academies and free schools, which signals an intention to atomise the teaching profession across all sectors. At a time when more and more is being asked of teachers and their expertise in the FE sector, it seems incongruous to undermine the professionalism of those who teach in it.

Suggested Further Reading

Ball S.J. (2004) *Education for Sale: The Commodification of Everything.* The Annual Education Lecture 2004. London: King's College London.

Gleeson, D., Davies, J. and Wheeler, E. (2007) 'On the making and taking of professionalism in the further education workplace', *British Journal of Sociology and Education*, 26 (4), pp. 445–60.

James, D. and Biesta, G. (2007) *Improving Learning Cultures in Further Education.* Abingdon: Routledge.

Moore, A. (2004) *The Good Teacher: Dominant Discourses in Teaching and Teacher Education.* London: RoutledgeFalmer.

Sachs, J. (2001) 'Teacher professional identity: Competing discourses, competing outcomes', *Journal of Education Policy*, 16 (2), pp. 149–61.

Whitty, G. (2006) 'Teacher professionalism in a new era'. Institute of Education, University of London. Paper presented at the first General Teaching Council for Northern Ireland Annual Lecture, Belfast, March.

CHAPTER 3

TEACHER EXPECTATIONS

This chapter will bring together secondary research on teachers' attitudes and prejudices to explore some of the more complex issues of equality and diversity. The relationship between teachers' implicit prejudices, teachers' expectations and educational attainment and achievement will be discussed. The terms 'attainment' and 'achievement' are often used interchangeably, but there is an important distinction: attainment is the standard of work reached compared with an expected standard, for example exam results, whereas achievement is the individual progress and success, i.e. the distance travelled. In this chapter, I mostly refer to achievement, because this ultimately has an impact on overall attainment.

This is no by means a definitive exploration of the literature on teacher expectations, but the intention is to draw some of the key themes emerging from this area of research together to encourage discussion and reflection on your own professional practice.

(Continued)

(Continued)

This chapter will cover the following:

- The importance of teacher expectations
- A summary of some key findings from research studies into teacher expectations with particular focus on ethnicity and social class
- Self-fulfilling prophecy and labelling
- The relationship between teacher expectations and learner achievement
- Assessment practices and issues for consideration

Potential is not a Number

The phrase, 'I've got a Level 2 learner who ...', has often been expressed by teachers and this seems innocent enough, until we start to unpick what this expression represents in terms of how we see and describe learners – by their level, or more accurately, by their perceived ability. This simple example of how teachers talk about their learners in reference to their 'level', is symptomatic of the education system in the UK, and in most Western countries. Learners are organised according to their ability, in levels, sets, bands or – dare it be said – streams. All of these terms contribute to how we think about learners, and for that matter learning. Standardised testing is pervasively used to group learners from a very early age in mainstream education in the UK, and this overshadows their schooling experience, because it influences how teachers work, and more importantly, think about learners and their achievement.

When learners enter further education, their prior attainment is used to signpost them on to courses, and there are good reasons for this, but as teachers we need to be aware that a grade, or a level, does not define a learner: it is merely a snapshot of achievement at a specific moment in time and does not represent a 'glass ceiling' of what an individual is capable of now, or in the future. What an individual is capable of is often beyond a learner's own imagining, let alone a teacher's. When talking about learners, what teachers should preferably be thinking is: 'I've got a learner on a Level 2 course who ...' In so doing, we see each learner as an individual and do not set limits on what they can achieve.

Year after year, national reports compiled by the Department for Education reveal continuing educational inequalities in data linked to ethnicity, social class and gender across the education sectors. Ethnicity is a persistently significant factor in the formation of teacher expectancies. For this reason, the relationship between teacher expectations, ethnicity and differential achievement has remained a recurring theme in education research and reform. Policy initiatives such as the Every Learner (Child) Matters (ECMs) agenda which was introduced in 2004, was intended to be a framework for promoting positive educational outcomes for all learners, but specifically those from disadvantaged backgrounds as educational achievement is seen to improve life chances.

FE has had a key role to play in addressing social inequalities particularly since the mid-1990s. Through widening participation it promotes social inclusion and community cohesion by giving opportunities for some of the more vulnerable and socioeconomically disadvantaged members of society to help them to progress in their studies, to gain employment and to integrate more fully into society.

In 2000, the government commissioned the Hay McBer Report, which outlined measures of teacher effectiveness and identified high expectations as an important attribute of effective teaching, stating that effective teachers communicate high, clear and consistent expectations with an appropriate level of challenge to all. Ofsted, however, have only started to seriously push this measure since the revised Common Inspection Framework (CIF) in 2012, which placed an increased emphasis and importance on teaching, learning and assessment. In judging the quality of teaching, learning and assessment, Ofsted inspectors are asked to consider:

- How well teaching and learning methods – including training, coaching and mentoring – inspire and challenge all learners and enable them to extend their knowledge, skills and understanding
- The extent to which teaching, training and coaching encourage and develop independent learning
- Whether high but realistic expectations are used to motivate learners (Ofsted, 2012: 48)

Since then, the mantra 'stretch and challenge' has emerged and which has affected how teachers plan, teach and assess; shaped lesson observation criteria; and influenced Ofsted inspections when making judgements about the quality of teaching and learning.

Activity 3.1

- What makes learning 'stretching and challenging'?
- What factors do you think limit opportunities for 'stretching and challenging' learning?
- Evaluate your own use of questions: in what ways are you stretching and challenging learners to think at a higher-level?

Self-Fulfilling Prophecy

According to Jussim and Harber (2005), after 35 years of research on teacher expectations and 'self-fulfilling prophecies', it is possible to conclude that self-fulfilling prophecies do occur in the classroom with modest effects most of the time, however powerful self-fulfilling prophecies are more likely to occur among learners from disadvantaged social groups.

First, a self-fulfilling prophecy must involve at least two people – we cannot have a self-fulfilling prophecy with ourselves. Second, put simply, a self-fulfilling prophecy is an idea which becomes reality because someone believes in it. Teacher expectations will affect how teachers interact with a learner, or group of learners, and this creates the conditions in which those expectations will be fulfilled. Hand in hand with self-fulfilling prophecy is 'labelling'.

Activity 3.2

- What labels do teachers use to describe learners? What labels do you use? Make a list of your ideas.

So, a self-fulfilling prophecy is a prediction that comes true because it has been stated, either consciously or unconsciously:

1. The teacher labels the learner (positively or negatively).
2. The teacher treats the learner accordingly.
3. The learner internalises the teacher's expectation, develops a positive or negative self-concept, and behaves accordingly.

Rogers (1959) suggests that the self-concept has three different components:

- Self-image – the view we have of ourselves
- Self-esteem or self-worth – how much value we place on ourselves
- Ideal self – the person we would like to be

Self-esteem can be seen as a continuum from low to high. Rogers believed that self-esteem develops in early childhood, but continues to be influenced by interactions with others beyond childhood. High self-esteem means that we have a positive view of ourselves, and therefore have more confidence in our own abilities, we have self-belief, and are more able to face challenges and accept failure. As teachers, self-esteem is not something we can give learners, rather we can create the conditions where learners can experience themselves positively.

Key Research on Teacher Expectations

Rosenthal and Jacobson (2003 [1968]) first claimed a relationship between teacher expectations and educational achievement in a controversial, and criticised, research experiment entitled *Pygmalion in the Classroom*. The study examined ways in which teachers interact with high-achieving and low-achieving learners, and how teacher expectations accordingly influenced learner performance and achievement. A group of learners was randomly selected and given a fictitious Intelligence Quotient (IQ) test. Teachers were given the results of the 'test', which supposedly indicated which learners were likely to be high-achievers, and which would make little or no progress. When the researchers returned to the school at the end of the academic year, results showed that those learners identified as high-achievers had made exceptional progress and the conclusion from the research study was that teacher behaviour differed according to whether they were interacting with low-achieving or high-achieving learners, which in turn affected achievement. The influence on achievement was explained as the self-fulfilling prophecy effects of teacher expectations: if teachers feel that learners can make exceptional progress, then learners are treated in ways that stimulate and encourage achievement. This conclusion was heavily criticised, one of the reasons being Rosenthal and Jacobson did not actually observe any classroom interaction between teachers and learners.

More recently, however, research has shown that teacher expectations can influence their interactions with learners and that teachers are less flexible in their expectations for black learners, female learners, and learners from low-income households (Ferguson, 2003). Whilst teachers may be unaware of the stereotypes or biases that have been created within their classroom, learners are extremely sensitive to these biases and stereotypes, and their implications.

Consequently, teacher expectations have a profound effect on learners' self-belief and achievement. Brophy and Good (1984) found 17 differing behaviours that teachers used with high-achieving and low-achieving learners that acted as self-fulfilling prophecies. These behaviours informed the learners of the teachers' expectations for them and as a result affected the learners' progress.

Jussim and Harber (2005) have challenged research which condemned teachers for their alleged role in creating inequality. Their research focused on the accuracy of teacher predictions and concluded that whilst a self-fulfilling prophecy exists, its effects are relatively insignificant because most teacher perceptions of learner achievement are accurate. In short, their research found that as accuracy increases, the potential of self-fulfilling prophecies decreases, and vice versa. However, research consistently shows that teachers behave differently with high-achieving and low-achieving learners, which increases the potential for self-fulfilling prophecies. Rubie-Davies (2008: 260) categorised these differences in teacher behaviour into the following five areas: grouping, materials and activities, the evaluation system, the motivational system, and classroom relationships. These identified variations in teacher behaviour create differing learning environments which affect the progress of learners.

Grouping, materials and activities

Ability grouping can provide learners with subtle messages about expected capabilities. Activities that learners are assigned, how they are paced, and how they are monitored, all provide learners with information about ability.

Evaluation system

Teachers who do not regard ability as fixed understand that the achievement of all learners will improve with appropriate support and feedback (this will be discussed in more detail in Chapter 4).

Motivational system

Teachers with low expectations of learner achievement focus more on extrinsic motivation so promote competition rather than collaboration.

Classroom relationships

Teachers with high expectations devote more time developing positive relationships with learners in order to create a positive learning environment.

These differing behaviours convey subtle, but powerful, messages to learners about how teachers feel about them and their ability.

Most learners are particularly perceptive and will pick up on all the verbal and non-verbal cues that teachers, often unconsciously, communicate and thus provide learners with information about teachers' expectations for achievement. Teachers' instructional behaviours, though, have a more significant effect on achievement, as learning is dependent on what opportunities to learn are given to learners by teachers.

As Rubie-Davies (2008: 261) states, learners are more 'likely to learn more in classrooms where learning experiences are challenging and exciting and where higher order thinking skills are fostered'. Interestingly, Rubie-Davies concludes that teachers' class-level expectations and the associated teacher behaviours within the classroom may be more significant for learning than expectations at the individual level.

Such research highlights classroom practices that can deny equal opportunities as a result of systemic discrimination. Learners from marginalised groups are particularly vulnerable to self-fulfilling prophecies. It must, however, be noted that this area of teacher expectation research is fraught with controversy and falls between two extremes: flawed and highly speculative, on the one hand; and conclusive in revealing the link between teacher expectation and its influence on learner achievement, on the other. That said, the majority of researchers agree that teacher expectations and teacher expectation effects do exist, but the strength and significance of these effects is still being debated.

Teacher Attitude and Prejudice

Teachers are also human, so we carry with us our own assumptions and preconceptions about people and groups in society, and these may, albeit unconsciously, come to influence how we interact with learners. These opinions may be based on knowledge, or biases, passed onto us by other teachers, on appearance, family background, socio-economic status or ethnicity. By raising this thorny issue, the idea is that we can be honest with ourselves and be more self-aware of how our own views and stereotypes may have an impact on the learning, and achievement, of the individuals we teach. This is not to say that all teachers are biased, but does highlight the fact that ethnicity or social class may lead a teacher to attribute a generalised perception of expectation to a group of learners, which can make it difficult then for individual learners to separate themselves from the generalised expectation of the teacher. Smith and Smith (2008) raise another point to consider, namely a teacher's ability to relate to, or understand, the diverse cultures or backgrounds of learners, which in turn then influences the teacher's interaction with learners. Teachers often report that learners' cultures, attitudes, influences (peer and media) and behaviours are poles apart from their own, which can act as a barrier between them and their learners.

Activity 3.3

- What differences in culture, attitude or behaviour between you and your learners do you find difficult to relate to?
- How could you try to understand your learners better?

Ethnicity

Disparity in educational achievement between groups of learners, particularly groups defined by gender, ethnicity and socioeconomic status, is referred to as the achievement gap. The ethnic achievement gap has been, and continues to be, a persistent problem. It often appears when schooling starts and continues, if not widens, throughout the education system and more often than not persists into adulthood (Paik and Wahlberg, 2007; McKown and Weinstein, 2008). Differences in educational achievement based on ethnicity have therefore been extensively researched and this is increasingly relevant if continuing social inequality is to be seriously addressed. Extensive studies by Dusek and Joseph (1983) and later, Tenenbaum and Ruck (2007), concluded that ethnicity is a significant factor in the formation of teacher expectancies. This is clearly an uncomfortable truth for some teachers. Through the use of Implicit Attitude Tests (IAT), teachers' prejudices have been researched and relationships between teacher expectations of ethnic minority learners and differential achievement gaps have been found.

Activity 3.4

- Search on the Internet for an Implicit Attitude Test. Take the test and reflect on the results.

Overall, the theoretical conclusion from the wide-ranging research carried out is that the differential expectations of teachers and the ethnic achievement gap are related to the implicit prejudiced attitudes of the teachers. Van den Bergh et al. (2010) carried out a large-scale study into the differential expectations of teachers and the ethnic achievement gap in primary schools in Holland. Although the size of the achievement gap between ethnic and non-ethnic learners differed across classrooms, it was found to exist in every classroom. Their research concluded that the differential expectations of teachers and the ethnic achievement gap were both related to the implicit prejudiced attitudes of the teachers.

Research consistently reveals that unconscious discrimination results in teachers devoting more time and resources to non-ethnic learners, creating supportive and challenging environments with increased opportunities to respond in class and more frequent feedback, which in turn suggests that the prejudiced attitudes of teachers may also affect the achievement of non-ethnic learners, but in a positive way. On the other hand, teachers with prejudiced attitudes are more likely to stereotype the intellectual ability, and the future prospects, of learners from ethnic minorities. Learners from ethnic minorities, therefore, are often given fewer opportunities to respond and receive less positive feedback, which have negative effects on their learning.

Activity 3.5

- Go to the Department for Education website and search for attainment by pupil characteristics: you can search for early years, Key Stage 2, GCSE and A level. What does the data reveal?
- Carry out some research into ethnicity in Higher Education. What data can you find about ethnic minorities progressing onto university and their achievement on graduation?

Social class

The link between low social class and low educational achievement is undeniable. Most researchers agree that social class affects teachers' expectations. Teachers tend to have higher expectations for middle-class learners than they do for learners from poor backgrounds. Where researchers are divided is over whether ethnicity plays a more or less relevant role in teachers' expectations than social class. There have been a variety of reports and publications related to the underachievement of white working-class learners in recent years, in particular male learners. A research review commissioned by the Department for Education revealed that the attainment of white British learners is polarised by social class to a greater extent than any other ethnic group. White British learners from managerial and professional homes are one of the highest attaining groups, while white British learners from working-class homes are the lowest attaining group (Strand, 2008).

Ofsted have attributed this to 'a poverty of expectation' which starts within the home environment but is then perpetuated by the education system, and by teachers' expectations and subsequent classroom practices. On the other hand, research carried out by the Joseph Rowntree Foundation (2011) reported that low aspirations were not a key cause of lower achievement among white British learners from low socioeconomic backgrounds, and suggested that aspirations were actually very high across all social groups. Instead, the Joseph Rowntree Foundation argued that the difference between those from richer and poorer socioeconomic backgrounds lay in the strength of their respective belief that they would be able to achieve their aspirations.

Activity 3.6

- What are the potential barriers to achievement for learners from a low socioeconomic background?

Assessment Practices

One of the guiding principles of assessment is reliability, and in order to ensure that this is upheld, assessment needs to maintain fairness and consistency. In 1973, Harari and McDavid carried out research into name stereotypes which indicated that teachers' expectations may be associated with implicit stereotyped perceptions of names. The research suggested that teachers may make more favourable judgements of work linked with common or frequent names and less favourable judgements of work linked with unusual names; teachers may also correlate names with social class and ethnicity. Despite many studies examining the reliability of marking, it is difficult to make conclusions about the factors that influence reliability. One of the reasons why the research on the issue of bias in assessment is contradictory is because the studies differ in many important respects: the training of the assessors, the type of assessment, the mark scheme, the subject/topic assessed and so on.

Gender bias has often been linked to subjects. For example, Punter and Burchell (1996) found that female learners were graded more favourably in history because this subject is often assessed by essays and female learners are thought to be better at extended writing. A similar finding was revealed by research undertaken by Goddard-Spear (1984) in science, where work was graded higher if the markers perceived that it was written by a male learner. Belsey (1988) looked at English degrees awarded before and after blind-marking was introduced. Before blind-marking was introduced, 27 per cent of women got 'good' degrees (firsts and upper seconds) compared to 45 per cent of men. After blind-marking was introduced, 47 per cent of women were awarded first and upper second degrees, while for men it was almost the same at 42 per cent.

The wholesale use of blind-marking for eliminating bias and improving reliability in assessment is nevertheless debatable. In some studies, blind-marking does seem to have overcome gender bias, whereas in others it seems to have had little, if any, effect.

Activity 3.7

- Make a list of some of the advantages and disadvantages of blind-marking.
- What measures are in place at your institution to ensure that assessment practices are fair and impartial?

Babad (1980) first revealed the possibility of ethnic bias in marking. Research conducted by the DfES (Broecke and Nicholls, 2007) showed that being from a minority ethnic group was found to have a statistically significant, and negative effect, on degree attainment. More recent data evidence shows that 66.5 per cent of white students studying first degrees received a first or upper second class Honours degree, with only 49.2 per cent of ethnic minority students achieving this, and only 38.1 per cent of black students (Equality Challenge Unit, 2011).

A study of blind-marking in GCSE English conducted by Baird and Bridle (2000) concluded that anonymising learners' names does not completely eliminate bias, because handwriting style, and the content and the style of the language used, all reveal learners' personal characteristics. It would seem, therefore, that the most effective solution to eliminate bias is to have clear marking criteria. This reduces opportunities for bias because it is more difficult for assessors to justify any differences in grades awarded.

Education and Social Inequality

Pierre Bourdieu (1930–2002) was a French sociologist who suggested that education produces and reproduces social inequality in society. The body of Bourdieu's work was dedicated to exploring class inequalities in educational achievement and the broader question of class reproduction in industrialised societies. Bourdieu claims that the education system has a key role in maintaining the status quo by legitimising social inequalities:

> [education] is in fact one of the most effective means of perpetuating the existing social pattern, as it both provides an apparent justification for social inequalities and gives recognition to the cultural heritage, that is, to a social gift treated as a natural one. (Bourdieu, 1974: 32)

According to Bourdieu, cultural capital consists of familiarity with the dominant culture in a society, especially the ability to understand and use 'educated' language. The possession of cultural capital varies with social class, yet the education system assumes the possession of cultural capital.

This makes it very difficult for learners who are brought up in families who do not possess this cultural capital, primarily working-class and ethnic minorities, and particularly those who have English as a second language, to succeed in the education system, but this is not to discount the fact that some learners from poorer socioeconomic backgrounds do go on to do well. Possession of cultural capital enables learners from the dominant culture, those from richer socioeconomic backgrounds, to maintain their social position.

Clearly, teachers do not set out with the intention of reproducing social inequalities, but evidently there are aspects of the education system that contribute to these inequalities which often have lasting effects on the lives of those learners disadvantaged by the education system.

Activity 3.8

- Revisit data collected in Activity 3.5. What evidence is there to support and/or dispute Bourdieu's theory?
- What aspects of your practice and institution do you think might contribute to social inequality?

Of course, there are many factors which can influence learners' educational achievement, the principal factor being the learners themselves. Hattie (2003) suggests that what a learner brings to the table accounts for 50 per cent of the differences in achievement between learners, but in institutions, Hattie found that the teacher accounts for 30 per cent, and is therefore a key influence on learning, and subsequently achievement. Increased achievement is brought about by setting challenging goals for all learners which ask them to do more than 'just your best'. This is why having high expectations of all learners is so important, not only to succeed educationally but also to avoid perpetuating social exclusion for marginalised groups in society. It is our responsibility as teachers to recognise and understand this issue so as to ensure that we do not perpetuate the problem.

Activity 3.9

- Find some recent achievement data for your subject area within your institution. What do the results show? If there is any disparity, what could you do to address this?

- It might also be possible to find the achievement data from across your institution. If so, do the same analysis and reflect on how any disparities could be addressed within your institution.

Conclusion

This chapter has highlighted some issues around inequality in educational achievement, and, also shared some key findings of research that has been carried out into teacher expectations in order to raise awareness of how teachers can influence learning and achievement in both positive and negative ways. When thinking about causes of social inequality it is important to remember that as teachers we play a significant role in addressing social inequality, but it is equally important to acknowledge that there are many external factors, such as home-life and social structures, including socioeconomic status and employment, which also contribute to social inequality. This chapter intends to raise awareness of how teachers influence learning and to encourage reflection on our own preconceptions and potential biases as teachers so that we can ensure that we have high expectations of all the learners we teach.

In FE, we meet learners at a pivotal point in their educational experience, and many may have not had a positive experience of schooling thus far, so having high expectations in their regard is of paramount importance to ensure that they have every possible opportunity to achieve their aspiration, whatever that may be. As teachers, we cannot alone overcome the effects of social disadvantage on individuals, but through our commitment to education and our learners we make an important contribution towards trying to create a fairer and more just society.

Action Research Link

- Is this an area that interests you? Has it raised some issues that relate to your own practice and institution?
- If so, then this could be an interesting area for an action research project. Go to Chapter 11 for further guidance and support on action research.

Suggested Further Reading

Bourdieu, P. (1974) 'The school as a conservative force: Scholastic and cultural inequalities', in L. Eggleston (ed.), *Contemporary Research in the Sociology of Education*. London: Metheun.

Joseph Rowntree Foundation (2011) *The Influence of Parents, Places and Poverty on Educational Attitudes and Aspirations.* York: Joseph Rowntree Foundation.

Paik, S.J. and Wahlberg, H.J. (2007) *Narrowing the Achievement Gap: Strategies for Educating Latino, Black, and Asian Students.* New York: Springer Publishing.

Rogers, C.R. (1969) *Freedom to Learn: A View of What Education Might Become.* Columbus, OH: Merrill.

Rosenthal, R. and Jacobson, L. (2003 [1968]) *Pygmalion in the Classroom: Teacher Expectation and Pupils' Intellectual Development.* Norwalk, CT: Crown House Publishing.

Rubie-Davies, C. (2008) 'Teacher expectations', in T. Good (ed.), *21st Century Education: A Reference Handbook.* Thousand Oaks, CA: Sage.

Smith, D. and Smith, B. (2008) 'Urban educators voices: Understanding culture in the Classroom', *Urban Review*, 41, pp. 334–51.

Strand, S. (2008) *Minority Ethnic Pupils in the Longitudinal Study of Young People in England: Extension Report on Performance in Public Examinations at Age 16.* DCSF Research Report. London: Department For Children, Schools And Families.

CHAPTER 4

ATTITUDES TO LEARNING

This chapter will outline the history of the notion of intelligence and go on to explore attitudes to learning using research stemming from Carol Dweck's theory of fixed and growth mindsets. This will critically examine the notion of 'intelligence' and how this can create a glass ceiling for learners by reinforcing the idea that ability is innate rather than developed through effort. This chapter stems from the need to challenge deterministic views about ability and ends with points to consider for inclusive practice.

This chapter will cover the following:

- Notions of intelligence from past to present
- An overview of attribution theory
- Fixed and growth mindsets
- Mindsets and praise
- Developing growth mindsets in a learning environment
- Creating a 'can-do' ethos
- Mindset issues for inclusive practice
- Resilience and disengagement

Definitions of 'intelligence'

Within education, the notion of intelligence is still a hotly debated area amongst academics and educationalists. There is very much a 'nature versus nurture' dispute as to what constitutes a person's ability, or potential ability. The core of the debate centres on the extent to which particular aspects of ability are a product of genetic or learned attributes. The dictionary definition of intelligence is: 'the ability to acquire and apply knowledge and skills' (*Oxford Dictionaries*, 2014).

During the Age of Enlightenment, there were philosophical meditations on human knowledge and the mind as thinking in this era started to separate from religion. Philosophy is one of the key influences on the schools of psychology, which have in turn influenced educational theory. In Figure 4.1, we can see how the three main schools of learning theory are rooted, to different degrees, in the nurture side of the debate. Behaviourism views learners as *tabula rasa*, a blank slate or empty vessel, which will be filled with what they are taught; whereas a cognitive view

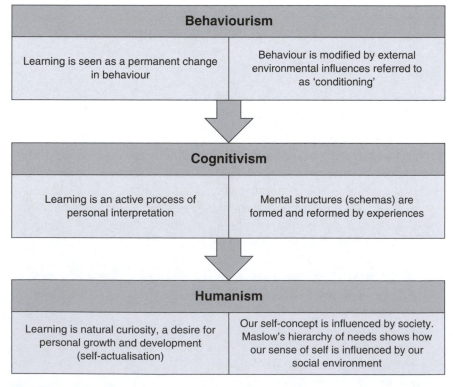

Figure 4.1   Representation of three main schools of learning theory within the nurture debate

suggests that learners create their own meaning; and humanism that learning is a process of self-discovery, not an end in itself, and given the right conditions we all have the ability to improve. These learning theories do not necessarily dismiss the role of innate intelligence, they maintain, however, that the greatest influence on learning is the environment.

This differs from the nature debate, which believes that genetic factors influence a person's ability. The 'nature' point of view has at various times been used to sanction notions of intellectual superiority which in turn legitimised the slave trade, supported eugenics, and promoted racial stereotyping which has fuelled and perpetuated social inequalities. However, instead of polarised debates, recent advances in genetic research and neuroscience have moved towards accepting that both genes and environment are mutually constitutive of a person's ability.

There is also a long history of debate about what constitutes intelligence. For some it is a single, general ability, for others it is a range of skills, aptitudes and talents. In 1905, Alfred Binet first designed a psychometric intelligence test as a tool to help identify at-risk learners. The idea of being able to measure human intelligence, and modern IQ testing, have both developed from Binet's early test designs. However, Binet was concerned with using these tests to identify learners who were at risk of failing school in order to provide the appropriate educational intervention to help avoid this, rather than to use this as a measurement of biological, innate, intelligence. Binet was evidently aware of the limitations of the test and challenged the idea that intelligence could be defined by a number, but rather proposed that intelligence was influenced by a range of factors and could change over time. However, this test proved popular and generated much interest due to the Western obsession with categorising individuals according to their intellectual ability, which cemented the link between intelligence and academic achievement still prevalent today. Stanford University developed and standardized a test, known as the Stanford-Binet intelligence test, which uses a single number as a measurement of intelligence, known as the Intelligence Quotient (IQ). The use of intelligence tests has significantly influenced education, and educators, in the USA, and, in turn, the UK. Psychometric tests are extensively used in schools to assess learners' mental capacities – Key Stage 2 SATs and the 11+ exam are further examples of standardized intelligence tests. These tests have been used to stream, band, group and set learners by ability for decades.

It could be argued that this has made the structuring of education, and its provision, more efficient. It could also be argued that this has created a deeply entrenched view of what counts as intelligence, but more importantly, that intelligence is shaped by internal genetic factors and can be inherited – the biological view. In this way, education is primarily concerned with the acquisition of skills and knowledge which can be measured, and, therefore, has become focused on performance goals, which rewards level of achievement; or in other words the end result rather than the process of learning. This has worked well with both of the favoured theories in mainstream education, specifically behaviourism and cognitivism, with the latter being the dominant view of learning currently. Behaviourism is concerned with the product of learning, and cognitivism assumes learning is the possession of the individual, and therefore both of these theories work well with an education system that uses standardized assessments to test achievement. Performance goals are a prediction based on current abilities and can only ever give short-term benefits. The flip side is that failure to meet performance goals can leave learners feeling helpless, inadequate and disengaged with deleterious effects on their attitude to learning, and ultimately educational outcomes.

It is fair to say that many learners who come into FE, whatever their age, have not had a particularly positive experience of schooling and the emphasis on performance goals prevalent within the education system has undermined their self-belief by perpetuating the notion of intelligence as a fixed entity. Therefore, demotivation, lack of self-belief and a negative attitude to learning are common attributes for many learners when they embark on a course in FE.

Activity 4.1

- What strategies do you use to engage learners when you first meet them on your course(s)?

Attribution Theory

Motivation to learn is key and 'motivation depends as much on the attitudes of the teacher as on the attitudes of the students' (Rogers, 1986: 66). Weiner (1974) developed a theoretical framework for attribution theory, founded on Heider's (1958) proposed theory of attribution, which examines how an individual interprets success or failure. This theory attempts to interpret how people explain their actions, and other people's actions, and the way people attribute different causes to different actions. When things go well and we succeed, we attribute this to something within ourselves or an external force, what Heider referred to as internal attribution or external attribution.

For example, if you pass an exam, you may attribute this to an internal factor such as ability (you're good at the subject) or effort (you revised/practised a lot), or an external factor such as luck (everything you revised for was in the exam) or task difficulty (the exam was really easy). This theory suggests that how we attribute success and failure is a key factor in learner motivation. According to the theory high-achieving learners believe that their success is due to internal factors: ability and effort. This belief in their responsibility for their own success would boost their self-esteem. For these learners, external factors such as bad luck or a difficult task would be the causes attributed to failure and would not, therefore, affect their self-esteem. In turn, attribution theory suggests that low-achieving learners attribute success to external factors such as good luck or an easy task as they do not believe in their own ability or effort. This is significant, as even if they do experience success, according to attribution theory, these learners would not be given a boost to their self-esteem as their success is attributed to external factors rather than confidence in their own ability and effort.

In Carol Dweck's research (2006), the internal factors, ability and effort, have been separated and researched as individual factors. In this way, how people view intelligence, fixed or changeable, and the attribution of success or failure has been studied. Therefore, belief in ability relates to ideas about intelligence being something we are born with, as a fixed entity. Dweck is a professor of psychology at Stanford University and her research has focused on motivation, personality and development, and she has developed attribution theory further. In 2006, her theory of mindsets was published in the book *Mindset: The New Psychology of Success*. Dweck describes two attitudes to learning: fixed mindset and growth mindset. According to Dweck, these two mindsets not only influence our attitude to learning, but also play a significant role in all aspects of our lives.

Learners will typically not be aware of their mindset, but teachers can identify this from observing their behaviour and being mindful of learners' attitudes to learning. Dweck proposes that we can assess a learner's mindset by using the following types of questions:

- Is intelligence something you are born with?
- Is it possible to change your intelligence level?

Fixed Mindset

Learners with a fixed mindset believe that their success is due to an innate ability. These learners thrive on success as confirmation of their intelligence, but fear of failure means that they are vulnerable to failure and therefore less willing to undertake more challenging tasks as making a mistake would reflect badly on their intelligence. In this instance, these learners would try to avoid a task if they fear failure and/or showing themselves up, and would simply give up. Of course, this is likely to manifest itself as disruptive behaviour in a learning environment.

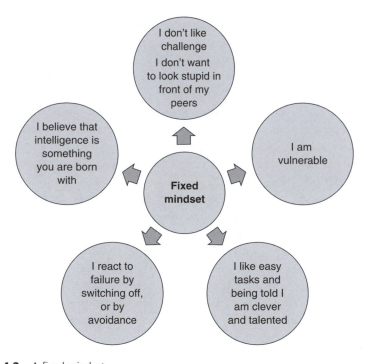

Figure 4.2 A fixed mindset

Source: Adapted from Dweck (2006)

Growth Mindset

Growth mindset learners attribute their success to hard work and effort. What is important with this attitude to learning is that from research, Dweck has found that these learners do not fear failure, or making mistakes, instead they see that this part of the process of learning and recognise that through effort, and perseverance, they can improve, and they recognise that mistakes, challenges and sometimes even failure are all part of learning. Ultimately, they have self-belief and resilience.

Figure 4.3 A growth mindset

Source: Adapted from Dweck (2006)

Activity 4.2

- Think of a few questions that you could use in an induction session with a group of new learners that would help you determine whether your learners have a growth or fixed mindset.

Mindsets and Praise

Dweck has also carried out research into the use of praise and warns how this can reflect a fixed or growth mindset view of intelligence. Teachers give feedback, routinely in the form of verbal praise, to learners and this sends messages about their intelligence that affect learners' self-concept, which includes self-esteem. Creating situations where learners can always succeed and then praising their success has been misleadingly thought to encourage self-esteem. According to Dweck, this is not the case, since all that this does is to reinforce the idea that their success is attributable to their innate intelligence. Dweck also asserts that learners with a fixed mindset will consider a challenging task a shortcoming in their level of intelligence.

Dweck and Mueller (1998) carried out a research study into the use of praise for intelligence, and its effects, with over 400 participants. They provided a range of tasks and praised intelligence on successful completion with a third of participants; another third were praised for their effort; and the other third were praised on their performance but without any indication as to why. Researchers then gave the participants a choice of tasks, a challenging one or an easier one. They found that the majority of those who had been praised for their intelligence chose a less challenging task. In the final part of the research, participants were all given challenging tasks. Those who had been praised for their intelligence, quickly lost confidence and motivation; whereas those who had been praised for effort persevered in the face of challenge, and maintained their motivation and confidence.

Dweck (2006) has repeated a research trial with undergraduates and found similar results, but importantly her research concludes that learners' beliefs about their ability can be influenced by the messages they receive about their learning, so their beliefs are not irreversible.

Activity 4.3

- Reflect on the praise you give your learners. Do you praise effort or intelligence?

Developing a Growth Mindset Learning Environment

Dweck suggests that teachers should focus on the following aspects of learning in order to modify learners' beliefs about their ability and to develop and/or sustain growth mindsets in a learning environment:

- Instil the belief that all learners have the potential to learn and succeed
- Learning is challenging, and sometimes we make mistakes, but that is all part of learning
- Help learners develop strategies to overcome difficulties and challenges. Reinforce the idea that learning requires effort

Activity 4.4

- What do you do to develop learners' self-belief and to foster growth mindsets in a learning environment?

These are some ways in which you can help to develop learners' self-belief:

- Believe in all your learners
- Create a 'can-do' ethos
- Make a safe space for learners to make mistakes
- Ensure that learners value their learning – giving them more autonomy in tasks will help to develop this
- Foster opportunities for learners to overcome challenges
- Help learners to develop resilience by helping them develop different strategies to approach tasks
- Praise effort, as effort builds resilience and ultimately success

The real challenge with learners with a fixed mindset is developing an attitude where they appreciate that learning is rewarding, that it is worth the effort. This may take time with some learners, but it is possible to persuade them that learning is worth the effort.

Creating a 'Can-Do' Ethos

There is a tendency to praise ability as it has been believed to boost self-esteem and motivate learners. The use of praise after success has been well-researched, but there has been little focus on how learners cope with challenges and failure in their learning. Dweck has shown that person-orientated praise needs to be avoided as it limits what individual learners believe about themselves, can lead to demotivation and disengagement if learners experience challenges or failure, and essentially does not help learners to develop resilience in their learning. It is important to encourage learners to think of the brain as a muscle that gets stronger the more we use it.

Using praise is a powerful way to communicate a 'can-do' ethos, but it needs to focus on the process, not the person:

- Give process-orientated praise (effort)

For example, 'You have made a really detailed essay plan, well done, keep up the good work.'

- Use task-orientated praise

For example, 'I like the way you have highlighted the key words on your diagram.'

Both of these types of praise avoid inferring that success comes from personal attributes but instead focuses on the effort and/or strategies needed to succeed:

self-esteem is something students experience when they engage in something fully and use their resources fully, as when they are striving to master something new. It is not an object we can hand them on a silver platter, but it is something we can facilitate, and by doing so we help ensure that challenge and effort are things that enhance self-esteem, not threats to the ego. (Dweck, 2000: 129)

Other incentives could include:

- Role models – it can be inspiring for learners to see other learners who have succeeded and to talk about their learning experiences on a course, and how they overcame any challenges
- Peer tutoring – this is an effective way to use peers to show that intelligence and ability can be developed through effort and using effective strategies
- Self- and peer-assessment – this helps to show learners that success is determined by what they do; that they can identify areas they need to work on and through effort can improve

---

Activity 4.5

- Reflect on your own attitudes and beliefs about learners and their potential to achieve.
- Have you ever thought that a learner was not able to achieve?
- What were the circumstances?
- What was your approach at the time?
- What was your institution's approach?
- What happened to the learner?
- Could anything have been done differently to help this learner achieve?

Mindset Issues for Inclusive Practice

To develop practice that is truly inclusive it is important to move away from fixed notions of intelligence, and teaching and learning approaches that are based on assumptions of a normal distribution of intelligence. As Florian asserts: 'a pedagogy that is inclusive of all learners is based on principles of teaching and learning that reject deficit views of difference and deterministic views of ability but see differences as part of the human condition' (2009: 49). Most organisation of teaching and learning within the education system currently is based on a hierarchy of ability, which constitutes practices based on judgements about inherent potential and undermines the reality of constructing and sustaining inclusion. This also relates to the discussion on teacher expectations in Chapter 3, where it was shown how assumptions about ability can be founded on socioeconomic status, ethnicity, language and gender. According to Slee:

> inclusive education is an ambitious project given that we seem to be commencing with an oxymoron as an organizing concept. Schools were never really meant for everyone. The more they have been called upon to include the masses, the more they have developed the technologies of exclusion and containment. (2001: 172)

Resilience

When faced with difficulty, fixed mindset learners will give up because they perceive it is a deficit in their own ability, or intelligence. Meanwhile, growth mindset learners will view difficulty as a challenge and not fear to try, as they do not fear failure. Instead they see mistakes as part of learning, as opportunities to learn and develop.

If we are to stretch and challenge learners, then they need to be resilient so they can cope with the risks of being taken out of their comfort zone. Learners will push back if they feel vulnerable, but resilience is an important life skill because we all have to face difficult and challenging situations at some point in our lives. Jarvis (1987) refers to this as disjuncture, when learners are put in a position where they have to discover a new way of doing something or thinking about something, i.e. learn. From this perspective, learning is defined as:

> the combination of processes throughout a lifetime whereby the whole person – body (genetic, physical and biological) and mind (knowledge, skills, attitudes, values, emotions, beliefs and senses) – experiences social situations, the perceived content of which is then transformed cognitively, emotively or practically (or through any combination) and integrated into the individual person's biography resulting in a continually changing (or more experienced) person. (Jarvis, 2006: 134)

This perspective of learning as transformative will be discussed in more detail in Chapter 9.

Activity 4.6

- Reflect on a time when you have taken learners out of their comfort zone. What happened? What would you do differently?
- How could you take your learning from this experience and develop resilience in your learners?

Disengagement

What has been discussed in this chapter relates to what was described in Chapter 3 as the long-standing history of grouping learners by ability, transmitting messages about intelligence being fixed, and therefore setting limits on potential achievement.

Disengagement from learning, and education, in the UK has been a persistent problem; young people who are not in education, employment or training are referred to as NEET. In 2014, in the second quarter, 955,000 people aged 16–24 were NEET, being approximately 13 per cent of people in this age group (ONS, 2014). There are a multitude of reasons for this situation, however it is significant that 'disengagement from full-time education, depending on how it is defined and measured can account for up to one-third or one-fifth of the total population of 14-16 year olds' (Stamou et al, 2014). This trend seems to begin as learners embark on their Key Stage 4 qualifications, namely GCSEs, at 14 years old. So, it is important to be aware of some of the attitudes to learning, and education, that learners bring with them, most significantly a state of indifference about learning largely attributable to previous negative experiences of education. The rationale behind raising the participation age in education, training or employment from 16 to 18 years old was to increase post-16 options and provide opportunities for young people's prospects for progression into further learning or employment.

Activity 4.7

- Think of a disengaged learner you have worked with. What aspects of a fixed mindset could you now recognise? What might you do differently now when working with disengaged learners?

Conclusion

This chapter is by no means suggesting that teachers are intentionally complicit in quashing learners' self-belief. Attitudes stem from a deeply embedded cultural belief about intelligence as a fixed trait, and this has resulted in endemic ability grouping within education which transmits powerful messages to learners about what the limitations to their achievement and aspirations are at an alarmingly early age. These are well-established structural factors in education that equally dictate the conditions in which teachers teach, and learners learn, respectively. The challenge for many teachers in FE is to change learners' perceptions about learning, to instil in them that learning is worth the effort, and that they 'can do it'. As Dweck (2000) suggests, self-esteem is not something we can give learners, we can only create the conditions in which learners can experience themselves positively, and in this way help them build a more positive self-concept. For many learners in FE, changing maladaptive beliefs about themselves and associated feelings of low self-esteem will be a process that will take time and requires opportunities for them to develop confidence and resilience in themselves and ultimately their learning. Part of this process is to stop defining educational difficulties as difficulties within individual learners, and this necessitates a cultural shift in teachers' perceptions about how we interpret ability and learning.

Activity 4.8

- What aspects of this chapter have been most helpful in raising your awareness about some of the issues that can affect learning, learners' attitudes to learning and their success?
- What aspects of your practice will you change in light of the discussions in this chapter?

Action Research Link

- What aspects of this chapter have been of interest in relation to your own practice and learners?
- This could be an interesting area for an action research project. See Chapter 11 for further guidance and support on action research.

Suggested Further Reading

Dweck, C. (2000) *Self-Theories: Their Role in Motivation, Personality, and Development*. Philadelphia, PA: Psychology Press.

Dweck, C. (2006) *Mindset: The New Psychology of Success*. New York: Random House.

CHAPTER 5

CHALLENGES TO EQUALITY AND DIVERSITY

Educational inequality will be examined using secondary research to explore some of the challenges in developing inclusive teaching and learning practice despite policy development in this area. Readers will be encouraged to reflect on aspects of their own inclusive practice in relation to Shulman's (2004) notion of three apprenticeships (knowing, doing and believing) and the future development of their inclusive practice.

The purpose of this chapter is to further examine the complexity of equality and diversity taking into account issues such as radicalisation and social constructionism.

This chapter will cover the following:

- Educational inequality
- Inclusive practice
- A critique of differentiation
- Radicalisation
- Social constructionism

Introduction

Educational inequality is a persistent issue in education in the UK, the USA and other countries in Western Europe. According to the data from the Department for Education, only 52.6 per cent of school-leavers achieved 5 GCSEs grade A*–C including English and maths in 2014 (DfE, 2014c). This in itself is reprehensible. If we examine further the data provided by the DfE, we find evidence for the reproduction of inequality within the education system. Educational inequality directly affects employment opportunities and earning potential. It also contributes to intergenerational inequality, and so becomes a source of inequality in its own right. However, if we eradicated educational inequality, it is doubtful that we would eradicate inequality in society. The data persistently show that for eligibility for free school meals (FSM), ethnicity, gender and learners with disabilities or learning difficulties all contribute to disparities in educational achievement. Although there has been some improvement in the outcomes for young people with these characteristics, the data repeatedly show that many slip through the net. Generally, these achievement gaps can be presented as girls outperforming boys; the lowest performing ethnic groups are Pakistani, white British from low-income backgrounds and Black Caribbean, although those from any black background remain the lowest performing major ethnic group; the substantial differential gap for learners with disabilities or learning difficulties; and those on FSM (Ofsted, 2013a). The most significant common denominator in achievement, however, seems to be socioeconomic status rather than ethnicity. Clearly, these disparities persist with young people as they enter FE, and often with adults who enter FE, which is seen by many as a second chance at education, but FE importantly also increasingly offers an alternative to the traditional academic routes.

Inclusive Practice in FE

Inclusion has become an all-embracing concept, whereas previously it was originally associated with provision for learners with disabilities or learning difficulties. The Tomlinson Report (1996a) found that learners with disabilities or learning difficulties were underachieving in FE and this report became an important move towards access to the wider curriculum and mainstream opportunities for such learners in FE. Although the Tomlinson Report was an important aspect of the widening participation agenda in FE, the term 'widening participation' was primarily reserved for learners from other under-represented and disadvantaged groups as detailed in the

Kennedy Report (1997). This report was published at a time when funding was directly linked to the successful achievement of qualifications that had been in place since the Incorporation of the FE sector following the 1992 Further and Higher Education Act. There was concern that initiatives to engage more people from working-class backgrounds, more disaffected young people, more women, more people from ethnic minority groups, refugees and ex-offenders were losing momentum due to the unyielding financial implications of the funding system which did not take into account the challenges that learners from these groups often faced when returning to education and which consequently impacted on outcomes. This per-qualification funding was criticised in the Wolf Report (2011), which recommended funding per programme and a given level of funding per learner that should follow the learner.

Tomlinson was adamant that inclusive learning was not synonymous with integration into mainstream provision, and stressed the importance of active engagement in the learning process and defined inclusive learning as: 'the greatest degree of match or fit between the individual learner's requirements and the provision that is made for them' (Tomlinson, 1996a: 2). However, Tomlinson also states that:

> a key element in reconceptualising provision for students with learning dif-ficulties is the recognition that their needs are cognate with those of all learners. Ensuring that all pupils or students make progress demands that teachers do not treat them uniformly, but differentiate their approaches. (1996b: 5)

This recognises that teaching and learning must be differentiated to accom-modate the previous experiences and needs of all learners, not just those with disabilities or learning difficulties. This has had a significant impact on the creation of an inclusive learning culture within FE. Following this report, government policy focused heavily on social cohesion and the role of FE in its promotion, in addition to economic regeneration, and FE became pivotal in supporting the achievement of these interconnected ambitions:

> Education has always been a source of social vitality and the more people we can include in the community of learning, the greater the benefits to us all. The very process involves interaction between people; it is the means by which the values and wisdom of a society are shared and transmitted across the generations. Education strengthens the ties which bind people, takes out the fear of difference and encourages tolerance. It helps people to see what makes the world tick and the ways in which they, individually and together, can make a difference. It is the likeliest means of creating a modern, well-skilled workforce, reducing levels of crime, and creating participating citizens. (Kennedy, 1997: 6–7)

Activity 5.1

- Is there evidence that exclusionary practices exist within your institution?
- To what extent is provision discrete and inclusive?

Inclusion in Practice

A key issue when considering inclusive practice is how we understand the concept of intelligence in relation to the learners with whom we work. One aspect of the notion of fixed intelligence that needs to be raised is that it tends to have a deficit view of learners with different abilities. This is of particular concern for learners with disabilities or learning difficulties. Quite often, when praise is being given, those who have perhaps worked the hardest and put in the most effort are overlooked. This may be because the task has not been completed as successfully as the teacher would expect, but nonetheless considerable effort has been put in. Perhaps learners with a learning disability or difficulty, or those with a perceived difficulty in learning, are the most vulnerable learners to deterministic beliefs about ability which sees individual differences as a deficit. This has significant implications for inclusive education, and inclusive approaches used by teachers in the learning environment. This is an area where policy initiatives in FE are incongruent; the drive for quality and raised standards counters policies of social inclusion and equity. As performativity and the policy-driven obsession with educational statistics and testing demand more and more audit trails as measures of quality, so educational inequalities become heightened.

Shulman (2004) discusses the need to ensure that induction into all the professions has three essential elements. He refers to these as the 'three apprenticeships'. The first is the 'apprenticeship of the head', which means the cognitive knowledge and theoretical basis of the profession. The second is the 'apprenticeship of the hand', which includes the technical and practical skills that are required to carry out the essential tasks of the profession. The third is the 'apprenticeship of the heart', meaning the ethical and moral dimensions, the attitudes and beliefs that are fundamental to each particular profession and its practices.

According to Rouse (2007), developing inclusive practice is about knowing, doing and thinking. Rouse has used Shulman's framework to come up with the essential components of inclusive practice focused on disability or learning difficulty. I have added equality and diversity to ensure a holistic framework of inclusive practice which underpins good practice in valuing individuality and which enables learners to be fully involved in their learning.

Knowing includes:

- Teaching strategies
- Disability and special educational needs
- Different cultures and backgrounds and individual differences of learners
- Learning theories
- Curriculum and subject knowledge
- Classroom institution and management
- Where to access support
- Identifying and assessing learning difficulties
- Assessing and monitoring learners' progress
- The legislative and policy context (principally the Equality Act, 2010)

 Activity 5.2

- How much training and support have you had, and do you now receive, in your work with learners with disabilities or learning difficulties?
- The first step of inclusion is to acknowledge and value differences, but not to lose sight of commonality. How do you ensure that this is part of your inclusive practice?
- What aspects of 'knowing' can you identify as areas for improvement in your current inclusive practice?

Doing includes:

- Using knowledge in practice – to promote individuality, to support individual needs and to challenge prejudice
- Moving beyond reflective practice – an understanding of the wider context: its social dimensions and political functions to move beyond individualised versions of reflective practice
- Using evidence to improve practice such as current and previous research or undertaking action research
- Working collaboratively with colleagues
- Becoming an 'activist' professional which is characterised by expertise, altruism and autonomy (Sachs, 2000). An activist professional identity is in response to teachers being deskilled and their workloads increased and involves being committed to taking action on behalf of learners, especially disadvantaged learners. (See Chapter 2 for more on this).

Activity 5.3

- Evaluate how you work with other colleagues to support learners' individual needs.
- What could potentially improve cross-curricula support for learners?
- What aspects of 'doing' can you identify as areas for improvement in your current inclusive practice?

Believing includes:

- That all learners are worth educating
- That all learners can achieve
- That you have the capacity to make a difference to learners' lives
- That all of the components of knowing, doing and believing are part and parcel of your role and your responsibility as a teacher and not only a task for specialists

Activity 5.4

- In what ways can you make a difference to learners' lives?
- Do you consider that all learners can achieve? Justify your answer.

The learners we work with in FE come from a vast array of backgrounds and many face significant challenges in their learning, be it from previous negative educational experiences or factors stemming from social, emotional, medical, psychological or behavioural needs. Above all, the time and energy we invest in developing positive relationships with all our learners can help them to overcome negative perceptions of themselves and is such a vital step towards helping them to develop a positive self-concept, which can be a life-changing experience for learners. Often the managerial systems we work in seem to operate against the culture of inclusion and equality, but we must continue to believe in all our learners and do all the invisible work that makes such a difference to so many learners in FE.

Differentiation

Although differentiation is a principled notion and an essential component of inclusion, it is complex and often confusing for teachers to implement.

Its pursuit of accommodating the differences, and resultant needs, of every individual learner is a huge challenge. It does not just encompass learners with learning difficulties or disabilities, but is also about all the differences among our learners, some more visible than others. Ways in which teachers differentiate to meet the individual needs of learners typically involve adapting curriculum material and teaching approaches, including activities and assessment methods. Simply stated: these are the content, process and product of learning.

With regards to content, differentiation is quite often interpreted as adding on a few extra activities for the more able or confident learners to complete in the form of extension activities. Alternatively, it may involve reducing or simplifying the content for some learners. However, this sets up a premise for lowering expectations for some and not others, which reinforces the notion of fixed intelligence and low expectations, and can communicate messages of potential which limit learners and which can contribute to self-fulfilling prophecies (see Chapter 3 for further discussion on this). In addition, these differential expectations may also lead to some learners feeling resentful about being given extra work and to others feeling 'different', which can result in tensions between learners, and between teachers and learners. The contentious issue with differentiated content is one of equity in its deficit view of reducing content for those deemed less able, and challenging those deemed more able, which only contributes to these differences rather than closing the gap. To avoid perpetuating inequality, differentiation must be focused more on processes than on content, in this way the same content can be covered by all learners, but with differentiated levels of support. In order to achieve this, the teacher needs to create a supportive and collaborative learning environment.

Another popular route is 'learning styles' which have spread like an epidemic to differentiate processes of learning. Learning styles are nothing short of a pseudo-scientific attempt to address a perceived deficit in differential learning outcomes for individual learners, and a tokenistic attempt at individualised learning to improve attainment and retention which panders to the commodification of education where teachers are individually accountable for performance indicators (Coffield et al., 2004; Coffield, 2005). In addition, their evidence base is anecdotal, meaning that there is no scientific evidence to support their impact on teaching and learning and research by Hattie (2008) has shown their impact on learning is negligible. Nonetheless, their adoption in education is ubiquitous. The lack of a strong evidence base for learning styles aside, the contention with learning styles also resides in how different types of learning and knowledge are valued and promoted in the education system:

> A high value has been put on knowledge, on academic learning, and on ways of studying which emphasize linear and logical thought. 'Approved' academic knowledge has a higher status than experience. Verbal, and especially written, communication has a higher status than, say, the visual medium. (Smith, 2002: 64)

In my own practice with trainee teachers, we explore how learning styles can simply be a tool to start the discussion about how we learn, perhaps as an induction activity, to promote metacognition which is the most empowering learning of all (see Appendix 1 for questions compiled by Coffield, 2008, which can usefully progress the discussion on how we learn).

Differentiating the processes of teaching and learning is probably the most effective and most used approach by teachers. In this way, they can differentiate how they communicate and interact with learners. This involves how learners are grouped, the levels of support given to individual learners, adapting teaching approaches, using different ways to explain key concepts or information, giving more individualised examples to help learners contextualise key ideas, differentiated questioning and individualised feedback and encouragement.

Differentiation by product is something I explore with trainee teachers. Some teachers have heard of a 'must, should, could' approach to planning learning outcomes, but again this perpetuates a deficit view of ability and low expectations, and makes differences between learners more pronounced. Learners will always complete tasks differently, and to varying degrees of quality and quantity. So, expecting less from some learners and more from other learners in assessment again raises issues related to differential expectations and a self-fulfilling prophecy. If we expect less then we are very likely to get less. We need to be encouraging and supporting all learners to do more, not less. As Hattie surmises in his book *Visible Learning*, 'any school with the motto "do your best" should immediately change it to "face your challenges" or "strive to the highest" … anything you do can be defined as your best' (2008: 164).

Planning outcomes that promote diversity and variations in the way that learners can demonstrate their learning means that all learners work towards the same goal, and it is less divisive. This approach to differentiation is where the same activity leads to open-ended, or divergent, responses, and in this way differentiates the learning outcome. It requires teacher intervention, namely facilitation, to assess and extract key learning. One way in which this can be achieved is by using expressive objectives which were developed by Eisner (1967), who was a student of Bloom's and continued to work on his taxonomy, in particular the cognitive domain and higher-order thinking. By using verbs such as 'interpret', 'develop', 'examine' and 'discuss', we plan learning experiences which afford opportunities for meanings to be more personalised, and to produce outcomes that are divergent:

> Consequently the evaluative task in this situation is not one of applying a common standard to the products produced but one of reflecting upon what has been produced in order to reveal its uniqueness and significance. In the expressive context, the product is likely to be as much of a surprise to the maker as it is for the teacher who encounters it. (Eisner, 1967: 18)

Activity 5.5

Reflect on your own teaching:

- What difficulties do you experience with differentiation?
- How do you differentiate – content, process, or product?
- Can you think of any ways in which you could develop this aspect of your practice?

This discussion is not intended to disagree with the concept of differentiation or to suggest that differentiation is something to be avoided. Clearly we must take the diverse needs of our learners into account to enable them to succeed, and especially to make reasonable adjustments wherever necessary and possible. Instead, we should question the pragmatics of differentiation and whether we can ever really take all individual needs into account in teaching, learning and assessment. This emphasis on the individual learner is to be celebrated, but also seems to contrast with the current instrumental view of education where all learners are assessed against the same rubric. Perhaps a better term to define the concept of differentiation is 'scaffolding'; this can be defined as the use of strategic support during the learning process tailored to meet individual needs which is then gradually removed so learners become more independent in their learning. The focus is therefore more on the process and more intuitive. Planning for differentiation can also mean that teachers presuppose what their learners will learn based on assumptions about their ability. However, much of differentiated learning happens as a lesson evolves and the use of questioning and discursive approaches are key tools in successful differentiation.

Radicalisation

Now, very much part of our remit in FE is to be vigilant about radicalisation. This is clearly a safeguarding issue, but it also raises some important issues about the surveillance of our learners, and also about how we interact with learners as professionals. Radicalisation is all too often associated with Islam, especially in the media. However, we need to be aware of far-right fundamentalism, particularly prevalent in current debates about immigration both nationally and in the majority of Western countries.

Radicalisation is a process of change: a personal and political transformation. The most widely used definition of radicalisation is that is it a: 'social and psychological process of incrementally experienced commitment to extremist political or religious ideology' (Horgan, 2009: 152), and the government definition for it is: 'the process by which a person comes to support terrorism and forms of extremism leading to terrorism' (Home Office, 2011: 108). However, it is important to remember that 'radical' is not synonymous with 'terrorist': throughout history there have been radicals. A radical wishes to transform the existing social order, and sometimes this necessitates using methods that are deemed extreme, anti-social and illegal. Being radical can lead to positive social change, such as the changes campaigned for by Martin Luther King and the Civil Rights movement, so it is important to remember the nuances of radicalisation (Lentini, 2009).

Radicalisation is a gradual process, a progression through distinct stages, which does not happen easily or quickly (Horgan, 2005; Silber and Bhatt, 2007). A study carried out by the New York Police Department (NYPD) shows that the radicalisation process takes on average two to three years, whereas with the Madrid bombers the process of radicalisation took over ten years (Silber and Bhatt, 2007).

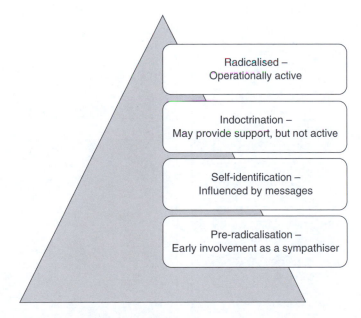

Figure 5.1 A model of the radicalisation process

Source: Adapted from Silber and Bhatt (2007)

Key findings from a classified MI5 research document (reported by *The Guardian*) concludes that there is no single pathway to radicalisation, and no typical profile of a terrorist, in fact terrorists are often marked by being 'demographically unremarkable' (Travis, 2008). As we know from recent attacks, the significant threat of terrorism in the UK is home-grown, potentially from a 'lone wolf', and the pathways to radicalisation and terrorism are multiple and diverse. However, according to Moghaddam (2005), despite the lack of commonality, these pathways will involve the following: individual (dispositional factors), institutional (situational factors) and environmental (sociocultural, economic and political forces). So, whilst the motives for radicalisation are varied, there are some common themes emerging from research:

- Perceptions of deprivation and injustice
- Personal grievance
- Political grievance
- Crisis of personal identity in Western society, and globalisation
- Personal discrimination (Cole and Cole, 2009)

It is possible to further explore these themes as push and pull factors, as shown in Figure 5.2.

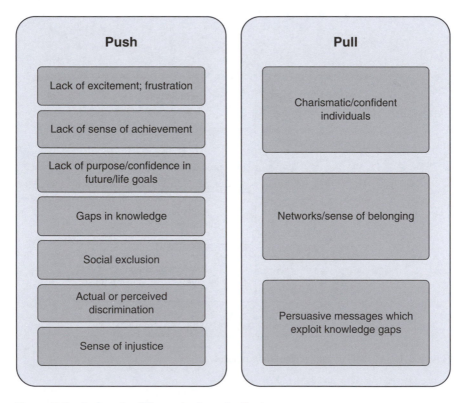

Figure 5.2   Push and pull factors in the radicalisation process

Source: Adapted from Silber and Bhatt (2007)

As teachers, we need to be aware of potential signs of vulnerability, as we would with any other safeguarding concern. These signs could include:

- Emotional vulnerability – feelings of anger, alienation, disenfranchisement, marginalisation
- Dissatisfaction/disillusionment with mainstream politics and society
- Identification with victims of 'injustice' or experience of personal victimization (loss of a loved one/racism)
- Belief that violence can be justified
- Religious naivety (Travis, 2008; Horgan, 2008)

Activity 5.6

- Come up with a strategy to create a safe space for dialogue and positive interaction.
- What do you need to do to be able to do this successfully?
- What are the potential challenges to creating a safe space?

One of the keys to creating a safe space for dialogue is to create some ground rules to help deal with conflict and ensure sensitivity to all learners, but also to create a no-blame atmosphere. We need to allow learners to express their thoughts and feelings in their own terms, even if we do not personally agree. Research findings from a large-scale study show that if we do not respect these preconceptions, then learners will disengage from discussions and positive interaction (Bonnell et al., 2011). Once views are aired, as teachers we can begin to challenge and show multiple perspectives, using education, not confrontation.

Some approaches that have been used to facilitate discussions on complex and sensitive issues suggested by Bonnell et al. (ibid.) are:

1. To create some key words, for example:

   'Ouch' acts as shorthand for saying, 'I found that offensive.'

   'Oops' means 'I acknowledge I've caused offence' or 'I take back what I said.'

2. For challenging a learner respectfully, the following DEAL framework has been found useful as an assertive technique to help learners challenge each other safely and respectfully in four clear steps:

   D – Describe the problem

   E – Explain how it makes you feel

   A – Ask them to change their behaviour

   L – Learn from the experience

Activity 5.7

Reflective questions:

- Can you think of an occasion where these techniques may have been helpful to you when dealing with a sensitive issue?
- Can you think of how you could use/adapt these techniques within your own practice?

These techniques are facilitated by learners and encourage respectful challenging, both of which can empower learners, but can also contribute towards maintaining a safe space. Without opportunities for learners to engage in dialogue about issues which affect their lives, and all of us essentially, we cannot begin to deconstruct and challenge the complexity of controversial issues such as extremism. We need to promote discussion where learners can share their views and encounter people who hold different ideas.

Activity 5.8

- What are the potential benefits, and potential challenges, of encouraging learners to critically explore issues?

As Table 5.1 shows, Bonnell et al. (2011) summarise some of the possible impacts of exposing learners to a multiplicity of views and experiences and to engaging them in critical discussion on emotive and often divisive areas.

Table 5.1   The impact of open debate to critically interrogate controversial issues

Potential benefits	Potential challenges
Greater respect for different points of view	Having time in an over-crowded curriculum
Increased readiness to discuss controversial issues	Teachers' willingness due to lack of training; it may take time to feel confident enough to facilitate an open debate on contentious issues
More open-mindedness	Anxiety about causing offence
Increased educational performance as ability to think critically and independently are used in other areas of their learning	Accessibility to relevant expertise that may be able to contribute different perspectives

It is suggested in the research that having open debate, where learners can be exposed to multiple perspectives and engage critically with differing points of views, builds personal resilience. The research further suggests that open debate can help learners to interrogate extremist views and, for example, the myriad of messages on the Internet as claims to truth because they have developed the disposition to critically engage with different world-views and are therefore less likely to endorse a binary world-view (ibid.). Clearly, there is also a link here to social cohesion within our communities, when there has been an overall rise in race, religious and homophobic hate crimes in the UK (CPS, 2008).

Action Research Link

- How confident do you feel to facilitate a discussion on a sensitive topic? How would you deal with an inflammatory, prejudicial or deeply offensive comment?
- Is this an area that could form part of an action research project? Perhaps some continuing professional development (CPD) could help support teachers within your institution to develop the skills needed to facilitate discussions on sensitive topics.

Social Constructionism

From a constructionist perspective, all ways of understanding the world around us are historically and culturally situated. Knowledge is the product of human thought, not external reality, and constructionism attempts to expose how reality is shaped by social forces. This theory 'cautions us to be ever suspicions of our assumptions about how the world appears to be' (Burr, 2015: 3).

If reality is socially constructed, then it can also be deconstructed. Language is an essential resource for constructing different accounts of the world and events. Constructionism has done a lot of work challenging how notions of race, class and gender are products of social forces.

'What we call "race" is not an invention of nature but of our social institutions and practices' (Graves, 2001: 2). This quote aptly encapsulates the theory of social constructionism and the fallacy of race as a genetic component. The fascination with skulls in the eighteenth century, their dimensions and anomalies, created an opportunity for the concept of race to become a reified entity; however, the history of racial classification is the history of white supremacy. The American essayist and novelist James Baldwin, said that there was no such thing as '"whiteness", "blackness" or "race". No one is white before he/she came to America … it took generations and a vast amount of coercion before this became a white country' (cited in Okihiro, 2001: 46).

When the human population was categorised into racial groups by erroneous science, it occurred at a time of colonialism and slavery and the race issue was influenced by the privileged position of white leaders, which evidently motivated how human diversity was studied and hypothesised. The original anthropological categories were Negroid, Caucasoid and Mongoloid. These groupings included people from different regions of the globe and so, in terms of physical characteristics, varied immensely. The terms Negroid and Mongoloid are now defunct due to dubious usage and hence negative connotations. The exception is Caucasian, which if you enjoy your crime dramas you will undoubtedly associate with meaning 'white'. However, when the categorisation was first introduced, it comprised people from Northern Europe, Southern Europe and even further into parts of Northern Africa, the Middle East and Northern India (Blumenbach, 1940 [1795]). This exemplifies how the categorisation has been adapted over time.

When researchers completed the Human Genome Project in April 2003, they confirmed that human beings were 99.9 per cent genetically identical (National Human Genome Research Institute, 2006). By discrediting biological classification, we are then left to explore what social and historical factors lead to the development of race as we know it today, and, if race has no biological basis, then racist thinking and practices become an ideology, so, we can say that race is a social construct.

So, when we examine inequality between different groups in society, then we must also examine the political and social contexts within which these inequalities came about and exist. And, as Graves goes on to argue, because we now have the evidence that no biological races exist in the human species, this does not mean that socially defined racism has not existed, and does not still, exist (2001: 197).

    Activity 5.9

- Reflect on how gender, class and disability have been socially constructed in different historical and cultural contexts.
- What assumptions, norms and values created these realities? In so doing, you will see how context-dependent these constructions are.

Conclusion

This chapter has covered a lot of ground, and has presented some opportunities for you to reflect on your own inclusive practice, as well as provoking thought about some broader issues regarding equality and diversity. Education clearly has a role to play in promoting the social values of equity and justice in society but there are considerable structural challenges, not only within wider society, but within education itself. Sometimes, it may feel as if the social goals of education are at odds with institutional processes, with market values taking precedence over social values of equity and justice. However, this is no reason for us to be complacent, particularly when we are faced with widening inequality in an age of extremes, where political rhetoric espouses a 'survival of the fittest' mantra within a capitalist system that rewards the few at the expense of the masses.

Suggested Further Reading

Bonnell, J., Copestake, P., Kerr, D., Passy, R., Reed, C., Salter, R., Sarwar, S. and Sheikh, S. (2010) *Teaching Approaches to Help Build Resilience to Extremism among Young People*. London: DfE.

Burr, V. (2015) *Social Constructionism* (3rd edn). Hove: Routledge.

Christmann, K. (2012) *Preventing Religious Radicalisation and Violent Extremism: A Systematic Review of the Research Evidence*. London: Youth Justice Board for England and Wales.

Coffield, F. (2008) *Just Suppose Teaching and Learning became the First Priority ….* London: Learning and Skills Network.

Graves Jr., J.L. (2001) *The Emperor's New Clothes: Biological Theories of Race at the Millennium*. London: Rutgers University Press.

Horgan, J. (2008) 'From profiles to pathways and roots to routes: Perspectives from psychology on radicalization into terrorism', *Annals of the American Academy of Political and Social Science*, 618 (1), pp. 80–94.

CHAPTER 6

QUALITY IMPROVEMENT, OBSERVATION AND PROFESSIONAL DEVELOPMENT

This chapter will concentrate on quality improvement, observation and professional development. Issues stemming from deregulation regarding Continuing Professional Practice (CPD) and Initial Teacher Education (ITE) provision for new teachers will be discussed. The role of observation in monitoring and enhancing performance will be examined. I will also explore teachers' experiences of grading, reliability and potential inequality in observation.

This chapter will cover the following:

- A discussion on Total Quality Management (TQM)
- A critique of the practice of formal graded lesson observations
- An evaluation of ITE and CPD since deregulation

Introduction

Neoliberalism can be well summarised by the words of Prime Minister Margaret Thatcher, when she famously declared in 1987 that: 'there's no such thing as society'. Neoliberalism is underpinned by a market-orientated ideology, and marked the rise of individualism alongside the fall of community and the notion of social good. The contradictory emphases on accountability and autonomy, which characterises neoliberal reform, have had a considerable impact on the education system in the UK since the 1980s, and continues to do so today. The Office for Standards in Education (Ofsted) was created as a government agency to regulate and monitor the quality of provision across all education sectors in the UK. Following Incorporation of the Further Education sector in 1992, decentralisation and deregulation, which are the cornerstones of neoliberalism, were coupled with increased state management from a distance in the form of inspection to hold individual institutions to account, top-down policy-making and stringent funding systems. Ball (2008: 43–4) argues that deregulation is in fact reregulation: 'the use of devolution and autonomy as "freedoms" set within constraints and requirements of "performance" and "profitability"'. This has fundamentally changed the education system in the UK as it introduced a new form of management, managerialism, into institutions with performativity as its core value to govern teaching and learning. Managerialism is a neoliberal approach to management which institutionalises market-led principles into the quality improvment systems of institutions. Performativity has created a target-driven culture; a culture of standards and audit in order to monitor the effectiveness of provision at an institutional level and an individual level. Ofsted makes judgements about how effectively institutions are performing and subsequently affect governance within institutions, namely in the form of performance management systems which determine the day-to-day practices of teachers, learners and managers. Ball (2003) writes about performativity as a mechanism to determine the productivity, quality and value of teachers and institutions, and the sense of terror that has been created as a result of neoliberal reform in education. In FE, quality-driven reform has been coupled with social inclusion policies to address inequalities in education and wider society. Equity and neoliberal reform create tensions which institutions, and their teachers, need to navigate to ensure that policy implementation upholds the equity ideal which runs deep in the veins of FE. The danger is that if the output of education is all that is valued, then those learners who do not meet the standards become devalued, and these tend to be learners with learning difficulties and other marginalised groups (Tomlinson, 2005).

This is not an outright denunciation of inspection. Inspection has a place in verifying self-assessment as a means of quality management and supporting institutions to be drivers of their own improvement, but current Ofsted inspection practice and grading judgements have recently been called into question and challenged by institutions, teachers and academics alike. The validity and reliability of observations for assessing the quality of teaching and learning is one key area of recent criticism.

Coe (2014) researched the accuracy of Ofsted grading judgements. He found that if a lesson is judged 'Outstanding' by one Ofsted inspector, the probability that a second inspector would give a different judgement is between 51 and 78 per cent. Furthermore, in reports, Ofsted have made specific comments on teaching styles on which judgements were based, despite assurances that Ofsted has no preferred teaching style. In their report, *Watching the Watchmen: The Future of School Inspections in England* (2014), Waldegrave and Simons went as far as to recommend the elimination of lesson observations as part of the fundamental redesign of how Ofsted conduct inspections. This, however, has not happened; the only change to the Common Inspection Framework (CIF) 2015 is the removal of individual grades for lesson observations.

Quality Improvement

Since decentralisation, accountability has been one of the key mechanisms to control individual institutions and this has been achieved through the implementation of quality improvement systems. Quality improvement is often defined as a systematic approach to improving quality. Total Quality Management (TQM) is a philosophy for managing an institution in a way which enables it to meet stakeholder needs and expectations efficiently and effectively; criteria favoured by managerialism. It is not a system, more of an approach to management, a way of thinking about quality and success which employs systems to achieve this end. One of the central tenets of TQM is the notion of continuous improvement. According to its proponents, adopting the TQM philosophy will:

- Make an institution more competitive
- Establish a new culture which will enable growth and longevity
- Provide a working environment in which everyone can succeed
- Reduce stress, waste and friction
- Build teams, partnerships and cooperation (Chartered Quality Institute, 2015)

> TQM as a management model, with its emphasis on leadership, strategy, teamwork, rigorous analysis and self-assessment, has a universal message. And it has always been a philosophy for the long haul rather than a short-term fix. (Sallis, 2005: xi)

More than ever before, a long-term vision is certainly now required in our world of rapid change in order to ensure sustainability. However, in a sense, this is a misnomer: in a sector that changes very rapidly, it begs the question as to whether it is really possible to have a long-term vision when policy reforms are so short-lived and so many changes within institutions are reactive as a result of such short-termism. Nevertheless, the introduction of TQM into the education system is probably the most significant change to professional practices and what it means to be a teacher. The value of teachers is measured by their individual accountability, and this creates a climate where self-regulation complements other regulatory mechanisms such as inspections and lesson observations.

Within managerialism, the cycle of continuous improvement, and its auditing through appraisals, lesson observations and performance indicators compel individual commitment towards its philosophy and the rewards and sanctions of the system ensures adherence to it. This system of management prioritises the knowledge of policy-makers and auditors, rather than the expertise of the professional teacher. This exerts external pressure on teachers, which is internalised as professional responsibility and can devalue their sense of self as it disregards their own personal values and professional knowledge in favour of auditable commodities in pursuit of economy, efficiency and effectiveness.

Alongside the development of managerialism has been the ascendancy of evidence-based practice in education (Hattie, 2008; Marzano et al., 2001). Managerialism is based on the principle that professional practice:

> should take the form of specifying goals explicitly, selecting strategies for achieving them on the basis of objective evidence about their effectiveness, and then measuring outcomes in order to assess their degree of success (thereby providing the knowledge required for improving future performance). (Hammersley, 2004: 137)

In this way it is clear to see that evidence-based practice, which aims to find the best possible input-output equation, neatly fits into the managerialist approach, but which Hammersley critiques as a misleading conception of the nature of professional practice.

Activity 6.1

- Make a list of the performance management systems in place to address quality improvement within your own institution.
- What are their strengths and weaknesses?
- Can you think of any situations where your professional knowledge has been compromised or overridden by performance management systems within your own institution?

Graded Observation of Teaching and Learning

I see the conceptualisation of the ideal type of teacher, of a good or outstanding teacher, as a social construction which suggests that teacher expertise is a fixed construct. Through this construct, effective teaching has become defined by a set of generalised and oversimplified normative practices which attempts to bring order and control over the complexity of teaching and learning. Teaching extends beyond pedagogic skills and knowledge, and beyond subject knowledge, referred to by Schön as knowledge-of-practice (1983). Ofsted have constructed the parameters which frame our conception of a good teacher, and the grading system used by Ofsted (2008) renders this social construction into an auditable commodity within a marketised education system; it also creates a performative mechanism for teachers to be judged and compared by. This conceptualisation of the good teacher is underpinned by the cognitivist assumption that teaching can be normalised and standardised regardless of its context. This instrumental view of teaching and learning within individual institutions has subsequently become the expectation in graded observations and this, therefore, defines what it means to be a good teacher, and shapes teachers' identities. Teachers are becoming increasingly aware of how this view of teaching and learning neglects their own values and sense of self, where transgressions from normative practices are countered with reprimands such as the notion of loyalty to the institution. Furthermore, observation of knowledge-of-practice is underpinned by the cognitivist assumption that there is a causal link between teaching and learning, and that learning is an observable entity. This enables focus on the teacher's role, which is easier to control, rather than identities which are dynamic and unpredictable. However, what I believe is that knowledge-in-practice (Schön, 1983), which is socially situated and distributed, is primarily what constitutes professional expertise. Knowledge-in-practice is characterised by high inference qualities such as enthusiasm, making on-the-spot decisions and motivational strategies such as being inspirational. Grading judgements are often value judgements based on high-inference qualities constitutive of a teacher's knowledge-in-practice, which Schön referred to as 'professional artistry' (1987: 13). Teachers face complex and unpredictable situations in their professional practice and therefore have a specialised body of knowledge-of-practice which results from negotiated experiences of knowledge-in-practice. These are not measurable behaviours and actions, so a reappraisal of how to conceptualise teacher expertise is required.

Activity 6.2

- Can you think of any occasions when your own principles have been compromised by expectations of 'best practice' in an observation within your own institution?

The notion of teacher effectiveness came to the forefront of neoliberal reform in the 1980s when views of teachers as self-serving, monopolistic and radical were embedded in the minds of the general population in order to justify greater state intervention, albeit from a distance, in education (Ozga, 1995). The common sense belief was that teachers should be held to account and were subsequently subjected to increased surveillance. Graded observation of teaching and learning has become a key audit instrument in the neoliberal agenda. Furthermore, a culture of managerialism and performativity was advanced to monitor educational output and teacher performance (Ball, 2003), which initiated compliant teaching in order to meet accountability measures. To legitimise observation as a meaningful activity, the need to define teacher effectiveness became apparent. The current competency-based model for assessing teacher effectiveness was founded on the influential Hay McBer Report (2000). The report was commissioned by the government and used Ofsted categorisations of teacher performance to research teacher effectiveness and subsequently offered a checklist as guidance to judge the quality of teaching. The Hay McBer model of teacher effectiveness is divided into three interrelated dimensions: professional characteristics; teaching skills; and classroom climate. The teaching skills are categorised below:

- High expectations
- Planning
- Methods and strategies
- Behaviour management and discipline
- Time and resource management
- Assessment
- Setting of homework
- Time on task and lesson flow

This conceptualisation of the effective teacher is set within a narrow and mechanistic view of the expertise of teachers and has subsequently become the expectation of institutions when carrying out graded observations of teachers.

The cognitivist perspective sustains a particular set of beliefs about teaching and learning. Principally, cause and effect are assumed, which advances certain pedagogical orientations and prescribes specific criteria for what is considered 'best practice' in the teaching-learning interaction. Neoliberalism has promoted the notion of quality as output, measured by performance indicators such as observation grades and achievement data. Graded observation reinforces the formulaic expectations of 'best practice', resulting in normative teaching and learning practices which are risk-free and individualistic. Neoliberalism has capitalised on the prevailing dominance of the cognitive model of learning which theorises that learning is something that individuals do, that it occurs in their heads and is something they possess. In turn, this has placed considerable emphasis on the conception of learner achievement as a measure of good teaching. In an observation, teaching has become a staged and scripted performance that adheres to the institutional notion of 'best practice'. Compliance and submission in graded observation has become a powerful way to regulate and monitor teachers, yet teachers themselves are complicit in this 'subtle dance of the self' in order to conserve a 'liveable identity' (Wenger, 1998: 41).

Two areas of current 'best practice' promoted by Ofsted and the standardised ITE curriculum and assessment, are briefly critiqued to challenge observation within the cognitivist view of learning; behavioural objectives and learning styles.

Behavioural objectives are pre-determined by the teacher and used to check learning throughout a lesson; learning is thereby deemed to be the direct result of teaching. It is therefore assumed that these outcomes will be met by all learners; in this way, learning is deemed to be measurable and quantifiable. This differs starkly from the sociocultural perspective of learning, which argues that learning is a process of becoming that does not have a definite end and is socially, rather than individually, situated. This process may not necessarily occur within the artificial construct of a 50-minute lesson, or even a three-hour lesson. In reality, when objectives are being measured, typically in question-answer routines, it is more the measurement of how expertly learners perform in the official space of a learning environment rather than a measurement of learning. Bateson (1972, cited in Engestrom, 2001: 138) suggested that: 'students learn the 'hidden curriculum' of what it means to be a student: how to please the teacher, how to pass exams, how to belong in groups'. Observations are therefore an evaluation of the normative practices of teachers in creating expert learners. Hattie (2008) suggests that 70 per cent of what is taught is already known, so, in a graded observation what is being assessed is the teacher's knowledge-of-practice in how to achieve behavioural objectives in a lesson observation: in other words, 'professional expertise is primarily of a *technical* and *instrumental* nature' (Biesta, 2005: 2–3, italics in original).

The pervasive use of learning styles, which teachers feel compelled to demonstrate in their planning and teaching, is underpinned by the cognitivist view that learning is internalized and therefore the possession of individuals. Furthermore, it plays into the hands of managerialism:

> This movement allows its disciples the pretence of student-centred teaching, and it neatly transfers the responsibility of students' failure to learn to tutors, e.g. 'You didn't match your teaching style to their learning styles.' (Coffield, 2008: 32)

Essentially, learning styles are based on the cognitivist presumption that the transmission and absorption of knowledge can be organised through instructional practices and is therefore an unproblematic process (Lave and Wenger, 1991).

Ofsted observes teaching and learning in order to make a judgement about the overall quality of teaching across an institution during an inspection. The inspectors further claim to focus on the impact of teaching on learning, and the impact of ITE on teaching and learning. I argue that in actuality, observers are observing more the high inference qualities of teachers, in how they respectfully relate to their learners, and how they show care and compassion, which are constitutive of their own values and ethical commitment to their learners. These are not attributes that can be measured.

Randle and Brady (1997) found that FE teachers share a commitment to public service values of altruism which are fundamentally opposed to the culture of managerialism, performativity and accountability derived from the neoliberal agenda. The inner dedication of teachers is important here as it is often a conscious action to play the game, whereby teachers comply with the prescribed notions of 'best practice', and in so doing become complicit in maintaining the status quo. Teachers' commitment to their learners commonly renders their participation in the observation process submissive and compliant. Increasingly however, with the marketisation of education, the needs of the learners become subordinate to the financial needs of the institution, and teachers are finding their own values of inner commitment coming into conflict with corporate values of economy, efficiency and effectiveness. In an era of austerity, where finances and physical resources are sparse, the increased bureaucratic workloads which teachers are expected to fulfil, increasingly leave less time for learners. The own values of teachers, consequently, are being conflicted by the mismatch between what they believe and the bureaucratic requirements of their institution. In the past, teachers perhaps had more opportunity to use their professional expertise to exert influence, but the room for manoeuvre is increasingly constrained by economic imperatives and managerial systems which frame the working lives of teachers. The 'audit-managerial monolith' (Ball and Olmedo, 2013: 91) of neoliberalism has changed the stakes, yet these stakes conversely rely on the emotional investment of teachers.

Initial Teacher Education, Professional Development and Deregulation

Initial Teacher Education (ITE) is an essential part of developing a sense of identity as a community of FE professionals. It brings with it a sense of belonging, as well as opportunities for collaboration and support in what can otherwise be quite an isolating working environment. In Chapter 2, I discussed the struggle for FE to have an equitable status with other education sectors in the UK. It also outlined a brief history of the professionalisation of the FE workforce from 2001 to 2007. Despite issues with the complexity of the 2007 regulations, which mandated that all teachers in FE be qualified, it did have a significant impact on the sense of professional identity that teachers developed. ITE provision was central to creating a sense of collegial unity within the profession and it brought professionals together in one space, gave them opportunities to collaborate and share, and fostered positive and supportive working relationships. Furthermore, it gave them a professional knowledge base, thereby supporting their professional autonomy.

The FE sector is unique in many ways. It has long endured a low professional status; the majority of its learners come from disadvantaged socioeconomic backgrounds; a significant proportion of learners have had negative experiences of schooling which is sometimes shared with teachers' own biographies; and most teachers have dual professionalism, meaning that they are experts in their own vocational subject before entering FE as well as being experts in teaching and learning. This means that new teachers cannot be viewed as a *tabula rasa* because they often come from industry with considerable vocational expertise; so, potentially, the vocational expertise of new teachers could change and enhance subject specialist practice within an institution. Another important aspect of FE, is that teachers undertake their ITE in-service. This means that their professional identities can be split between their sense of belonging as an employed teacher within their specialism, but at the same time they need to actively embrace the conception of what it means to be a good teacher as they complete their ITE qualification and endeavour to establish themselves as part of the wider institutional community. They have to juggle the bureaucracy of their teaching role alongside their ITE programme (Orr and Simmons, 2010), and so what a good teacher does is accordingly conveyed. Current ITE programmes prescribe the normative practices which are deemed 'best practice'. This discounts the particular context of the learning environment, as well as its own unique ecology. This is problematic, especially in FE where the diversity of provision ranges from 14 to 19, re-engagement programmes for excluded young people, offender learning,

Foundation learning, learners on a wide range of vocational and Higher Education programmes, as well as the diversity of learners on these programmes. Normative practices also reduce the willingness of teachers to take risks in their practice.

Part of what trainee teachers go through on ITE programmes is a process of identification with what it means to be a good teacher. The new suite of ITE qualifications, following the Lingfield Report (2012) includes the requirement for all observed teaching practice to be graded. This is, however, potentially problematic for FE teacher educators as it substantially threatens the professional development of teachers as they embark on their teaching careers. If teachers are discouraged from taking risks in their developing practice, or at any stage in their teaching career, then teaching loses its creative and bold edge. As Miles Davis suggested, playing it safe is the antithesis of creativity:

> The brilliance comes in your mistakes – that's how you discover new things. And the only way to make mistakes is to stretch and take chances. If you play it safe, you'll never progress. (Cited in Swann and Pratt, 2003: 3)

This further destabilises the professional identity of FE teachers who predominantly train as they teach, by making performative demands of their developing practice and reducing ITE to a potentially technocratic exercise in the restrictive pursuit of the competent practitioner notion of professionalism (Moore, 2004).

Graded observations are a key mechanism for negotiating forms of membership and maintenance of membership within an institution, because grading signifies loyalty to normative practices, and whether you are accepted into that community as a 'good teacher' and therefore seen as a respected and professional member of the teaching community by colleagues and managers. Grades are appraised and converted into prestige or shame which contributes to authorised professional practice and is ultimately the gateway to, or exclusion from, being seen as an expert. Furthermore, this plays an important part in the identification process, and could partly explain why observation is such a stressful and pressurised experience for many teachers. The pressure of being accepted, or not, into the community as an expert lies at the root of the stress and anxiety surrounding observation. Moreover, Keltchermans (2005) suggests that fear of criticism comes from teachers' normative isolation in their professional practice which perversely therefore relies on validation and approval from others. Being judged against a set of normative criteria and given a grade, which validates or invalidates expertise, puts an exceptional amount of power in the hands of the observer. Making judgements about a teacher's performance is notoriously rife with subjectivity and bias (O'Leary, 2006).

An observer's grading decision can only ever be regarded as a subjective interpretation of a lesson and is largely based on inaccurate assumptions about the teaching-learning interaction.

In 2002, the Commission for Black Staff in Further Education reported that the proportion of FE teachers from minority ethnic groups was 7 per cent of the total, with the majority of FE colleges then employing less than 5 per cent. This was under-representative of the BAME population of England at the time. The percentage of BAME teachers in the FE sector for 2011–12 was 8.2 per cent (LSIS, 2013). Research into observations of teaching practice on ITE programmes found that by the final observation, 67 per cent of white trainees achieved a Grade 1 in contrast to 35 per cent of BME trainees (Noel and Waugh, 2014).

Beck and Young (2005) suggest that the narrow and prescriptive content of ITE curricula, where theoretical content has been diminished in favour of a more competency-based model, is in effect 'silencing' teachers by severely limiting their critical awareness. Where the division of labour is a hierarchal one, as in the observation process, this is of particular concern especially as new teachers are coming into the profession at a time when ITE is deregulated, so potentially there will be a whole generation of FE teachers who have been silenced, with ideas of what it is to be a successful teacher based on more 'instrumental assumptions' (ibid.: 194).

 Case study 6.1   Evaluation of the new revised ITE curricula in FE

The Diploma in Education and Training (DET) has been a whirlwind roller coaster of a ride: fast and furious, with some unexpected bumps, but ultimately it has introduced me to the world of Further Education and guided me through my first days of teaching. From a bleary beginner where I was unsure of what was expected of me, the DET has prepared me for my future career. It has clarified the role and responsibilities of a FE teacher, taught me how to plan and teach inclusive lessons and how to reflect upon and so improve my own teaching. During this year, I have studied learning theories, been introduced to emerging technologies and engaged with behaviour management strategies. In this sense it has been highly practical, as the skills that I have learnt in the DET classroom one day I have deployed in my English classroom the next.

In addition, the course has encouraged me to become more critically aware, and to pay close attention to education news and policies and the impact they have upon the FE sector. In particular, I have experienced first-hand the difficulties of enforcing the compulsory English agenda on 16–18-year-old learners. Some of the challenges I have faced in my placements have been directly related to this. They include: low attendance levels, low levels of motivation, disruptive behaviour, short and often insufficient teaching time (especially for the re-sit GCSE class), and a persistent drive for learners to achieve a Grade C at GCSE.

Whilst I have seen the reality of working in an environment controlled by policy and financially constricted, during my placement I have also been lucky to work with some experienced and creative teachers. I have shadowed their practice, borrowed resources, shared ideas and got constructive feedback. In particular, I have watched as they walk the tightrope between implementing education policies and supporting learners' holistic development.

The main thing that I will take away from the DET is a growing sense of confidence: whilst I am still a fledgling teacher, I am not afraid to have a go, try new things, learn from my mistakes and celebrate my successes.

Source: Case study kindly contributed by Jess, DET student and English specialist on the graduate bursary scheme

Reflective question:

• How does this experience compare to your own ITE experience? Do you feel that you have developed a critical awareness of the FE sector, with regard to both policy and practice?

This evaluation by a trainee teacher demonstrates that despite the parameters of the overly prescriptive revised ITE curricula for FE teacher education, teachers can still develop a critical awareness of the sector and the issues related to both policy and practice. This gives optimism for a new generation of critically aware teachers in FE, but also reiterates the importance of teacher education as a vital process to support new teachers, not just with the practical expertise they need to do the job successfully, but also with the critical acumen needed to be a teacher in this era of top-down policy implementation and 'effective teacher' ideology.

Much of what FE teachers do is beyond the subject curriculum content. It is a process of building relationships, changing attitudes to learning, fostering the value of learning, untangling the fixed mindset view of intelligence (Dweck, 2000), and helping learners become a member of a more democratic learning community than they have perhaps experienced in their schooling thus far. This constitutes the tacit knowledge teachers use in their practice, within their specific contexts, and 'suggests a commitment to ensuring that students receive a "quality" education based on a definition of quality through *process* rather than just output measures' (Shain and Gleeson, 1999: 23, italics in original). Developing supportive relationships with learners provides the essential conditions for changing their self-concepts, perceptions of themselves as learners, and subsequently their attitude to learning.

The individualised approach to the observation process, where the lone teacher is observed by a lone observer, leaves a vast subjective space for observers to govern the boundaries of grading. Teachers want, and value, opportunities for more collaboration and professional dialogue, and yet this individualised system of performance management and accountability creates an atmosphere of competition, not collaboration, between professionals, especially amidst current realities such as job insecurity and redundancy. Teachers' emotions, consequently, become appropriated and those which are permitted, or not, become a significant part of the institutional culture. This renders inner dedication potentially as self-interestedness, and engenders individual 'feelings of pride, guilt, shame and envy' in response to the torrent of 'performance information' to which teachers are subjected (Ball, 2003: 221). Teachers' emotions are a key part of their professional values, and engaging these emotions contributes to a sense of identity and self-expression. By focusing on a teacher's role, feelings, thoughts and behaviours are constrained and determined by the institution. Teachers' values comprise an inner dedication to their learners, meaning that they have an emotional investment in their learners, and the corporate appropriation of teachers' emotional investment prevents them from being a whole person when working with their learners.

Teachers then become engaged in a staged performance that is contingent on the demonstration, not only of technical skills but also sanctioned emotions. For example, a teacher could be supported in emotions related to the withdrawal of a learner and the impact on performance indicators, but not supported in the emotions felt regarding the personal circumstances of the learner that necessitated discontinuation of their studies. Ball (2003) discusses the emotional burden for teachers who feel that their practice has become inauthentic as the gap between the needs of learners and corporate goals widens: 'A kind of *values schizophrenia* is experienced by individual teachers where commitment, judgement and authenticity in their practice is sacrificed for impression and performance' (Ball, 2003: 221, italics in original).

The tensions experienced by teachers are further compounded by the current era of austerity, such as funding cuts, which helps to perhaps explain why many teachers continue to 'play the game' and do not voice their dissent. Significantly, the value that ensures that learners do have a positive learning experience, namely commitment to learners, is the value that is causing so much discord and unrest for teachers in FE. A sense of perpetual insecurity is sustained by annual observation cycles which focus on a teacher's role; this makes it easier to control professionals with a strong sense of purpose, and therefore identity. However, this is leaving many teachers feeling disillusioned and unable to reconcile the tensions between their own ethical values and managerialism that dislocates teachers' values and emotions. Keltchermans (2005) asserts that to neglect teachers' emotions is to put education at risk.

Continuing Professional Development (CPD)

The 2007 Regulations required all full-time FE teachers undertake at least 30 hours of CPD per year, and part-time teachers to undertake pro rata amounts of CPD of a minimum of 6 hours per year. A record of all CPD undertaken had to be maintained and declared to the Institute for Learning (IfL) annually. Along with deregulation in 2012, came the end to this statutory requirement to complete CPD. The IfL maintained that CPD, which supported teachers' expertise in their subject area and in teaching and learning, referred to as dual professionalism, was essential to maintain and improve the quality of provision in FE. Following deregulation, CPD opportunities have often now been used by institutions to provide whole-college training and development, often in line with implementing new policy or Ofsted requirements, which are important. Nonetheless, it then limits the autonomy, and time, for teachers to access CPD that would benefit their own personal dual professional development. Teachers who engage in CPD which enhances their own subject specific knowledge, or pedagogy, and which supports the development of their teaching repertoire, helps to enthuse teachers about their work, but also enhances the learning experience for their learners. With staffing being kept at the bare minimum due to current funding constraints, the opportunity for teachers to have time off is challenging, therefore quite often CPD that supports personal professional development is undertaken by teachers in their own time, and even self-funded.

Activity 6.3

- Take a moment to reflect on the CPD you have undertaken recently. Has this been for your personal professional development, or has it been more cross-college CPD?
- What opportunities are there for you to undertake CPD that supports your own personal professional development at your institution?
- What barriers are there to you undertaking CPD that supports your own personal professional development at your institution?

Case study 6.2 Deregulation and ITE

The government deregulated FE by removing mandatory membership of the professional body Institute for Leaning (IfL), minimum CPD requirements, and the necessity to hold, or be working toward a teaching qualification. This happened three years before I began my teaching post, however deregulation has had a fundamental impact on my practice.

Whilst many of my peers were required to have membership of a professional body such as the IFL, this has not been the case for me. Whilst this may save me having to pay a membership fee, professional bodies serve a very important purpose in maintaining standards of teaching, learning and assessment. Whilst I am not formally a member, I attempt to adhere to the Education and Training Foundation (ETF) Professional standards, covering professional skills, values and attributes and knowledge and understanding. I find that combining these standards with being a member of a vocational professional body, in my case The Chartered Institute for IT, is ample for me to maintain my professional standards.

Whilst I am not officially obliged to hold or be working towards a teaching qualification nationally, it is actually an institutional policy where I currently teach. So I was fortunate enough to be one of the last cohort to be supported in gaining the Diploma in Teaching in the Lifelong Learning Sector (DTLLS) Level 5 qualification, and this serves a greater purpose than just simply ticking a box to confirm that I hold, or am working towards a teaching qualification. DTLLS has allowed me to greatly enhance my teaching practice, by teaching me about key underpinning theories of teaching, learning and assessment. The course has allowed me to identify and explore my teaching role, and use the knowledge of this to further refine my practice. As well as this, this opportunity has allowed me to work collaboratively with my peers, many of whom are in their first year of teaching. As well as being a chance to partake in CPD, DTLLS has allowed me to develop a useful support network that has been a really effective learning tool.

Again, whilst I am not nationally obliged to undertake CPD, this is an institutional policy where I work. I am encouraged by my line manager to seek 30 hours CPD during the course of an academic year, but there are time restraints in achieving this. In my opinion, CPD is fundamental to becoming an effective FE teacher, not only in developing new strategies for teaching and assessing, but also in keeping up to date with knowledge of industry.

As an IT and computing teacher, my goal is to prepare learners for industry, so there is a great importance in ensuring that I am up to date with industry standards and technology, and CPD provides an excellent opportunity to ensure that I maintain this currency. This is particularly relevant in the computing, where industry standards and technology are rapidly changing. Deregulation places greater emphasis on me now to update my skills and knowledge in my own time.

Source: Case study kindly contributed by Chris, IT and Computing Lecturer

Reflective questions:

- What is the policy at your institution regarding initial teacher education?
- In what ways have you benefitted from initial teacher education?
- What are its strengths and weaknesses?
- What impact has being a qualified teacher had on your own sense of professionalism?

Conclusion

The prevailing cognitivist approach to learning restricts teachers' development of their practice, constrains learning and prevents a more transformative education. Instrumental views of teaching and learning are perpetuated through constant surveillance of teachers' practice. Graded observations have become an instrument in the monitoring of teachers and suppress opportunities for teaching and learning to move beyond normative practices where transformation becomes possible (see Chapter 9 for further discussion on transformative education). With issues such as radicalisation coming into a teacher's remit, then education accordingly needs more dialogic spaces where the outcome is unknown and immeasurable. In order to meet the considerable economic, social, environmental and political challenges facing the local, national and global community now, and in the future, education has to be freed from the watchful gaze of Ofsted inspections which under the current regime has produced a culture of fear and compliance. We need to move to a system of inspection that promotes collaboration and support between institutions and its inspectorate so that transformative opportunities for learners, and teachers, can be nurtured.

This chapter has examined how graded observations play a key role in ensuring that teachers comply and adhere to what a good teacher is expected to do, which is aligned to a reductive view of teacher expertise. Cycles of continuous improvement are leaving even experienced teachers in a permanent state of limbo as they negotiate tensions in being expert, and the ramifications of compliance. More frequently, however, teachers are interrogating their own investment in the work of teaching; as the neoliberal stakes of the field become further estranged from their own sense of moral purpose they are increasingly less prepared to 'play the game'. Fracturing the link between moral purpose and practice is one way to manage the unruly nature of professional learning because teachers who make the links between their moral purpose and practice are more likely to be proactive in the enactment of their own identification of what it means to be expert (Sachs, 2003). The danger is that these teachers then are so disillusioned by target-driven performativity, which construct teacher identities at odds with their own personal and professional values, that they leave the profession. Research into this aspect of professional learning deserves urgent attention if we are not to have a teaching profession made up entirely of administrators.

Teachers want opportunities to work collaboratively, to be able to share their experiences and knowledge of teaching and learning, its complexities and challenges. Their inner dedication to their learners ensures that they will always endeavour to develop their practice, but this involves taking risks, and this cannot happen unless there is a good support system in place.

Action Research Link

- You may wish to investigate issues raised in this chapter regarding CPD, ITE and observation within your own institution. This could encompass quality improvement systems and issues regarding professionalism since deregulation.

Suggested Further Reading

Ball, S. (2003) 'The teacher's soul and the terrors of performativity', *Journal of Education Policy*, 18 (2), pp. 215–28.

Noel, P. and Waugh, G. (2014) 'Confronting the difference: Ethnicity and patterns of achievement in initial teacher education for the further education and skills sector', *Teaching in Lifelong Learning: A Journal to Inform and Improve Practice*, 6 (1), pp. 20–31.

O'Leary, M. (2014) *Classroom Observation: A Guide to the Effective Observation of Teaching and Learning*. Abingdon, Oxon: Routledge.

Randle, K. and Brady, N. (1997) 'Managerialism and professionalism in the Cinderella Service', *Journal of Vocational Education & Training*, 49 (1), pp. 121–39.

CHAPTER 7

WORKING WITH STAKEHOLDERS

The influence of stakeholders within FE, such as employers, awarding bodies, Ofsted, Governors, learners, parents and teachers, and their role within quality improvement, will be examined from a critical perspective regarding the marketisation of FE. The role of stakeholders in advocacy of FE, recognising its role and provision, as well the impact of a demand-led sector on provision will be examined. In addition, this chapter also offers practical guidance to support teachers working with stakeholders. The impact of accountability on institutional culture and subsequently on professional learning and practice will also be discussed.

This chapter will cover the following:

- An overview of the range of potential stakeholders in FE
- Accountability to stakeholders
- Institutional cultures and the impact on professional learning and practice

Introduction

According to government policy, a key driver amid all the recent policy change has been an attempt to simplify funding and give FE colleges greater flexibility to be responsive to the priorities of learners, employers and local communities. This has included devolution to new local and regional structures, such as City Deals and Local Enterprise Partnerships (LEPs), for planning provision that responds to the current, and expected future, demands of employers as well as local and regional communities.

The term 'stakeholder' is taken to mean those with an interest in further education in the UK. Stakeholders can be categorised into the following:

- Individual
- Institution
- Employer
- Government

Activity 7.1

- Draw up a list of as many examples of stakeholders as you can think of.
- What roles do these stakeholders have?
- Which stakeholder(s) do you have most contact with in your own teaching role?
- Now rank the stakeholders in their order of power or influence.
- Is there a tension between the stakeholder you have most contact with in your own teaching role and the ranking of power/influence of stakeholders?

Employers

In the 1970s, market-orientated forces began to infiltrate education in the UK, with notions of accountability to parents and employers being entered into the ensuing market-based neoliberal reforms. The power and influence of stakeholders is not evenly distributed, indeed there has been a steady decline in the power and influence of individuals such as the teacher, and institutions such as trade unions, whilst employers and central government have gained in power and influence.

Engagement with employers locally and regionally can allow institutions to move beyond its own walls and develop partnerships within the local community. These local partnerships provide employers with an opportunity to train their workforce at recognised educational institutions. In addition, local and regional employer engagement potentially allows employers to actively shape and contribute to the kinds of courses their local FE provider can offer, and the new innovation code (discussed in Chapter 8) enables this type of bespoke provision to be readily made available on demand. Employer engagement addresses the educational needs of local communities and businesses whilst also addressing the national economic and social challenges of upskilling young people and adults to meet the skills shortages, and to maintain global competitive advantage. However, employer engagement is not a choice for institutions, due to deep incremental cuts in funding to adult learning, institutions have had to make business decisions which divert provision away from adult learning and into learning for employability for 16–19-year-olds, in order to meet employer demands in an increasingly competitive labour market. This competitive labour market results from global economic changes resulting in fewer jobs, especially for those with low or no qualifications. This significant shift from a supply-led labour market to a demand-led labour market means that FE provision is increasingly responsive to employer demand and their priorities.

Over the years, the Confederation of British Industry (CBI) has successively, and repeatedly, claimed that further education frequently fails to equip people with the skills and knowledge for the modern workplace. The Association of Colleges (AoC), and others, have vigorously counter-challenged this with accusations that CBI members do not adequately invest in their workers' training, and some FE providers have suggested that CBI members, some of whom are private training providers, have a vested interest in undermining them.

Employers feel that there has been significant improvement in the relevance of FE college courses. A CBI/Pearson (2013) survey found satisfaction amongst business was up from 52 per cent in 2012 to 61 per cent in 2013. However, key findings from the same survey show that 55 per cent of businesses say young people lack the right work experience and key attributes that set them up for success, including:

- Self-management – 54 per cent
- Problem-solving – 41 per cent
- Attitude to work – 35 per cent

In addition, 32 and 31 per cent of businesses are dissatisfied with young people's basic literacy and numeracy skills, respectively; and 31 per cent reported that young people lack the technical skills they need for employment. The CBI suggest these findings stress the need for educational reform to produce young people who are rounded and grounded, as well as stretched academically.

The current emphasis from the CBI seems to suggest a definition of educational achievement that goes beyond exam results, and addresses social and behavioural aspects of education. Measures implemented by Ofsted such as stretch and challenge, character-building (a term which we may see replace employability skills) and productivity are three key examples of how the CBI influences educational policy. For further discussion on these findings and their impact on policy in further education please see Chapter 10.

Evidence from a study by the 157 Group (2014) highlights several key characteristics of institutions engaged in successful partnerships with employers:

- A clear purpose and role for the college in the economic community
- Creating college 'advocates' in key local employers and stakeholders
- Building credibility
- Talking business language

Activity 7.2

- Evaluate your own institution's effectiveness in engaging with employers locally and regionally.

Some curriculum areas engage well with local employers, but this is not systematic across all further education provision.

Activity 7.3

- Evaluate employer engagement within your own curriculum area and subject specialism.
- Can you identify any aspects that could be developed and improved?
- If you provide work experience as part of your curriculum area, evaluate how well this prepares learners for future employment. What do they learn from the work experience component of the course?
- Discuss employer engagement with your colleagues and peers who teach in different curriculum areas. How does it compare with your own curriculum area and subject specialism?

Working with the local business community can be both a rewarding experience for employers, colleges and learners alike, but sometimes there are conflicts of interest.

Case study 7.1   Employer engagement in hospitality and catering

I have been working with employers, businesses and stakeholders for the past five years. I have had both positive and negative experiences when working within the local community. There have been some exceptional high points, whereby the employer and learner have mutually benefited from the college course, its pace and content have satisfied the needs of both the employer and learner. Networking between the teaching team and employers has also proven successful, with employers visiting the college, seeing first-hand the catering facilities and sampling the learners' cooking. This is the college working at its best and contributing to the local economy. Research commissioned by the Association of Colleges (AoC) claims that every £1 spent by a college generates another £1.90 for its local community (NIACE, 2009).

However, there are also some pitfalls which I have experienced. One key issue that I have come across is employers sending a fully funded 16-year-old apprentice to college for pure financial gain. After 13 weeks on the course, the employer qualified for their entitlement of a £1500 government grant and once received by the employer, their commitment to the apprenticeship reduced, which then impacted on attendance and attainment. In these cases, the employer does not need to repay the government grant.

Another issue that I have encountered is employers being disillusioned with the college and the curriculum content. The qualification does not always meet the needs of learners' specific workplaces, for example we may have employees from a nursing home and a three-starred Michelin restaurant on the same course. To address this, we have a Sector Focus Group which meets three to four times a year. The meeting mainly focuses on the curriculum and how it could be improved, and discusses developments such as building a training hotel.

In our local area, demand for catering and hospitality employees outstrips supply, so one of the biggest successes of engaging employers with the college within our department has been inviting employers in to recruit from our pool of learners, for paid employment, as apprentices or for work experience. This benefits both employers and our learners.

Source: Case study kindly contributed by Neil, Catering Lecturer

(Continued)

(Continued)

Reflective questions:

- How do these experiences of working with employers compare to your own experiences? You may also wish to discuss this with colleagues from other departments within your institution.
- How does being accountable to stakeholders impact on curriculum design, teaching and assessment in your subject specialism?
- In what ways does your department involve local employers in events at your institution?
- What could be done to further promote employer engagement within your department and/or institution?

The study by the 157 Group (2014) also reported the challenges and success factors in building partnerships with employers, and can be seen in Table 7.1.

Table 7.1   Challenges and success factors in partnerships with employers

Challenges to successful partnerships with employers	Key success factors for partnerships with employers
• Engaging successfully with small-to-medium-size businesses • Competition with private training providers • Competition with other colleges • A lack of flexible funding to meet specific employer needs • Employer uncertainty about the role of colleges and how best to make contact • A lack of understanding of employers' training/skills needs • Employer perception of too much administration involved • Lack of time to build sustainable relationships • Hidden or unexpected costs for employers	• Taking a whole college approach to engaging employers • Adopting a creative/innovative approach • Not simply doing what has always been done • Having specialist teams/individuals • Understanding local employer skills needs • Working closely with key stakeholders • Having employer advocates to communicate/offer to wider networks • Having flexibility to deliver a bespoke service

Source: 157 Group (2014)

 Case study 7.2   Franchise partnerships

Working within an FE college as a lecturer within the teacher education team, I carry out various roles. One of those roles involves visiting different institutions in the locality, both private and public, to monitor and assure

the quality of their curriculum provision on behalf of the college. This quality assurance forms part of their contractual obligation with the college agreed franchise partnership. This annual franchise curriculum visit involves meeting with the designated individual training manager and/or teaching team.

From my experience to date, I often find employers are unaware of the constant changes within the education system, and I find that during my visits I have to update them about these changes. A good example of this is a large public health institution in the region that is responsible for provision to numerous cohorts of Health Care Workers employed within the institution. On visiting the lead tutor of the education team at the institution, it was clearly evident they were not aware of the choice of English and maths courses available which would allow them to develop and update their own essential skills, which in turn would also enable them to embed English and maths into the design of the current curriculum at their institution.

In my opinion, to engage with employers and create successful partnerships between colleges and employers we need the following:

- More responsive training providers with well-regulated awarding institutions
- Vocational qualifications have to be relevant to the needs of individuals and employers
- The future vision should be employer ownership of skills making vocational qualifications integral to business growth and individual prosperity

Source: Case study kindly contributed by Theresa, lecturer in Initial Teacher Education/Lead IQA and course manager for TAQA

Reflective questions:

- Which local employers has your institution successfully developed partnerships with?
- How does your institution keep local employers informed of changes and opportunities within education and training?

On the whole, stakeholders are positive about further education and see that it is strategically important for social inclusion, community cohesion and economic productivity and competitiveness:

Colleges generate a wide array of benefits, many of which are not fully appreciated: learners benefit from higher lifetime earnings; society benefits from avoided social costs; taxpayers benefit from an expanded tax base; local businesses benefit from increased consumer spending; local employers benefit from a more productive local workforce. (157 Group, 2015: 6)

Research repeatedly shows that further education adds significant economic value to local communities, but also to learners' lives and society as a whole.

Perhaps the most striking findings on employer contribution to the upskilling of the employed workforce comes from recent work by Mason and Bishop (2010), which, using Labour Force Survey data, indicates that across the UK workforce as a whole, average levels of job-related training tended to decline from about 2000 onwards, and have now returned to levels last witnessed in 1993. This clearly has a significant impact on the government's flagship apprenticeship scheme. The proposed future funding of apprenticeships through a system of vouchers in 2017, which puts employers in full control of the funding, is one way in which the government hopes to encourage employers to participate in the apprenticeship scheme.

Institutional Cultures

The culture of an institution establishes the values and behaviours that are considered to improve overall institutional performance, and will have considerable influence on how we work and the relationships that we develop with those we work with. The culture created by an institution is largely determined by the institutional structure, but can also be captured in the mission statement.

Activity 7.4

- What is the mission statement of your institution?
- What requirements and expectations does this place on your teaching roles and responsibilities?
- What requirements and expectations does this place on curriculum and practice in your subject specialism?

An institutional structure determines lines of communication, policies, authority and responsibilities. It shapes how authority is disseminated within an institution, as well as how information flows within it. Typically, institutions will adopt a flat or hierarchical structure. A flat structure has few, or even no, levels of management between senior management and frontline staff. In this structure, frontline staff are more involved in decision-making and, commonly, there is less supervision by senior management. In contrast, a hierarchal structure assumes a pyramid model, with multiple layers of management between senior management and frontline staff. Each layer of management has a narrow and specific focus, with decisions made by senior management being passed down the hierarchy.

Activity 7.5

- Come up with a list of advantages and disadvantages for a flat and a hierarchal institutional structure. You might want to consider the following to get you started:

  o   Communication and relationships between different roles
  o   Decision-making
  o   Response to change

- What type of institutional structure do you work in?
- Evaluate the effectiveness of this structure.

I have discussed the individual accountability of teachers in Chapter 6, but collectively institutions are accountable to stakeholders. These stakeholders all have a vested interest in an institution and this will have an effect on how an institution is managed, its policies, practices and processes.

Activity 7.6

Revisit the list of stakeholders and their roles from Activity 7.1:

- How does being accountable to these stakeholders impact your institution?

You might wish to consider the following:

  o   The culture and ethos of your institution
  o   Policy, practices and processes within your institution eg quality improvement, continuing professional development (CPD)
  o   Your roles and responsibilities eg teaching-related, administrative and institutional (Gould and Roffey-Barentsen, 2014)

- How does being accountable to these stakeholders impact learners' experience within your institution?

An institutional culture determines the fabric of an institution in terms of its dynamics, how it promotes professional practice and how it supports its staff. As discussed in Chapter 2, this can influence our sense of professional identity; in terms of how we are viewed by colleagues and managers, which shapes our sense of professional self.

Activity 7.7

- Go to Appendix 2 and complete the questionnaire: 'Is yours a learning institution?'
- Discuss the results with peers/colleagues and come up with suggestions for improvement based on your findings and discussion.
- Evaluate how frontline staff at your institution can make suggestions and contribute to decision-making.

Ofsted

The role of the Office for Standards in Education, Children's Services and Skills (Ofsted) is a particularly contentious issue in education in the UK and has seen sustained criticism recently: complaints that its judgements are unreliable and arbitrary; charges of political bias; accusations of poor leadership; and unions, and recent research, warning that the system is causing unnecessary stress on the profession and learners (Hutchings, 2015).

The origins of Ofsted as an independent inspectorate can be traced back to 1839 when the first two of Her Majesty's inspectors were appointed. Ofsted, as we know it today, was created by the Education Act 1992, and since then a national scheme of inspections has been in place. Under this scheme, Ofsted regularly inspect each state-funded educational provider in the country, and publish its reports so they are available to the public, namely parents, instead of reporting directly to the Secretary of State as was previously the mechanism for oversight of state-funded education in the UK. The development of an inspection framework in 1992 was to ensure a rigorous and transparent inspection process that assessed all institutions against the same criteria to make judgements about quality of provision. Since 2007, Ofsted has been the single inspectorate for schools, further education colleges, children's care services and teacher education providers. Their core mission is to improve education, and care, for children and young people through inspection. Ever since 1839, the key remit of a regulatory body has been to ensure that public money is spent effectively so that children and young people receive the best standards of education and that underperforming schools are improved. In a report which evaluated the work of

Ofsted, the authors concluded that 'a longitudinal view of all its frameworks shows a move away from a focus mainly on compliance towards a greater concern with effectiveness' (Whitty et al., 2004: 160). However, what has been heavily criticised, especially more recently, is the process by which its regulatory remit to improve educational standards through inspection has been executed. Successive revisions to inspection frameworks have sought to reduce the burden of inspections; but, in reality, the burden has intensified as the frameworks have become more demanding, and revisions result in continuous changes to policies and practices within institutions. In effect, the inundation of government initiatives and reforms, which principally focus on structures and systems of accountability in the drive for effectiveness, have amplified compliance and detract focus from educational improvement within current Ofsted inspections.

In 2007, uncertainty as to whether Ofsted was fit for purpose was raised by the House of Commons Education Select Committee. Other sector bodies such as the Association of Teachers and Lecturers (ATL) have criticised Ofsted for being over-reliant on performance data in its assessment of quality of provision and teacher effectiveness.

In 2014, the Policy Exchange (Waldegrave and Simons) published a report into Ofsted inspections titled *Watching the Watchmen* which focused on two key recurrent themes in the criticism levelled at the regulatory body: accuracy of judgements made by inspectors, both overall judgements as well as lesson observations, and the quality of the inspectorate itself. Evidence gathered from teachers of their experiences of Ofsted highlighted the following assessments:

- Variable quality between different inspection teams
- Inspection teams making decisions based on the data before they arrived at the institution
- Short lesson observations not allowing for accurate judgements
- Problems with the reliability and interpretation of data
- Some senior leadership teams very guided by 'what Ofsted wants'
- Pressure to adapt to teaching style when Ofsted are present
- Some teachers felt pressure to inflate levels to show better progress (Adapted from ibid.: 64)

Activity 7.8

- What is your view of Ofsted and their role as a regulatory body?
- If you have experienced an Ofsted inspection, do any of the themes reported by Waldegrave and Simons match your own experience?

(Continued)

> *(Continued)*
>
> - If you have not experienced an Ofsted inspection, what concerns you about it?
> - Which aspects of your teaching role and professional development are guided by 'what Ofsted wants'?

As from September 2015, observations of teaching and learning during inspections will not be graded. This is a huge step forward in acknowledging the unreliability of observation to assess and validate the quality of teaching and learning. Waldegrave and Simons (2014) go one step further, however, and assert that the practice of lesson observations exemplifies the imbalance of power between the inspectorate and institutions and recommend the total abolition of all routine lesson observations during inspections.

> So long as inspectors are observing lessons, they will – in practice – still be making judgements on the teacher and on the quality of teaching … even if such individual judgements are not graded or even shared. (Waldegrave and Simons, 2014: 7)

The authors recommend that a new two-stage inspection model be implemented which would see the role of inspection to:

1. Assess the performance data of an institution off-site
2. A one-day on-site inspection to validate the self-assessment of the institution

This would be a significant shift towards a more democratic peer review model of inspection, where institutions lead quality improvement systems in partnership with Ofsted. This is very much the approach endorsed by the majority of the profession. In 2014, Ofsted carried out pilot inspection schemes and have tailored the inspection system in the 2015 Common Inspection Framework (CIF). However, whilst some advancements have been made, such as not grading individual lesson observations, the actuality of the much desired peer review model of Ofsted inspection has not yet been achieved.

Ofsted inspectors assess how the visions and values of senior leadership teams influence an institution's culture and ethos by checking whether the values and vision of senior leadership are known and shared by staff, learners and the local community.

Activity 7.9

- Evaluate the impact Ofsted has on the culture and ethos of your institution?
- What does your institution do to create a culture and ethos of ambition for learners to raise their confidence, aspirations and achievements?

The accusation that Ofsted is too closely aligned to political agendas is a common criticism regarding its fitness for purpose. Whilst this has been refuted by Ofsted, its future seems uncertain, in its current guise at least. The high-stakes nature of inspections has created a culture of fear which impedes innovation, creativity and collaborative partnerships within institutions, and between institutions across the education system. This is not a sustainable model of inspection, especially in the current climate of severe funding cuts where creativity and collaboration are key to the future survival of further education, but also to the provision of quality education which best meets the needs of learners in local communities. It requires an inspection model in which the locus of control for improvement is in the hands of individual institutions, which supports autonomy and innovation as institutions drive their own improvement, and whereby Ofsted check and validate this progress. In other words, a model which is based more on peer review and partnership with the inspectorate rather than on externally imposed improvement. As Waldegrave and Simons suggest: 'this would return Ofsted to being the hygiene inspector – someone who checks empirically to see if the kitchen is clean and the food is fresh – and away from being the food critic' (2014: 58).

Conclusion

The role of stakeholders is likely to become more significant in the FE sector, as creative and innovative ways to sustain provision in an era of severe funding cuts are found through mergers. Funding cuts and increased competition between schools, sixth form colleges, further education providers and universities means that mergers are an inevitable part of financial management for the future survival of many providers. Mergers ensure sustainability through increased scale and partnerships. This means that further education colleges can diversify their provision to better meet the needs of local communities and employers. The high-stakes of Ofsted inspections is another driving force behind mergers, as colleges have less and less resources due to cuts in core funding to meet the ever-increasing demands of Ofsted inspection, therefore, pooling resources is an effective approach to try to meet these demands as well as secure financial viability.

Suggested Further Reading

157 Group (2015) *The Economic Impact of Further Education Colleges*. London: 157 Group.

Hutchings, M. (2015) *Exam Factories: The Impact of Accountability Measures on Children and Young People*. Research commissioned by the National Union of Teachers. Chelmsford: Ruskin Press.

Waldegrave, H. and Simons, J. (2014) *Watching the Watchmen: The Future of School Inspections in England*. London: Policy Exchange.

Whitty, G., Matthews, P., and Sammons, P. (2004) *Improvement through Inspection: An Evaluation of the Impact of Ofsted's Work*, July. London: Ofsted.

CHAPTER 8

INCLUSIVE CURRICULUM

A brief overview of curriculum ideology and models will begin this chapter, which will encourage readers to critically engage with their own curriculum. This will continue the discussion of a demand-led sector, introduced in Chapter 7, and its impact on curriculum change. Influences on curriculum design, curriculum design as a cooperative activity and tensions between the principle of inclusion and curriculum will be explored. You will have the opportunity to analyse key features of your own curriculum area and be encouraged to use this to consider a topic, theme or area that you would like to introduce to your own existing curriculum, or a completely new course that you feel your institution is really well placed to offer.

This chapter will cover the following:

- An overview of curriculum theory – ideologies and models
- Inclusive curriculum – an examination of some issues
- Inclusion in education – its potential and its tensions
- Negotiated curriculum – possibilities and constraints
- Demand-led and supply-led curriculum – curriculum redesign and innovation in FE

Introduction

Awareness of curriculum, and curriculum theories, is an important component of a teacher's professional knowledge base, and one that has fortunately been maintained in initial teacher education programmes in FE. It is important because it also impacts on our practice, and therefore our role as a teacher, which is why it deserves critical exploration.

Teachers' engagement with curriculum often ranges from: (1) an 'off-the-shelf' approach, where teachers use ready-made materials and follow a prepared curriculum; to (2) teachers who follow a prepared curriculum but supplement it with some of their own materials; to (3) teachers who can plan and design a new curriculum and create their own materials to accompany it.

Activity 8.1

- From the range of 1–3, where would you place your own engagement with the curriculum you teach?
- Why do you think this is the case?

Most teachers in FE, I assume, would fall into the latter two categories due to the nature of their work and the diversity of provision in FE which is becoming more demand-led. Anyhow, before we go any further, let us define what 'curriculum' means.

Activity 8.2

- Come up with your own definition of curriculum.

'Curriculum' in Latin was a racing chariot, and *currere* was the verb meaning 'to run'. The imagery here I believe is quite significant, as it suggests that we are in a race to get to the end, but also we often use the expression, 'to roll out', when we are talking about teaching a curriculum, which suggests that the path from A to B is predetermined and all we have to do is keep our learners on track. This is all imbued with perspectives on knowledge, teaching and learning which we will explore further in this chapter.

First, before we explore it in more depth, it is important to clarify the distinction between 'curriculum', 'syllabus' and 'scheme of work', as these can sometimes be confused. What is of note in Figure 8.1, is that the focus is very much on the teaching, rather than on the learning.

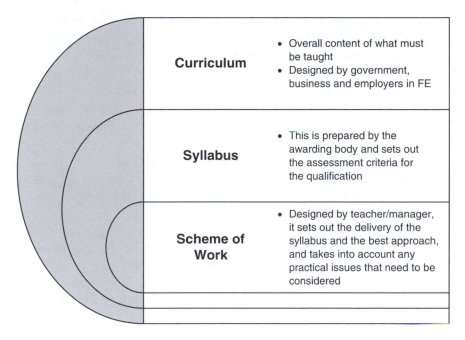

Figure 8.1   A diagrammatic representation showing how curriculum, syllabus and scheme of work all fit together in the planning of a course

Curriculum Theories

The transmission and acquisition of knowledge and skills has always been the primary goal of curriculum development. A curriculum, however, is not neutral – it is value-laden, or ideological: 'Every curriculum represents a set of fundamental beliefs, assumptions and values' (Armitage et al., 2012: 207), and manifests ideological conceptions of knowledge, teaching and learning.

From Table 8.1, it is possible to discern that each ideology has a very different set of ideas and beliefs about the purpose of education. The underpinning beliefs of each of the four ideologies will now be briefly explained.

Table 8.1   Four curriculum ideologies

Liberal humanism (Hirst, 1974)	Instrumentalism (Bobbit, 1918; Tyler, 1949)	Progressivism (Dewey, 1916; Stenhouse, 1975)	Reconstructivism (Freire, 1970; Lawton, 1983; Skilbeck, 1984)
The use of the intellectual disciplines in developing individuals and, thus, a fairer and more equal society	A curriculum delivering a specific type of product, such as the development of a skilled workforce	Meeting individual's needs and aspirations so as to support their personal growth and strengthen a democratic society	Education to change society and its existing injustices. Education should help people become critical thinkers and to transform existing society

Liberal humanism emphasises the importance of intellectual development through academic knowledge and the transmission of cultural heritage. The possession of culture and civic spirit gained through learning a canon of subjects will ensure people become better human beings. Such subjects would include study of literature, arts, the classics and other traditional academic disciplines. It believes that education has a key role to play in the moral development of learners, and that developing free thinking, responsible individuals will ensure active participation in a democratic society. Some critics argue that liberal humanism has led to elitism.

Instrumentalism serves to maintain the status quo in society by providing everybody with a job, or meaningful role, and therefore a place in society. Having a highly skilled and educated workforce will enable competition and economic advantage. Currently, subjects such as maths, science, technology and English are valued as they are seen as essential to achieving this end. Vocational education plays a key role in achieving economic competitiveness with many curricula, such as Business and Technology Education Council (BTEC) qualifications, focused on behavioural outcomes and work-related competencies.

Progressivism emphasises individual growth and development. Dewey (1916) believed that it was better for society if people grow and develop together, and so he argued that education should promote cooperation and learning to think. He theorised this would promote democratic values and strengthen a democratic society. The learners, and their needs, are the source of content for the curriculum and personal development is the goal of education rather than formal qualifications.

Reconstructionism aims to address inequality and bring about change in society. It assumes that society is unequal and unjust and therefore should be reconstructed. In this reconstruction process, teachers and learners are active agents of social transformation. Reconstructionists believe in:

> the ability of education … to educate learners to understand the nature of their society in such a way that they will develop a vision of a better society, and then act so as to bring that vision into existence. (Schiro, 1978: 12)

 Activity 8.3

- Think about a curriculum you are currently teaching. Which ideology do you think it stems from?
- What are the potential implications of this underpinning ideology on your role, your practice and your learners?

These curriculum ideologies, and their differing interests in the role of education, have resulted in three models of curriculum: the product model (means–ends learning); the content model, or sometimes referred to as the transmission model (the what of learning); and the process model (the why of learning). These models have a direct impact on the planning and assessment of teaching and learning.

Tyler (1949) had a considerable influence on curriculum, and teaching, after the publication of his book *Basic Principles of Curriculum and Instruction*. It prompted a significant shift in the aims of education and redefined what it meant to be an educated person.

Table 8.2 A summary of the product model (Tyler, 1949)

Product model (Tyler, 1949)
Focus on the aims/objectives of the curriculum, i.e. exam or qualification

Advantages	Criticisms
• Clear statement of intent which helps to structure content • Skills/knowledge to be mastered clearly defined • Assessment is more specific	• Too content- and qualification/exam focused • Fosters behaviourist approaches such as behavioural objectives/teacher-led/passive learners • Does not foster creativity (for teachers or learners)

Source: Tyler (1969 [1949])

Tyler's 'product model' views curriculum as a means to an end, where the aims and objectives are specified in advance of teaching (Table 8.2). This implies a technical view of education – in its pursuit of achieving these ends, or in other words, it is instrumental. It is a linear model of curriculum planning, whereby the objectives are the basis of curriculum design. Tyler's model is based on four fundamental questions:

1.   What are the aims and objectives?
2.   Which learning activities meet the aims and objectives?
3.   How can these learning activities be organised into a curriculum?
4.   How can the aims and objectives be assessed?

The technical view of curriculum epitomised by the Tyler's focus on measurable, quantifiable outcomes was criticised by Stenhouse (1975) as being too prescriptive, too teacher-centred and inadequate to deal with the complexities of teaching and learning. Stenhouse's own 'process model' encapsulates this critique (Table 8.3).

Table 8.3   A summary of the process model (Stenhouse, 1975)

Process model (Stenhouse, 1975)	
Focus is on the learning, how it is organised, the learning activities and the conditions for learning created by the teacher	
Advantages	**Criticisms**
• Learner-centred, therefore learners are active and contribute to learning • Emphasis on learning and a more individualised approach • Not all learning activity focused on end result – sometimes just important for life	• This approach is not always easy to apply in all areas • Can lose sight of appropriate content • Relies more on formative assessment which needs to be closely monitored and recorded

According to Stenhouse (1975), a curriculum needs to be flexible and open-ended, rather than predetermined, so that the potential for the learners' growth and development is maximised. Therefore, a process curriculum is fundamentally based on more democratic values, and intrinsic principles rather than extrinsic objectives, which means that the outcomes are unpredictable.

Hirst (1974) proposed that there are particular forms of existing knowledge and ways of thinking that everyone should experience, not just the elite. He favoured the same knowledge-base as the liberal humanist tradition, but in the form of a curriculum for all. He suggested that everyone should be introduced to the ways of knowing these distinct forms of knowledge thus providing the rationale for a common curriculum in education. In effect, education is a form of initiation into the types of knowledge defined as relevant. However, some argue that classifying these distinct forms of knowledge is exclusive (Pring, 1976). The 'content model' is concerned with the transmission of knowledge in distinct subjects, namely maths, science, literature, art, religion, history and philosophy (Table 8.4).

Table 8.4   A summary of the content model (Hirst, 1974)

Content model (Hirst, 1974)	
Focus is on the transmission of existing knowledge, structured around subjects and with a focus on intellectual development	
Advantages	**Criticisms**
• Content is sequential and cumulative, resulting in proficiency and achievable outcomes • Can be helpful in differentiating content by level of learner	• Little individualisation • Content is the same whoever you teach, just the pace of delivery can be accelerated • Can focus on quantity of content rather than quality of learning experience • Decisions about essential knowledge remain fundamentally political and ideological

Activity 8.4

- Can you match the curriculum models to each of the four ideologies?
- Which model(s) do you think your curriculum has used in its design?

Many modern curricula tend to conflate the content and product models by specifying content as objectives. The process curriculum has been increasingly difficult to offer when teachers are constrained by assessment regimes, reduced guided learning hours (GLH) and quality improvement mechanisms, including external inspections, and where education has become in many ways an 'impossible practice' (Edwards, 2007: 4).

Sir Ken Robinson is an outspoken educationalist and advocate of creativity in education, and stipulates that creativity is as important, if not more important, than literacy. He makes a powerful case for transforming the education system into one that nurtures, rather than undermines, people's natural creative capacities. He argues that to prepare learners for an unknown future we need to transform education by 'empowering passionate and creative teachers and by firing up the imaginations and motivations of the students' (Robinson, 2009: 247). In order to do this, we need to change the current dominant ideological paradigms of liberal humanism and instrumentalism, and move towards a more progressive curriculum which would foster creativity and innovation.

> We need to evolve a new appreciation of the importance of nurturing human talent along with an understanding of how talent expresses itself differently in every individual. We need to create environments – in our schools ... – where every person is inspired to grow creatively. (Robinson, 2009: xiii)

Activity 8.5

- Watch Sir Ken Robinson's 2008 TED talk on *Changing Education Paradigms*, animated by the Royal Society of Arts (RSA). (NB: a 'paradigm' is another word for a model or pattern.)
- As you watch, make a note of the principles he argues should underpin our educational system.

Robinson suggests that changing the education paradigm towards a progressive curriculum would:

- Prepare learners for an unknown future
- Foster creativity and innovation
- Embrace technology and the arts
- Stimulate learners *aesthetically*, i.e. wake up their senses
- Involve learning in groups, with opportunities to work in pairs or alone
- Have extremely well-trained teachers

 Activity 8.6

Each of the ideologies, and their associated model, has implications for our practice in relation to:

- Knowledge
- Learners' role
- Teachers' role
- Resources
- Organisation of learning
- Assessment
- Educational outcomes

Come up with a few ideas as to how you think the 3 models of curriculum (product, content and process) may affect some of the aspects of your practice as listed above. You may find it helpful to refer back to Activity 8.5 and Robinson's argument for a more progressive curriculum.

From exploring four key ideologies and three models of curriculum, it is perhaps clearer why curriculum theory warrants its inclusion within teachers' professional knowledge base. A curriculum has a very profound effect on what we teach, how we teach and on how learners are positioned in learning experiences. Pinar (2012) appeals to teachers to know what they are teaching, to understand, not just implement or evaluate the curriculum.

Inclusive Curriculum

In Chapter 5, we explored inclusion as an underlying principle of all educational contexts.

Activity 8.7

- What is your definition of an inclusive curriculum?

Powell and Tummons provide the following definition:

> all the ways by which … education and training can be made more accessible to any groups of potential students who might otherwise face structural, financial or cultural barriers to participation. (2011: 71)

Activity 8.8

- Which groups in society are likely to be the object of exclusion and what are the social or economic consequences for them?
- Do you have any learners that fall into any of these groups?

Tennant (2006: 101–3) has identified four basic concerns in the adoption of objectives in curriculum design, namely: that these objectives can rarely be determined in advance; that the emphasis on outcomes undervalues the importance of the learning process; that not all learning outcomes are specifiable in behavioural terms; and that learning may be occurring that is not being measured.

Activity 8.9

- Consider Tennant's objections and reflect on the aims and objectives of your curriculum in light of these objections. What issues of inclusivity are raised in your reflections?

Principles of inclusive curriculum involve every stage of the planning process; the curriculum content, the planning of teaching and learning and assessment. It is worth considering the learners recruited on to courses; there may be some particular learners who need consideration, and this therefore needs to be taken into account in planning. Learners are usually recruited from a wide range of diverse backgrounds: some may have English as a second language (ESOL); some may be unfamiliar with the ethos of FE; others may be mature learners returning to study after a considerable break from education. These are all factors which need to be considered, alongside other specific needs of learners, such as learning difficulties or disabilities, to help pre-empt any potential barriers accessing the curriculum. This can then be built into the curriculum before its implementation, so that provision is inclusive from the outset. Table 8.5 sets out some areas for consideration when planning to ensure that a curriculum is inclusive.

Table 8.5   Elements of an inclusive curriculum

Content	Teaching and learning	Assessment
<ul><li>All groups within society should be represented positively, and curricula should include groups which have previously been excluded</li><li>Course content should relate as closely as possible to learners' backgrounds, ethnicity and age as well as motivation to study and prior experience</li><li>Use inclusive language; avoid gender pronouns *he/her*, avoid labels like 'dyslexic learners', 'weak learners', replace with 'learners with dyslexia', 'less confident learners'</li><li>Seek to raise learners' awareness of other cultures, traditions and multiple perspectives</li><li>Ensure content is drawn from significant current social issues where appropriate</li></ul>	<ul><li>Raise the profile of the teaching of equality and diversity: the subject itself can have a low status</li><li>Provision for learners with disabilities: reasonable adjustments must be made</li><li>Draw on learners' prior knowledge, experience and interests as a routine part of the delivery</li><li>Raising learners' awareness of other cultures, traditions and multiple perspectives will help them to understand where their own views come from and evaluate them</li><li>Experiential learning and collaborative learning opportunities help learners to reflect on their own and others' experiences or perspectives which leads to an understanding of the application of theory within a given context</li></ul>	<ul><li>Blind marking</li><li>Ensure access to word-processing facilities</li><li>Awareness of different perspectives, use of non-standard English</li><li>Provision for learners with disabilities during summative assessments: reasonable adjustments must be made</li></ul>

Activity 8.10

Reflective questions:

- How inclusive is your curriculum? In your reflection, consider content, teaching and learning and assessment.
- What could you do to further develop an inclusive curriculum for your course?

Inclusion in Education

The seismic shift in education with regards to the inclusion of learners with learning difficulties or disabilities into mainstream educational provision came about due to a change in society's perceptions of disability, or model of disability. There are two models of disability: medical and social.

Table 8.6 Medical and social models of disability

Medical (deficit) model of disability	Social (difference) model of disability
• Disability is a deficiency/abnormality • Being disabled is negative • Disability resides in the individual • Remedy for disability-related problems is cure or 'normalisation' of individual • The agent of remedy is the professional so the disabled individual can 'fit into society'	• Disability is a difference • Being disabled is in itself neutral • Disability derives from interaction between individual and society • Remedy for disability-related problems is change in interaction between individual and society • The agent of remedy is the individual or an advocate which affects arrangements between the individual and society

The medical model focuses on what a person can or cannot do, in other words, what is 'wrong' with the person and the best treatment or cure for them. The emphasis is placed on the individual, with no regard for their potential. In contrast, the social model views disability as a social condition and focuses on the attitudes and structures of society and the barriers this creates. The social model attempts to address these barriers and the ways in which these can be either removed or reduced by society.

Although the social model of disability underpins the principle of inclusion following the Warnock Report (DES, 1978), the medical model has informed the development and structure of legislation, and is still reflected in some people's attitudes towards disability and can be associated with negative educational outcomes experienced by some people with disabilities. In addition, aspects of the Equality Act 2010, in relation to disability discrimination, follow the medical model of disability as it focuses on what a person is unable to do as a result of their disability. So, despite considerable changes in societal attitudes towards disability, it is important to acknowledge that there are still aspects of the medical model that continue to affect everyday experiences for people with disabilities. An inclusion policy that focuses predominantly on individual deficits, even if done with good intention, can create negative consequences due to its adoption of deficit-difference approaches to inclusion, in both the diagnostic identification of need and its treatment. So, perhaps we need to ask ourselves who benefits from the practice of inclusive education.

However, as discussed in Chapter 5, inclusion now incorporates the unique characteristics, interests, abilities and learning needs of all learners.

The evolution of a knowledge base prescribed in a curriculum accompanied with national standards and accreditation requirements has to be taken into consideration when exploring the notion of inclusive curriculum. As mentioned earlier, curriculum and decisions about knowledge and skills are not neutral, they are value judgements. Currently, we have curricula designed outside of the contexts in which they are taught, and curricula drive the educational process and define what it means to be 'educated'. The majority of curriculum within further education currently will be a combination of product and content models:

> This ends-orientated understanding of the educational curriculum (made possible by a linear understanding of process) underpins every form of education where the end or intention of the educational intervention is pre-defined. (Osberg and Biesta, 2010: 601)

Osberg and Biesta go on to discuss the dominant assumption that for learning to be classed as educational, there has to be a predetermined end before education can take place and 'that the choice for such a trajectory is indeed a choice which has to be made by someone – it will always reflect particular interests and values' (ibid.: 601). In summary, Osberg and Biesta argue, this means–ends approach renders an educational curriculum a tool to secure a predefined set of norms, which obstructs 'inclusive education' because it specifies what is normal. In so doing, educational curriculum problematises the concept of inclusion, as it pathologises difference and therefore becomes an instrument for normalisation rather than inclusion.

How curriculum is conceived is embroiled in specific social and political interests, and creates barriers to cultural pluralism. The initial commitment of multiculturalism was assimilation in order to bring social cohesion through the development of a shared pluralistic culture. Time, however, has shown how minority cultures in the UK have become subordinate to the dominant Anglo-European culture, making it difficult to achieve equity among the cultures because the dominant culture does not reflect the cultural diversity of the UK. In an ideal world, the entire curriculum in the UK needs to be redesigned to promote multiple ways of perceiving and evaluating so as to be aware of our own cultural perspectives, but to raise awareness of multi-ethnic perspectives in an increasingly interconnected global world in which issues such as terrorism, climate change, immigration and scarcity of natural resources are interdependent global issues which require novel and collective solutions. Curriculum change needs to include the removal of racist and ethnocentric bias in its content and in associated materials, and include global multi-ethnic perspectives. This will undoubtedly require teachers to develop new knowledge, especially in understanding current knowledge and its origins that are socially, culturally and historically situated. If education is to seriously address social justice, then historical contributions, both individual and institutional, to prejudice and discrimination need to be studied and understood. Only by exposure to a wide diversity of people, ideas and perspectives can teachers help guide their learners to respond to current and future situations with compassion and respect. It is evident that the current educational curriculum is not inclusive. The polarisation of minority communities and those from socially disadvantaged backgrounds is ever-present and exacerbated by exclusionary practices within the education system and wider society. Events such as the London Riots in 2011 and the current concerns regarding radicalisation stem from disenfranchisement caused by lack of equity and social justice. Education has transformational potential as an agency of social change, and curriculum change which promotes learning that is non-discriminatory and emphasises positive attitudes, such as compassion and respect, is one step towards bringing about a more equitable society.

Activity 8.11

- Evaluate your own curriculum for potential bias.
- How could you redesign your curriculum to be less biased and more non-discriminatory?

Negotiated Curriculum

The lack of congruence between the specifications of a predetermined curriculum and the learners' actual needs can make its implementation difficult. Furthermore, the external decision-making about the specifications of a curriculum before its implementation, or encounter with learners, invokes significant preconceptions about education, its purpose and assumptions about learning. As discussed in the preceding section, it also is imbued with cultural bias.

The negotiated model of curriculum (Clarke, 1991) allows full learner participation in selection of content, teaching, learning and assessment. In this way, it embodies the principle that learners' needs are of paramount importance. A negotiated curriculum model, involving full learner participation, is not only unimaginable within the current market-orientated education system, but also perhaps unrealistic. However, the concept of negotiation is an extremely valuable one, intrinsic to the idea of democracy and inclusion, so it is worth considering, at the very least, how a negotiated component might be incorporated into existing curriculum. In this way, learners can collaborate with teachers in the design of a curriculum.

According to Clarke (1991), curriculum design then becomes part of the learning process rather than being external or prior to it. The process of negotiation also gives learners responsibility for their own learning, and can motivate learners to engage positively in making decisions about how to achieve the goals they have helped to determine.

Activity 8.12

- Consider some of the potential advantages and disadvantages of a negotiated curriculum within your own subject specialism.

The key to successful implementation of a negotiated curriculum perhaps rests in being able to anticipate some of the potential drawbacks, and as a democratic activity we, as teachers, must be ready to allow for learners to make mistakes about their educational needs, as this is all part of the learning process. It is in this way that the curriculum becomes part of the learning process, as it empowers learners to be actively involved in the ongoing development of the curriculum.

Demand-Led and Supply-Led Curriculum

In further education, curriculum design has historically been supply-led. Colleges plan the supply of training, and in turn learners supply skills to employers. One of the problems of supply-driven programmes was the centralisation of decisions about provision. This limited its responsiveness to changing forces in the labour market, which subsequently led to criticisms that it was inefficient and incapable of meeting the dynamic needs of a labour market in a globally competitive economy.

High unemployment, particularly youth unemployment in the UK since 2008, and the ongoing mismatch between supply of skills and labour demand has resulted in a more demand-led curriculum in further education. In demand-driven curriculum, the underlying idea is to create competition, namely for funding among institutions and business, and for employers to participate in planning provision for identified demand within the labour market in order to increase employability of the workforce in training. Employers may also demand training, for example through traineeship programmes currently available within further education. One of the ways in which this has manifested itself is in the introduction of the 'innovation code' by the Skills Funding Agency in 2011. This enables institutions to draw down funding for bespoke programmes that meet the needs of local employers and learners without having to wait for the development of new qualifications to be developed by the Qualification and Curriculum Authority (QCA), and to give greater flexibility to meet the needs of local communities and employers more rapidly.

Activity 8.13

- In your institution, what examples of customised programmes of learning under the 'innovation code' are you aware of, or have been involved in the development of?
- Within your own subject specialism, what changes to the curriculum are needed to better meet the needs of local employers and learners? Ideas could include:

  o   A completely online component to your current curriculum.
  o   Develop a series of 'one-off' workshops to offer to the public as full-cost courses.
  o   Work through an improvement to your current curriculum.
  o   Propose a new way of ensuring that all learners improve their English and maths in your own subject specialist curriculum area.

The increased accountability for further education colleges to respond to local community needs was reviewed by Ofsted in their report, *Local Accountability and Autonomy in Colleges* (2013b). This report concluded that the cumulative effect of funding driven by qualifications and quality measures focused on success rates have limited the opportunity for creativity and risk within the sector and that the capacity for implementing curriculum change is in need of development as a result. According to a 157 Group project, capacity for curriculum change in the further education sector may be constrained by a range of factors including:

- A lack of appropriate staff skills and attitudes – staff have over the years become accustomed to delivering a prescribed, supply-led curriculum
- A lack of appropriate college infrastructure to enable colleges to respond swiftly and rapidly to new demands – colleges are large institutions, often with bureaucratic processes for decision-making, meaning that quick responses can be a real challenge

- Inadequate quality and intelligent interpretation of market information
- Inflexible staff contracts and structures, with drives to maximise staff utilisation, leaving little scope for involvement in new opportunities (Green, 2013: 8)

These factors may help to explain why, despite the political attention given to the need for demand-led provision, it has not yet been truly realised within the further education sector.

Activity 8.14

- Evaluate your institution's capacity for curriculum change.
- Can you identify with any of the factors highlighted by the 157 Group as constraints within your own institution with regard to curriculum change?
- Can you find any examples where your institution has been rapid and innovative in its response to local community and/or employer needs?

Conclusion

This chapter has provided an overview of curriculum theory, outlining the different ideologies which underpin curriculum design. For some time now in FE, personal development in conjunction with knowledge and skills to meet the needs of the economy has been its principle mission. However, more recently it is evident that greater pressure is being exerted on the sector to meet national economic goals and in particular its mandate to develop desirable characteristics in future employees through the ambiguous notion of employability (this is discussed further in Chapter 10).

Whilst the notions of an inclusive curriculum, and inclusion, are noble, this chapter has deliberated whether fostering inclusive attitudes can effectively be achieved when exclusionary practices in society continue to impact on the most vulnerable and disadvantaged. Despite the political rhetoric about a 'meritocratic' social order, in such a society it is unsurprising that young people from disadvantaged backgrounds or with learning difficulties or disabilities believe that they cannot hope to achieve their aspirations, no matter how hard they work (see St Clair et al, 2011). At the time of writing, *The Guardian* reported that Debrett's 500 list reveals more than 40 per cent of the UK's most influential people went to fee-paying schools, confirming lack of diversity and showing the trend of Britain becoming 'less meritocratic' (Siddique, 2015). Surely, to be inclusive, we need a firm political commitment that goes beyond idealism. The marketisation of further education, and education across all sectors in the UK, has also made it difficult to create or sustain inclusion-friendly environments and increasingly makes education less hospitable for learners and teachers.

Action Research Link

- Examine the curriculum you are currently teaching and identify an element that could be negotiated and designed in collaboration with your learners.
- Alternatively, revisit Activities 8.8 and 8.9, develop your initial ideas and put them into practice. You could then plan this, implement it and evaluate it as an action research project.

Suggested Further Reading

Powell, S. and Tummons, J. (2011) *Inclusive Practice in the Lifelong Learning Sector.* Exeter: Learning Matters.

Robinson, K. (2009) *The Element: How Finding your Passion Changes Everything.* London: Penguin Books.

Ken Robinson has given several TED Talks which may also be of interest to you, see: www.ted.com/talks

Tummons, J. (2012) *Curriculum Studies in the Lifelong Learning Sector* (2nd edn). Exeter: Learning Matters.

CHAPTER 9

EMPOWERING LEARNERS AND THE VALUE OF LEARNING

Ken Robinson has long been vocal about the crisis of marketisation in education, with particular emphasis on creativity, and in his latest book written with Lou Aronica, *Creative Schools* (2015), puts forward a compelling argument about the failure of the current education system to meet the needs of learners in the twenty-first century and calls for fundamental transformation in the how we educate young people in a complex era with significant socioeconomic and environmental challenges.

> The aims of education are *to enable students to understand the world around them and the talents within them so that they can become fulfilled individuals and active and compassionate citizens.* (Robinson and Aronica, 2015: xx, italics in original)

The key principle of learner participation in democratic education and its relationship to Education for Sustainable Development (ESD) will be explored in this chapter, presenting case studies to exemplify the use of learner voice in FE to enact change at an institutional, a curriculum, a pedagogical and an individual level. The contribution that learning can make at an individual and societal level will be discussed in conjunction with the transformative potential of education.

This chapter will cover the following:

- An introduction to Education for Sustainable Development (ESD)
- A discussion on how transformative learning can contribute to ESD
- Case studies to discuss how learner voice in FE can be a force for change at an institutional, a curriculum, a pedagogical and an individual level
- Learner voice – its potential and its limitations
- Learner voice and teacher professionalism

Introduction

The education system in the UK is perhaps one of the most politicised compared to America and other countries in Western Europe. In the UK, education is rife with elitism and its tradition of separatism has resulted in a longstanding hierarchal structure between academic and vocational education, which still blights the FE sector, for both those who study there and those who work within it. Particularly since the 1988 Education Reform Bill, the education system has become subject to relentless neo-liberal reform and its associate managerial discourse has prevailed in educational policy-making and intensified the marketisation of FE, and education across all sectors. The emphasis is consequently on the measurable outputs of education and performance indicators such as success rates, rather than on the process of learning. Our education system is dominated by cognitivist assumptions about how learning happens, primarily the notion that learning is something that happens to us individually in our heads and is therefore the possession of the individual learner. This view ignores the social aspect of learning, the idea that through social interaction we jointly construct new learning; that learning is a social activity. However, this requires a very different approach to teaching and learning, it necessitates a more dialogic learning experience where the outcomes are less predictable and certainly less measurable in quantitative terms. A dialogic space for learning is one where learners co-construct knowledge through dialogue, whereby ideas, values, beliefs, emotions and assumptions are exchanged and critically explored. This model of learning clearly challenges the current climate where accountability measures prioritise data over learners, teachers and subsequently the processes of teaching and learning.

We live in an increasingly interconnected, but also complex world. We face many challenges as a society, and as a global community, and a lot of the challenges we face need joined up thinking, but also a new way of thinking. Transformative education, which is attributed to the work of Mezirow (1978), is a critical component of ESD. In short, transformative education is the transformation of a person though learning and is rooted in the sociocultural view of learning. This view defines learning as a social process where social interaction plays a fundamental role in development.

Education for Sustainable Development (ESD)

ESD provides a way to transform the education system, and most importantly how we educate. The stakes are high, and so the guiding principles of ESD are ambitious, but they are not inconceivable. What is inconceivable, however, is that these principles can ever be achieved by using the traditional ways of thinking and educating which have ultimately led us into the socioeconomic and environmental predicament that we currently find ourselves in. A transformation, not reform, of education is needed to help confront these challenges head on.

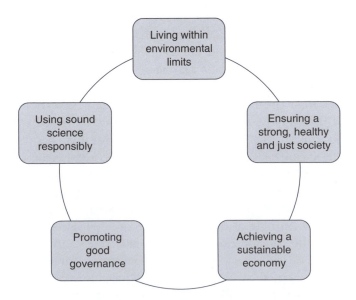

Figure 9.1   The principles of sustainable development

Source: Defra (2005)

Learner Voice

Learner voice initiatives stem from democratic ideals. At the heart of learner voice is reciprocal dialogue and participation to transform education from the bottom-up through collaborative cultures between learners, teachers and educational institutions. The definition of learner voice in this chapter is:

> the involvement of learners and potential learners in shaping the learning opportunities that are available to them. It means involving learners in reforming the lifelong learning system at all levels, by supporting them to act as partners with policy makers, providers, practitioners and other agencies. Learner Voice initiatives enable learners to express their views, needs and concerns and also ensure that institutions respond appropriately to the issues that they raise. (NIACE, 2001, cited in LSIS, 2012)

The concept of learner voice is important for all of the guiding principles of ESD to be realised, however this chapter will focus primarily on its role in ensuring a strong, healthy and just society. To this end, learner voice is about engaging learners in a democratic process as equal agents of change in the development of policy and the planning of provision in the diverse communities found within FE, which is essential for social justice, equality and inclusion. Furthermore, it is about providing opportunities for learners to have levels of social responsibility and personal freedom that they may, or may not, have in other aspects of their lives. In an educational context, learner voice gives learners the responsibility to shape their learning, thereby promoting relevant skills needed for the future. Research has shown that learner voice provides a rich environment for the following:

- Deeper engagement with learning
- Improved metacognitive skills
- Greater responsibility for learning amongst learners
- Better relationships between learners and teachers (Hargreaves, 2004)

Learner voice embodies the notion that a democratic experience is one where the voices of *all* learners are equally important; the aim being for learners to take ownership of their own learning. Learner democracy promotes opportunities for participation in active citizenry beyond the classroom and the educational institution. This concept of citizenship is essential to developing a vibrant, participative democracy and in encouraging personal development within a social context.

The current climate in which learners and teachers are working highlights the urgency of learner voice in education institutions. Chapter 1 discussed some of the issues regarding GCSE attainment, illiteracy and innumeracy, and disengagement in education that persists within the education system in the UK, all of which impact significantly on the FE sector.

It could be debated as to why and whether the gold standard of 5 GCSEs is what is needed to participate fully in today's society, however this is beyond the scope of this chapter, but suffice it to say that poor English and maths contribute to social inequalities. Issues of youth unemployment have been a recurrent issue in the UK: between August and October 2014, as many as 16.6 per cent young adults aged 16–24 were unemployed, with almost a third of these being unemployed for more than twelve months, and so are classified as long-term unemployed (Hough, 2014). Disengagement from learning is an increasing fact within the education system and one of growing concern in Western society. Not only is there disengagement in the education system as it currently stands, but more significantly perhaps is the research finding by the Electoral Commission (2010) which revealed that 56 per cent of 17–25-year-olds were not registered on the electoral roll. Disengagement from political processes and parliamentary democracy in the UK signifies a worrying disconnect between young people and the political representatives who make decisions about their everyday lives, and their futures. Further, this contributes to the lack of active participation in society, which can lead to the polarisation of communities and the individuals within them. The danger then being that polarisation results in exclusion and builds mistrust and disenfranchisement, which Cantle (2011) suggests led to the riots in 2011 in the UK. Disillusioned young people who live in deeply segregated and deprived communities, alienated from much of society, in no way contributes to the ESD principle of a strong, healthy and just society.

It is telling that the National Curriculum consultation in 2013 did not extensively seek learner voice in any significant manner: of over 17,000 respondents, only 50 were young people (DfE, 2013b). Although it is acknowledged that curriculum is ideologically laden and therefore that education can function to empower or control, when teachers are preparing learners for an uncertain future with challenging problems at a local, national and global level, educating learners for jobs that do not yet exist, for encroaching social and environmental problems we do not have the solution to, it is even more pressing that learners are involved in their learning and the decisions that affect their lives now and in the future.

A top-down government approach does not only impact on learners and how they engage in, or disengage from, their learning, it also affects teacher professionalism. Teacher professionalism is increasingly undermined as 'educational policy increases its control over classroom practice and education metrics and reduces autonomy' (Strike, 2004: 107). This is where learner voice and democratic professionalism become intertwined in counteracting topdown policy by engaging learners and teachers in participative and dialogic learning. In this way the traditional power dynamic of teacher-learner, teacher-manager, learner-institution becomes obsolete and education is no longer imposed on learners, it is shaped by them, their teachers and institutions.

Transformative Learning

Mezirow (1978) theorised that transformative education is whereby learning transforms a learner's frame of reference. Illeris defines this as life-history, which is 'the story one has about oneself and which constantly develops and is interpreted anew, is the red thread running through life, self-understanding and learning' (2007: 62). Our life-history is the accumulation of all our previous experiences which we use to interpret new experiences and to make sense of the world around us. It is who we are as individuals at a particular point in time, how we see ourselves, how we see others, how we position ourselves in the world, and how we act in response to different situations. Morrell and O'Connor define transformative learning as:

> Experiencing a deep, structural shift in the basic premises of thought, feelings and actions. It is a shift of consciousness that dramatically and permanently alters our way of being in the world. Such a shift involves our understanding of ourselves and our self-locations; our relationships with other humans and with the natural world; our understanding of relations of power in interlocking structures of class, race, and gender; our body-awareness, our visions of alternative approaches to living; our sense of possibilities for social justice and peace and personal joy. (2002: xvii)

A disjuncture, or disturbance, occurs when we encounter a situation that we cannot assimilate into our frame of reference or life-history: 'we are faced with a situation that we cannot take for granted and we have to stop and think and learn' (Jarvis, 2009: 83). Disjuncture is an experience which triggers a process that leads to the reformation and the reconstruction of our previous learning into new meaning which reshapes our personal frame of reference. Each learner brings their own frame of reference to the learning process and it 'constitutes a starting point for discourse leading to critical examination of normative assumptions underpinning the learner's ... value judgements or normative expectations' (Mezirow, 2000: 31). The impact of uncertainty and unfamiliarity, and the decisions that accompany disjuncture are the building blocks used to reconstruct our personal frame of reference that determines new ways to interpret experience. Through the transformation of the frame of reference, an individual is actually changing the way in which they make meaning in order to interpret their life experiences. This process is significant, since, according to Jarvis (2009: 69): 'meaning ... is a very complex phenomenon and making meaning is certainly crucial to our understanding of both learning and personhood'. Engaging learners in critical debate on topical, and sometimes sensitive issues facilitates disjuncture and, therefore, the transformation of learners' perspectives on issues that will affect their lives now, and in the future.

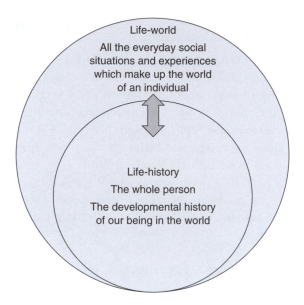

Figure 9.2   The relationship between life-history and life-world

Source: Jarvis (2006)

Further education colleges are social hubs and 'incubators of social value' (Sharp, 2011: 12) which enables teachers to position learners as citizens. Critical thinking and dialogue can influence disjuncture by actively involving learners in challenging their innate assumptions and meanings through social interaction, creating their own resolution and ultimately changing a learner's individual world, or life-world. Transformative learning recognises that learners are more than cognitive beings; it takes into account the whole person – mind and body. Our mind includes knowledge, skills, emotions, values, attitudes and senses; and our body is biological, genetic and physical. When we learn we are therefore transformed cognitively, physically, emotionally and practically (Jarvis, 2006). So, in the transformative learning process we change who we are as a person; this in turn changes how we interact with the world and how we experience events, and, so our individual world changes. Indeed, Jarvis suggests that it is 'through emotions that thought can be transformed into action' (ibid.: 11). Illeris asserts that: 'it is not enough to discuss and consider, the thoughts must also be manifested in action' (2014: 7). Through raising an individual's consciousness, social action ensues and this is at the core of transformative learning. As Schumacher writes: 'too often we communicate at the level of the word, we don't change the world if we leave it there; unless the word, our message, our understanding, becomes incarnate, becomes flesh and dwells among us, nothing happens' (1997: 30).

There are three possible ways in which a person can change in transformative learning, as shown in Table 9.1.

Table 9.1   Three ways in which a person can be changed by transformative learning

The self	New meaning	More experienced
• We change mentally • We change emotionally • Self-esteem • Self-confidence • Self-understanding • Our identity	• We perceive events and the world differently	• We are more able to cope with similar situations • We are more able to cope with problems

Source: Jarvis (2009)

Transformative education offers an important alternative to the current education system as it challenges the status quo in its pursuit of its guiding principles, and in so doing facilitates creativity, critical thinking, debate and opportunities for learners to be agents of positive and sustainable social change.

Learner Voice in Action

This next section will explore learner voice in further education and how it has enacted change at an institutional, a pedagogical, a curriculum and an individual level. Learner voice is about expression of identity, self-esteem and personal development, where institutions and teachers collaborate and transform with learners. Knowing their voice can effect social change, be it within their classroom, at college or within their community, is a powerful realisation for most young people today.

Case study 9.1   Engineering and exclusion in society

Within the Engineering curriculum, it is essential that sustainability becomes a part of every concept taught. It is through engineering design that technology change is driven and this is explicitly linked to the cost of achieving climate change targets with the Oxford Economics modelling giving a 13 per cent lower cost of change by 2020 when design is driven by sustainable and energy-conscious thought. By recognising that life-worlds are social places, the paradox of spatial separation can be

(Continued)

(Continued)

challenged, so environmental impact becomes part of learners' social interaction which promotes critical thinking.

Giving learners the opportunity to travel abroad and visit structures that have been used to segregate and exclude such as the Berlin Wall promotes critical debate about embedding ethnicity, race, religion and faith into social structures to help reduce segregation and exclusion in society. By providing enrichment opportunities, learners can experience at first-hand the impact of structures in society and their use to either liberate or oppress people in society, thereby challenging exclusion in future design.

Source: Case study kindly contributed by Andrew, Mechanical Engineering Lecturer

Reflective question:

- In your own subject area, how could you embed more critical debate on issues of social exclusion, segregation, discrimination and oppression?

Current educational policy and its advocacy of a market-model of education where 'value replaces values' (Ball, 2004: 10) has proven to be a means for the social reproduction and maintenance of inequalities. As Sterling states: 'advocates of a market model of education talk of choice: their notion of choice is a little like choosing deckchairs on the Titanic' (2009: 87). Transformative education supports the realisation of the ESD principle of social justice, as it envisions education and society in a process of continuous co-evolution in which learner voice and active citizenry are central. In this way, it would be possible to: 'create a curricula that is both meaningful, and produce modes of critical pedagogy that truly embrace education as a practice of freedom and young people as critical agents and engaged citizens necessary for making democracy meaningful and substantive' (Giroux, 2014).

Learner voice could potentially provide opportunities for the more powerful, and serve to maintain exploitation and exclusion (Hildyard et al., 2001) rather than promote active democratic participation. So, the question of whether participation is directed by the more outspoken learners, the powers that be, or whether *all* learners truly have the power to challenge existing structures of decision-making as equals within the participatory process, is of critical importance when discussing learner voice. If the institution controls the participatory process, then the implication is that it becomes tokenistic or, worse, a mechanism for containing learner voice and unsolicited discontent and thereby 'allows the have-nots to hear and to have a voice, although they lack the power to ensure that their views will be heeded by the powerful' (Arnstein, 1969: 217), and ultimately it is the interests and perspectives of the institution that are served. This tokenistic approach to participation corresponds to the 'consultation' rung of Arnstein's (1969) Ladder of Citizen Participation (see Figure 9.3) and does not equate to genuine democracy that would challenge the status quo. Arnstein provides a useful framework for depicting the differing levels of participation between power-holders and learners. The bottom rung is non-participative, and further up the ladder the degree of participation increases. The mid-rung is consultation, which Arnstein regards as tokenism, and the top rung is a redistribution of power so that full participation can take place.

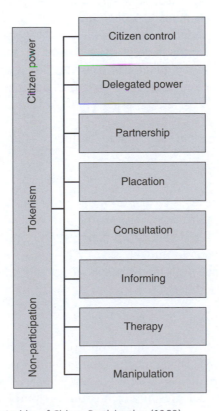

Figure 9.3 Arnstein's Ladder of Citizen Participation (1969)

Case study 9.2   Course representatives

Course representatives are a key mechanism by which learner voice is promoted by most colleges, but often it is the college which is still very much in the driving seat when it comes to resolving issues raised by course representatives which go beyond general repairs.

One example, cited by course representatives at a college involved the price of the same brand of fruit juice which differed across the three outlets where it was sold (80 pence, 90 pence and £1); the college listened to the issue raised at a termly meeting and then two meetings later the college informed the reps that the situation was resolved and the cost was now £1 across all three outlets. Although their voice had been heard, the reps were angered that the decision had been made to increase the price to the maximum rather than a median price or even better the cheaper one.

A further issue sometimes raised by reps is that when minutes of meetings are distributed, sometimes where an issue had been raised at a meeting, the minutes had been altered slightly to make an issue sound more unreasonable than it was if the college was less willing to see the suggestion through. Reps usually have no mechanism to make amendments before the minutes of meetings are distributed to the relevant members. Reps also feel that college staff predominantly pushed the agenda when it comes to making significant changes.

Source: Case study kindly contributed by student representatives

Reflective questions:

- Where on Arnstein's Ladder does this experience of being a course representative sit?
- How similar or different is this experience of being a course representative at your institution?
- How does your institution disseminate changes brought about by course representatives?

Experiential learning is not a new concept, with Dewey (1938), Rogers (1969) and Kolb (1984) laying much of the groundwork. It is defined by the Association for Experiential Education (2007: 13) as a: 'philosophy that informs many methodologies in which educators purposefully engage with students in direct experience and focused reflection in order to increase knowledge, develop skills, clarify values and develop people's capacity to contribute to their communities'.

Experiential learning is also referred to as learning through action, learning by doing, learning through experience, and learning through discovery and exploration. According to Usher et al., experiential learning is when: 'educational practitioners, rather than being the source/producers of knowledge/taste, become facilitators helping to interpret everybody's knowledge and helping to open up possibilities for further experience' (1997: 105). Meaning-making is central to experiential learning and is the process which turns experience into learning, where self-understanding is reached through 'observing the reactions of others, and listening to their evaluations' (Illeris, 2007: 72), and these insights into ourselves are used to reconstruct ourselves many times over.

Case study 9.3   Pedagogy and curriculum-level change

The Level 3 Business and Technology Education Council (BTEC) Health and Social Care course is a vocational course which requires a large amount of theory and academic content to be taught. The challenge with a course of this type is to ensure that the indicative content is covered whilst providing the opportunity for the practical application of theory.

Learners regularly had the opportunity to provide feedback to teachers and managers on all aspects of their course, and through this approach, learners were able to bring about a pedagogical change to the course as well the development of their own curriculum. Learners requested the opportunity for their practical skills lessons to continue into the second year of their course, when previously it had been removed to allow more contact time for teaching of theory. The learners felt that these practical skills allowed them to apply their knowledge and to learn new skills which would make them more sustainably employable in the sector, and give them an 'edge' when applying for vocational degree courses.

Once this change had been implemented, learners also requested the addition of First Aid and Manual Handling courses to be incorporated into their curriculum. This development of a broad range of practical skills has been showcased with learners competing in the Worldskills Advanced Caring Competitions regionally and nationally, where they apply their practical skills and knowledge to live care scenarios.

This curriculum change brought about by learner voice also provided pedagogical changes, namely the incorporation of more experiential learning opportunities wherever possible. This included the use of science laboratories to carry out pig-heart dissections, microscope work

(Continued)

(Continued)

to examine tissues, external trips and visits where appropriate. Due to these substantial changes, learners were significantly more engaged and motivated through these experiential and problem-solving activities, which also encouraged the development of higher order thinking skills.

Learner voice had a beneficial effect for these learners who were able to influence their own curriculum and learning experiences and they have been able to include these additional skills on their CVs and personal statements for university applications.

Source: Case study kindly contributed by Sally, Health and Social Care Lecturer

Reflective questions:

- In what ways have learners influenced your pedagogical practices and curriculum development on your course?
- How effective are your mechanisms for gathering learners' feedback on your course?
- What are the potential constraints of implementing learner feedback in your own practice?

This case study highlights the importance of creating the contextual conditions where learners feel part of the learning process rather than just being a recipient of teaching. They are active participants in the issues pertaining to the improvement of their overall learning experience from the macro level of curriculum design to the micro-level of teaching and learning approaches. The process of collecting learner feedback on professional practice and course design is highly dependent on the teacher-learner relationship and whether it is based on democratic educational values or managerial values. However, the constraints of implementing learner feedback may be practical, financial and at times managerial. By creating the conditions where learners feel that their voice has worth, learning becomes a process of social participation rather than simply cognitive acquisition. Opportunities for democratic dialogue between teachers and learners encourages the development of communities of practice (Lave and Wenger, 1991), which can develop into larger entities and move beyond the immediate community of the classroom. Communities of practice provide the conditions of respect, reciprocity and collaboration, which are the cornerstones of democratic education and democratic professionalism. In this way, Wenger argues that as a 'locus of engagement in action, interpersonal relations, shared knowledge, and negotiation of enterprises, such communities hold the key to real transformation' (1998: 85).

 ### Case study 9.4   A curriculum perspective

The Animal and Land-based section is a well-established team consisting of lecturing and technical staff that possess a wealth of industry and practical experience. A wide range of courses are offered ranging from animal studies, horticulture, countryside management and a foundation degree in Animal Science. The curriculum on offer and the resources available present many opportunities to embed sustainability and meet the needs of a wide range of learners.

The section conducts weekly feedback sessions with its learners and promotes engagement in extracurricular activities which promote sustainability and aim to engage learners with the natural environment. Extracurricular activities are often put together based on the needs of learners and cover topics which they have an interest in. Each year the college hosts 'Go Green' week: the focus of this event is sustainability. Land-based learners play a key role during this week and cover a vast range of subjects which are not covered in-depth by the curriculum but were identified by learners as being important. These subjects have included: sustainable fishing, marine litter and pollution, ethical food production, insects as a protein source, food miles and palm-oil production. Promoting these themes led to learners setting up petitions and campaigning to change things within the college which resulted in the college offering more locally-produced meats and an increased use of free range eggs in their eateries. During 'Go Green' week, learners also managed to secure a radio interview with a researcher who works in Borneo assessing the impact that palm-oil production is having on the environment. This experience allowed learners to increase their understanding of a subject and drive their passion for the natural world.

The Animal Management course lacks embedded links with horticulture, to the team's surprise a large number of learners wanted to expand their knowledge of horticulture and see how it links to animal husbandry. This feedback from learners allowed the team to embed horticulture by growing, making and analysing our own silage. The project was managed by the learners and enhanced sustainable skills that otherwise they may not have had the opportunity to develop, such as communication, leadership and collaboration.

(Continued)

(Continued)

Learner feedback has led to field trips from Scotland to Africa, where learners have been able to develop a wide range of sustainable employability skills and work with a range of leaders within the field. Learners have also requested visits from experts within the field so that they can seek career advice and listen to how these experts developed their own career. This feedback led to a visit from a leading naturalist and television presenter who was able to spend a day sharing their experiences. Learners used this visit as an opportunity to present some of their own research and demonstrate their own skills and ability.

Source: Case study kindly contributed by Stuart, Animal Management Lecturer

Reflective Question:

- In what ways could you embed sustainability in your curriculum in a way that empowers learners to participate in democratic processes to effect changes in their:

  o College community
  o Local community
  o National community
  o Global community

This case study exemplifies the current challenges of working under conditions of rapid global change, ambiguity and uncertainty which directly impacts on what it means to be an FE teacher in contemporary society with the considerable challenges faced by future generations. This gives rise to the issue of teacher professionalism and the conflict between managerialism, which shapes teacher identities through market forces such as accountability, efficiency and effectiveness, and the notion of democratic professionalism which promotes collaborative cultures, and facilitates participation between teachers and learners. Democratic professionalism is founded on emancipatory aims, in alignment with the key ESD principles of equity and social justice, which can only be achieved through engagement in democratic processes to effect change.

Research reveals that learners report the following outcomes when democratic ideals are successfully embedded in institutions:

- They feel that views are taken seriously and makes learners feel respected
- They see how their views can be translated into positive outcomes for their own learning and/or educational establishment
- They are more inclined to discuss and reflect on their learning (Fielding, 2001a; 2001b; 2004)

Case study 9.5   Travel plan

In 2011, the abolition of the Education Maintenance Allowance (EMA) was announced. The college relocated to a business park and transport links had to be negotiated with a local transport provider. However, the college serves a wide surrounding area, serving many rural communities as well as nearby towns and has several campuses, as well as working with some high levels of deprivation in the locality. Rural transport networks are patchy at the best of times, but also considerably expensive in fares. The provision of free travel for learners who meet the means-tested criteria is essential to widen participation, but also to support learners access further education in the local area.

Historically, transport had been funded by the local authority, but the introduction of the EMA meant that there was a shift to learners making contributions to transport costs out of this payment, as well as contributions from the college, which reduced the funds from the local authority for transport.

So, the abolition of the EMA created a funding shortfall that needed to be addressed. The college's main intention was to protect free bus passes for learners, however the five-day free bus pass was not going to be feasible with the current funding gap. Learners were consulted, through the course representatives, and some focus groups were set up to discuss the situation and find some alternative solutions to be able to achieve this aim. A meeting was set up with the college, the course representatives, the local authority and the transport provider to explore the possible alternatives. This was a productive meeting, where open roundtable discussions were held, where voices of learners were listened to, in particular access to transport in some of the more remote and outlying communities.

The outcome of this meeting was a free 3-day bus pass for every learner who meets the threshold criteria, but also to support learners who did not meet the criteria to be able to buy a bus pass at a nominal rate, and additional incentives were agreed such as a £1 fare during holidays. The development of new routes being laid on by the transport provider, also benefited the local community and is based on a principle of sustainability as the links now serve communities which had previously not been able to access public transport and also builds a sustainable infrastructure which becomes attractive to investment in the area which helps to regenerate the community in the longer term.

The challenge now, however, is that with the introduction of the 16–19 Study Programme, and additional curriculum time being devoted

(Continued)

(Continued)

to English and maths, means that the historical three-day college attendance is now five days for the majority of learners. This now presents another challenge at a time of considerable funding pressures on the college, but free bus travel needs to be safeguarded.

Source: Case study kindly contributed by Alex, Advice and Guidance Manager

Reflective questions:

- What issues currently concern learners at your institution?
- What are the mechanisms to voice these concerns with management at your institution?
- How effective are these mechanisms?
- Can you find any examples of where learners have brought about significant changes at your institution?

Teacher professionalism is a shifting phenomenon and one that is threatened by marketisation where policies are intended to achieve the economic values of efficiency, quality control and output. The purpose of a market-driven education system conflicts with the social values of equal opportunities, community and social cohesion and undermines teacher professionalism. Persistent pressures on teachers to meet targets dictate the use of normative approaches to teaching, learning and assessment. This is now endemic in FE as a result of successive government policy, and the result is diminished professional autonomy and reduced opportunity for teachers to take risks and be creative in their own practice. Despite decades of political rhetoric regarding quality, raising standards and social inclusion, education has alienated many young people from learning and shattered their hopes, due to the over-emphasis on market values. As Whitty (2006: 1) states: 'market-based policies … are already demonstrating their limitations, especially in relation to social justice'. Regrettably, all too often, FE teachers regard themselves as part of the system, not as critics of it and those that do speak out are vilified rather than regarded as innovators of change.

Traditional conceptions of professionalism have been criticised as elitist, paternalistic and authoritarian. However, within FE, professional status is something that has been long-battled for within the sector, and is now threatened by the repercussions of the Lingfield Report (2012) which recommended the deregulation of initial teacher education in FE. Currently, there exists a 'narrow technicist model of professionalism' (Whitty, 2006: 12), which stems from decades of mistrust of the teaching profession. Sadly, mistrust breeds mistrust and so teachers are less likely to welcome learner voice in a climate of inspection and accountability.

However, it is important to remain optimistic that there exists an opportunity for a new style of professionalism to develop from the bottom-up with both teachers and learners collaborating in new ways of working within contemporary conceptions of citizenship and democracy. This is what Whitty (2006) calls 'democratic professionalism' and is integral to overcoming the effects of social disadvantage on educational outcomes. Sachs, however, goes a step further, calling for an activist professionalism:

> Activist teacher professionalism is essentially about a politics of transformation. Its spheres of interest are concerned with changing people's beliefs, perspectives and opinions about the importance of teaching, the social location of teachers and the role of competent and intelligent teachers in various education institutions. A politics of transformation is not self-interested; its concern is with wider issues of equity and social justice. (2003: 12)

Whilst democratic professionalism encourages the development of collaborative cultures and spaces for learner voice, the potential for this to be appropriated by managers limits its influence as does the undertow of mistrust of teachers by the system, and by teachers of the system. The activist identity suggested by Sachs is a more progressive way forward as it mobilises the teaching profession politically 'to regain control and to establish its power in setting education agendas that are for the benefit of everyone in the community' (ibid.: 18).

Clearly, this notion of professionalism extends the responsibility of teachers beyond the learning environment, and promotes teachers' collective responsibility for a wider social agenda that encompasses the institution, the community, the education system and *all* learners. This requires collaboration and a collective identity for the teaching profession in order to be able to challenge the dominant forces and assumptions that control and regulate further education, indeed the education system as a whole.

Conclusion

This chapter has examined how the current education system is failing in its responsibility to uphold democratic ideals in order to maintain civic society, which has the social values of justice and equity at its core. The challenges are considerable, and require transformation on a grand scale if the issues discussed in this chapter are to be addressed in any meaningful way. The first step is to address the ways in which we think about education, and most importantly about learning, and create the conditions where its transformative potential can be realised. This requires teachers to become agents of change, as well as learners, so that the decisions made about education encompass the needs, aspirations and values of both, respectively.

 Action Research Link

This could be a potential area for an action research project. Some of the questions below may be helpful in starting to explore this topic for your own research project:

- How inclusive is learner voice in your institution?
- How do your colleagues feel about their professionalism? Is there any opportunity for teachers to be involved in institutional decision-making about policy and its implementation?
- How effectively is learner voice being used within your institution to uphold and promote democratic ideals?

Suggested Further Reading

Illeris, K. (2007) *How we Learn: Learning and Non-Learning in School and Beyond*. London: Routledge.

Illeris, K. (ed.) (2009) *Contemporary Theories of Learning; Learning Theorists in their own Words*. London: Routledge.

Jarvis, P. (2009) *Learning to be a Person in Society*. London: RoutledgeFalmer.

Mezirow, J. (1978) *Education for Perspective Transformation: Women's Re-entry Programs in Community College*. New York: Teachers College, Columbia University.

Robinson, K. and Aronica, L. (2015) *Creative Schools: Revolutionizing Education from the Ground Up*. London: Penguin Books.

Rogers, C. (1969) *Freedom to Learn: A View of What Education Might Become*. Columbus, OH: Merrill.

Sachs, J. (2003) *The Activist Teaching Profession*. Maidenhead: Open University Press.

Sterling, S. (2009) *Sustainable Education: Revisioning Learning and Change*. Dartington: Green Books.

Wenger, E. (1998) *Communities of Practice: Learning, Meaning and Identity*. Cambridge: Cambridge University Press.

CHAPTER 10

POLICY AND PRACTICE

This chapter will contextualise the role of further education in social policy. It will further focus on policy and professional practice using case studies as a reflective tool to examine how policy impacts professional practice and professionalism within FE. Issues of discretion (Lipsky, 2010), commitment to learners and performativity will be explored thematically in this chapter.

Policy in FE is principally aimed at tackling social exclusion and contributing to economic efficiency. Several measures have contributed to increasing participation in FE and the achievement of learners. However, there remain significant challenges in FE due to policy changes, particularly for adults as this provision has borne the brunt of recent funding cuts, leaving the needs of many of the most disadvantaged adults unmet. The other substantial challenge facing FE is the requirement for 16–18-year-olds, who do not have English or maths at grades A*–C, to continue studying towards them.

(Continued)

(Continued)

In 2005, Sir Andrew Foster famously described further education as the 'neglected middle child' of the UK education system. While it lacks the resources and status of schools and universities, further education has a unique importance in the UK. It is required to meet the skills and needs of the economy, provide opportunities for people with previous negative experience of schooling, and respond to the demands of employers as well as learners. Further education plays a significant role in community regeneration in deprived areas providing an array of opportunities for people to return to education, retrain or go on to higher education.

This chapter will cover the following:

- An overview of educational policy in FE
- Discussion on some recent educational policies in FE and their impact on curriculum and practice
- Professionalism in FE since deregulation
- Performativity and professionalism in FE

Introduction

FE is seen by governments as central to economic growth and as such has had to respond to employer demands and focus increasingly on employability skills as well as the personal development of learners. A churn of successive policy has ensued as a result: lifelong learning; 16–19 expansion; a renewed push on adult basic skills after the Moser Report (1999); funding for people working towards Level 2 qualifications and apprenticeships; and now a new focus on 14–19 growth which comes with increased competition with secondary school provision and significant funding pressures (TLRP, 2008).

According to UNICEF (2013), when the Coalition Government came into office in 2010, the UK ranked bottom of 29 rich countries in the proportion of 15–19-year-olds participating in education, and fifth from bottom in the proportion of 15–19-year-olds not in education, employment or training (NEET). There were also a significant number of low-skilled adults, employed and unemployed, and a high proportion of school leavers not achieving the 5 GCSEs A*–C, especially in English and maths, and therefore lacking the basic skills for work. The then Education Minister, Michael Gove, commissioned a report into pre-19 vocational education, known as the Wolf Report (2011). The report concluded that vocational education had weak employer engagement and a weaker apprenticeship system and was characterised by complex and unstable policy structures. The report made 27 recommendations, which were all adopted by the government. These recommendations fall into the following three categories:

- Curriculum
- Apprenticeships/workplace learning
- Funding

Curriculum

There is now an increasingly populated 14–19 educational landscape, including free schools, FE 14+ provision, sixth form colleges, studio schools, academies and university technical colleges (UTCs). This requires a concerted effort on behalf of all the providers to ensure that there is good information available to help learners, parents and employers to make informed choices.

The key development has been the 16–19 study programmes which were introduced in September 2013. These must now include a component of work experience, and since August 2014, all 16–19-year-olds who have not achieved GCSEs in English and maths at grades A* to C as part of their programme must pursue a course that either leads directly to these qualifications or that provides significant progress towards them.

Apprenticeships

The Coalition Government transferred funding from workplace learning to apprenticeships to revive efforts to get young people into work, and since 2010 over 2 million apprenticeships have been started (SFA, 2014b). However, since their introduction, most of the increase in apprenticeships has been among people aged 25 or over (ibid). Traineeships were introduced for 16- to 23-year-olds as a pre-Apprenticeship route. However, major reforms to improve the funding and quality of apprenticeships, such as funding being linked to achievement and co-investment from employers, remain to be fully implemented at the time of writing (BIS, 2014; House of Commons Library, 2015).

Funding

In 2009/10, total programme spending on 16–19 education, FE and skills was £12 billion, of which spending on 16–19-year-olds (approximately

£7.9 billion) accounted for 66 per cent of the total, compared to adult spending of £4 billion. Between 2009/10 and 2013/14, spending was maintained almost at its 2009/10 level but in real terms this equates to a 10 per cent cut in spending on FE (Lupton et al., 2015). Spending on 16–19 provision has been protected, and colleges have been on ardent recruitment drives to attract this age group since the Wolf Report (2011) recommended that funding be reformed from a per-qualification basis to a per-learner basis and the increased competition between schools and colleges due to the expansion of the 14–19 landscape. But it is adult education that has suffered the worst cuts, with a 26 per cent cut in funding thus far. Funding has been removed from a large number of qualifications for 19+ learners deemed to have low quality or poor take up, and a new funding system of 24+ Advanced Learning Loans for Level 3 (A level equivalent) qualifications has been introduced. As a result, there were 17 per cent fewer adult learners in 2013/14 than 2009/10 (Lupton et al., 2015).

Whilst the funding rate for 16 and 17 year olds has been maintained at £4000, for 18-year-olds this was cut by 17.5 per cent to £3300 in 2014–15. As part of this move, the government is seeking to extend the 24+ loan scheme, to 19+ loans for learners on Level 2 and Level 3 courses.

Raising of the Participation Age (RPA)

This was announced by the New Labour Government and then supported by the Coalition Government when they came to power. School leavers in 2013 were the first to be required to continue in education or training at least for one more year and from September 2015 this was extended to two more years. Although the Coalition enacted the RPA, it did so with remarkably little publicity or comment, and did not implement the fines for learners and employers for non-compliance that were proposed when it was first announced.

The Coalition Government reduced the financial support available to learners from low income backgrounds by abolishing the Education Maintenance Allowance (EMA) in 2011. The EMA scheme was intended as an incentive to encourage learners from low-income backgrounds to stay in education post-16. The maximum allowance per learner was £30 a week, depending on the household taxable income. The EMA policy cost £560 million per year at the time of abolition and its payment to learners was contingent on their attendance. This financial scheme was replaced with the 16–19 Bursary Fund at the reduced cost of £180 million. The government rationale behind this drastic reduction in funds was to provide more targeted support for disadvantaged learners. Providers are given £1200 per year for learners in care, leaving care or on Income Support, Employment Support Allowance or Disability Living Allowance. Additional funding is based on the number of learners who received EMA at the provider previously at a rate of £266 per learner, although this is a discretionary fund and it is up to each provider to support those who are most in need. A review of the 16–19 Bursary Fund in 2014 showed that around a quarter of a million (or around 40 per cent) fewer learners were in receipt of the bursary compared to the EMA (Callanan et al., 2014).

Professionalisation and Qualified Teaching and Learning Skills (QTLS)

In my opinion, the key change in recent FE policy is the deregulation of Initial Teacher Education (ITE) and therefore the requirement for FE teachers to be qualified. It is felt by many in the sector that the statutory requirement of ITE qualifications ensures that the professional status of all FE teachers in the sector remains intact. The historical and current context of deregulation has been outlined in Chapter 2.

The Lingfield Report (2012), which recommended the deregulation of ITE in FE, has been deemed deeply flawed on several fronts. Most importantly, however, is the lack of an evidence base on which the review panel based its inquiry, and furthermore, neglected to refer to research it had in its possession that contradicts some of the key recommendations made in the final report. This included research commissioned by Business, Innovation and Skills (2012: 27), which illustrated that the 'central ambition of the 2007 Regulations to raise the bar in terms of level of qualification required to teach is being met' which was ignored by the Lingfield inquiry.

One of the recommendations of the Wolf Report (2011) was to allow FE teachers with QTLS to teach in schools on the same basis as qualified school teachers, which is the first step towards the acknowledgment of FE teachers as being comparable with qualified teachers in the schools sector. This professional recognition has been maintained and is a major contribution to the professionalism of FE teachers and the legacy of the IfL.

Deregulation can only further undermine the pay and conditions of those teaching in FE at a time of increased workload pressures and continuing casualisation due mainly to funding cuts in the sector. The 2007 professionalisation strategy made significant progress towards securing parity of esteem for the FE sector and its workforce. Deregulation risks, once more, relegating FE to the 'Cinderella' of the education sector (Brooks, 1991).

Activity 10.1

- What ITE is available for teachers at your institution?
- What is your opinion of deregulation?
- What impact has it had/will it have on the profession and provision in FE?

Deregulation undermines the significant steps made in raising the status of FE teachers. Many fear that it will lower the status of the sector and its learners at a time when more and more pressure from high-stakes expectations is exerted on the sector and its learners through government policy to meet economic goals.

Case study 10.1   The impact of ITE on professional identity

When I started my teaching practice in further education, I wasn't quite sure what to expect. Some years ago, I'd been involved with teaching adults in a community college but that was in a night-school setting so I'd not had much (if any) contact with fellow professionals. At college, I found myself as part of a large maths team which had expanded dramatically due to the recent changes to conditions of funding. My first week coincided with an Ofsted inspection and so suddenly I was immersed in a culture which was very focussed and professional. It was all somewhat bewildering if I'm honest.

Over the next few weeks I gradually began to get used to college and make the connections between what we were learning on the Diploma in Education and Training (DET) course and what I was seeing in the classroom. I saw at first-hand just what an impact the requirement to study maths has had on the college and its learners. Many learners, particularly those doing functional skills, struggle to engage with maths or to see how it is relevant to their lives or careers. It's a challenge to try to build confidence and motivation while still keeping pace with covering material in the scheme of work.

During my teaching practice I had lots of discussions about how to teach maths and the maths team (and especially my mentor) encouraged the sharing of ideas and resources. For me this was an invigorating and supportive environment and has triggered an interest in finding out more about the how to teach maths in ways which encourage and motivate disenchanted learners.

During the DET course we looked at wider professional practice and I began to appreciate more fully the links between government policy, the organisation of the college and my classroom experiences. All this has helped me to realise that my professional identity extends beyond lesson planning and teaching (although of course that is important) to being part of a wider debate about the role of maths in our society.

Source: Case study kindly contributed by Ann, DET student, and maths specialist on the graduate bursary scheme

Reflective questions:

- What opportunities do you get in your current teaching role to discuss teaching and learning with your colleagues?
- In what ways has your own experience of ITE impacted on your professional identity?

From my own experience as a teacher educator over the past decade or so, the overriding value of ITE which teachers share as they come towards the end of their qualification is the opportunity for them to come together as professionals, to have the opportunity to share ideas, resources, challenges, in a supportive and collaborative environment. This collegiality and the development of positive working relationships, is something that continues beyond the structure of the ITE qualification and feeds into the culture and ethos of an institution. As professionals in our high-stakes, highly pressured teaching roles, we get very little time to come together and actually talk about teaching and learning. ITE creates these opportunities. It also creates a space where professionals can discuss their role as a teacher, something which many teachers are questioning within this overly prescribed and audit-driven culture which defines the work of teaching currently. Within the current climate in education, ITE may in fact be the only haven where professionals can come together and discuss their practice openly and honestly and challenge the practices expected of their increasingly bureaucratic job role. ITE may be the last vestige of resistance to the performative demands of our job role, the space for us to air our collective voice as professionals. Without this, we become fragmented as a profession, and I fear that this will result in our subservience to the normative practices that are being foisted upon us. Feedback from a new teacher who has just completed their ITE supports its value in developing autonomy as professionals:

Case study 10.2   A personal reflection on ITE

Undertaking initial teacher education gave me the opportunity to develop new skills and knowledge and embed these into my own teaching. I wouldn't say that my experience of the course was 'this is how teaching works' or 'this is what you must do', rather the course was a means for me to explore my own teaching practice as an individual and examine educational theories and experiment with the ones that I believed would work best in my practice to develop my own style of teaching. Of course, there have been practices which are referred to as 'better', but they were never deemed to be the definitive approach. At the beginning of the course, this open-ended approach frustrated me as I wanted to know specific answers to topics like behaviour and motivation. However, now I reflect back on my teacher education, I prefer this approach because it has allowed me to develop and hone my own skills as a reflective practitioner and develop confidence in my teaching based on my own professional judgements about what works best for my learners, my subject and my context.

Source: Case study kindly contributed by Matt, Marine Technology Lecturer

Reflective question:

- How does this compare to your experience of ITE?

A key concern regarding the deregulation of initial teacher education in FE is that it potentially denies teachers the opportunity to develop, and reflect on, their theoretical knowledge base, therefore the ability to link theory to practice and use this to make informed decisions about their own practice, to take risks, and more importantly in the current high-stakes climate to justify and defend their professional judgements about their own practice. Case Study 10.3 is a first-hand account of how important initial teacher education is.

 Case study 10.3   The impact of ITE on a new teacher entering FE

The combination of theoretical content, combined with practical exposure in the classroom right from the start has given me a fantastic grounding and helped me develop my personal and professional identity. The structure of the DET course has allowed me to examine different theories and principles of teaching and learning, as well as explore differ-ent philosophical and ideological perspectives on the role of education, and further education, within society. This was all taught at a steady pace, giving me time to experiment with different approaches in the classroom and reflect on this as my practice and teaching experience developed. Not everything worked, but it was a great opportunity to try techniques and approaches I would never have thought of using, and it has made me a far more rounded teacher. The support of my fellow teachers to let me make these mistakes and provide feedback afterwards has been invaluable. I now feel confident to start my career in FE teaching, not that I have all the answers or that I'm the finished article, but I have a wide enough range of tools in my repertoire, and the ability to reflect on my practice, which will give me and my learners the best possible chance of success.

Source: Case study kindly contributed by Tony, DET student, and maths specialist on the graduate bursary scheme

Reflective question:

- What aspect of your ITE has had the most significant impact on the following:

  o Your professional development
  o Your practice
  o Your learners
  o Your professional identity as an FE teacher

Employability

Diminishing youth labour markets are a feature of most Western countries, but the UK has been less effective than most in ensuring progression from education into the labour market. The continued mismatch between supply and demand in FE training and labour market vacancies highlights the per-sistent deficit in progression from education into the labour market in the UK (National Careers Council, 2013). Tackling this issue is the key driver for the employability agenda.

Employability has been a component of ITE qualifications since 2007. However, the fervent promotion of employability has really taken flight more recently. One key area that employability encompasses is what are referred to interchangeably as transferable skills, soft skills, character or personal development. Personal development is one of the key fields under the new 2015 Common Inspection Framework (CIF).

Employability can be defined as:

> A set of skills, behaviours, competencies and personal attributes – that make learners more likely to gain employment and be successful in their chosen occupations, which benefits themselves, the workforce, the community and the economy. (Yorke, 2006: 8)

In this era of rapid economic and technological change, nations need a workforce that is able to sustain the ever-changing demands of the labour market. Employability is therefore aimed at helping people gain and maintain employment as well as obtaining new employment as and when required.

So, there is now a march towards helping young people develop 'soft skills' beyond the normal competences and qualifications they need to secure employment and be sustainably employable in a changing labour market. With fewer job opportunities available, employers are being more selective in their recruitment of employees. Having the prerequisite vocational training and qualification is no longer sufficient. Employers are keenly looking for 'soft skills':

> Given the choice between someone with the desired mindset who may lack the complete skill set for the job, and someone with the complete skill set who lacks the desired mindset, a total of 96 per cent of employers picked mindset over skill set. (Reed and Stoltz, 2013: 7)

Activity 10.2

- Make a list of the components of employability developed within your own teaching.
- How could you further improve this aspect of your practice?

Knight and Yorke (2006: 5) provide the USEM model which encompasses four main interrelated components of employability:

- Understanding – subject understanding and application; understanding how organisations work
- Skills, or skilful practices which relates to awareness of, and responsiveness to, the work context, including a willingness to learn and team work, as well as key skills in maths, English, digital literacy and communication. These skilful practices relate to subject area, work and life in general
- Efficacy beliefs, self-theories and personal qualities – this includes problem-solving commitment, energy, self-motivation, self-management, reliability, cooperation, flexibility and adaptability (see Dweck, 2006 in Chapter 4 for growth mindset, self-belief and resilience)

- Metacognition (learning how to learn), which involves self-awareness regarding the learner's learning, and the capacity to reflect on, in and for action

The USEM model highlights the point that employability is not a simplistic set of skills, rather it is a complex myriad of personal qualities and beliefs, understandings, skilful practices and the ability to reflect productively on experience (Yorke, 2006:). Furthermore, Yorke's definition of employability affirms that employability is more than just about gaining and sustaining employment, it is also importantly about developing active citizenship. Employability, however, is not without its critics. Some argue that the notion of employability being transferable from one context to another is fundamentally flawed. Critics on the primacy of context include Wolf (1991). However, Hyland and Johnson's critique on the fallacy of transferability is well-summarised in the following passage:

> Is it reasonable to expect someone who has learnt to solve problems in, say, business studies, to be able to transfer this learning to other spheres such as counselling, engineering or town planning without acquiring a large additional body of domain-specific knowledge? Indeed, even with the benefit of this additional body of knowledge, the idea of generally transferable problem-solving skills is still highly suspect. There is no general routine, no one set of procedures, no algorithm that will at the same time facilitate the solving of a chess problem, show people the way out of difficulties in personal relationships, diagnose an electrical fault and help sort out a difficult passage in Hegel. (Hyland and Johnson, 1998: 169)

Further criticisms have been focused on the work-centric approach imbued in employability which promotes a simplistic dualism between work and dependency and which omits analysis of inequalities in society and therefore the working population (Patrick, 2012). The polarisation of those in work, and those who are not and are therefore reliant on benefits, has been promoted through recent welfare reforms and the valorisation of work as the primary duty and reward of being a good citizen. Therefore, those who are not employed are demonised, made to feel individually accountable for their own failure to find work, and this exacerbates issues of social exclusion for many individuals and communities. This contributes to the discourse on the deservingness of those in work, and the undeservingness of those not in work, according to Patrick (ibid.). Whilst work can be rewarding and can help lift people out of poverty, this is not as straightforward as politicians would have us believe. More than half of all working-age adults in poverty now live in families where someone is in paid work, moreover the type of work has a significant impact on people's well-being. The growth of insecure employment such as that based on zero-hour contracts can actually be harmful to individual well-being (ibid.).

According to research by the TUC (2014), just 1 in every 40 of the net jobs added to the economy between 2008 and 2014 has been a full-time employee job and 1 in 12 employees since 2008 in the UK are now in precarious employment. These findings clearly undermine the idea of sustainable employment which is embedded in the employability agenda.

Prevent Strategy and the Counter-Terrorism and Security Act 2015

Radicalisation and its implications on our role and practice have already been discussed in Chapter 5. In 2015, the Coalition Government introduced the Counter-Terrorism and Security Act 2015, which sets out the legal obligation for schools, colleges and universities to tackle non-violent extremism. This Act has caused an outcry from many in the teaching profession, as it is seen to conflict with the right to freedom of speech which is legislated in the Education Act 1986, and consequently places a duty on universities and colleges to 'ensure that freedom of speech within the law is secured for members, students and employees of the establishment and for visiting speakers' (DfE,1986: 46). The contention is the reference to non-violent extremism and what this constitutes, as the counter-terrorism strategy focuses more explicitly on ideology, and even non-violent ideology. According to Richards (2012: 22):

> the concern with non-violent ideology as a focus of a counter-terrorism strategy diminishes the prospect of opening up radical but non-violent avenues for democratic political expression as an alternative to the use of terrorism.

The new statutory duty for providers is to have 'due regard to the need to prevent people from being drawn into terrorism', and includes powers to charge individual principals in schools and colleges and university vice-chancellors with contempt of court backed by criminal sanctions if they fail to enforce the new statutory guidance (HM Government, 2015: 2).

So, not only does this impact on our role and responsibilities being teachers on the frontline in FE colleges, but the other requirement, albeit non-statutory, is that we promote mainstream British values in our practice to prevent extremism: 'democracy, the rule of law, individual liberty and the mutual respect and tolerance of different faiths and beliefs' (HM Government, 2011: 34). The Prevent Strategy defines extremism as: 'vocal or active opposition to fundamental British values' (HM Government, 2011: 107). The human rights organisation Liberty, gave a response to the Prevent Strategy, which criticised it on the grounds that it is a counterproductive policy, and that rather than tackling extremism, it has created discrimination and mistrust, especially amongst the UK Muslim community which has been the primary focus of Prevent as it noticeably ignores other forms of extremism, such as far-right ideology. In their response, Liberty also point out that this policy leads to self-censorship and alienation by outsourcing intelligence-gathering to teachers, because the professional responsibility to monitor learners risks pushing extreme views underground rather than creating safe spaces where they can be challenged:

> Teachers are uniquely well placed to encourage open debate on sensitive political and religious issues and make the case for mutual respect built on a system of common values. Such a vital role can only be performed effectively, however, if students trust their teachers and feel able to speak freely about deeply personal issues of morality. (Liberty, 2010: 5)

Most FE colleges see the risk of radicalisation, and the need to protect young people from radicalisation, identified in the Prevent Strategy, as another aspect of their duty of care to safeguard learners. According to the new inspection framework launched in September 2015, Ofsted will be looking at radicalisation and extremism as a safeguarding concern and will be looking to see it within policies and procedures. It will look to see how governors and managers address this as part of its judgement on effectiveness of leadership and management. Ofsted, furthermore, expect to see British values and radicalisation measures embedded in the curriculum in the same way that equality and diversity is, when making judgements about the other fields in the CIF.

Activity 10.3

- How vulnerable do you think your institution is to potential radicalisation?
- What is your institution's policy and procedure on radicalisation?
- What training have teachers, managers, governors and other staff at your institution had on the Prevent Strategy and the factors that may make some people vulnerable to radicalisation?
- How do you and your institution ensure the promotion of British values (democracy, the rule of law, individual liberty and mutual respect and tolerance for those with different faiths and beliefs) within the FE curriculum?

Performativity

Stephen Ball has written extensively on the ongoing shift towards marketised education in the UK. In FE, this really started following Incorporation in 1992. In short, productivity is the driving force of neoliberal policy, which prioritises economic goals over moral obligations. This has fundamentally changed education: learners are now positioned as consumers; there is an intensified emphasis on the outputs of education; and the quality of teaching and learning is measured by a set of standardised practices (Ball, 2004). The reverence for performance data by which individual institutions and individual teachers can be judged and compared by sets the parameters of educational processes, professional practice and how institutions are managed. Increasingly, we choose and judge our actions in terms of effectivity and appearance. 'Beliefs and values are no longer important – it is output that counts. Beliefs and values are part of an older, increasingly displaced discourse of public service' (ibid.: 9).

As mentioned in Chapter 2, teachers in FE have a strong inner dedication to the learners they work with, and tensions between teachers' own ethical commitment to their learners and the requirements of performativity are an increasing struggle for many teachers. Where economic imperatives in policy prevail over the needs of learners, teachers are often making decisions that are not always in the best interests of their learners. Compliance with implementing these policy directives is how teachers are judged to be doing a good job, thereby further compounding these tensions. Lipsky suggests that teachers, as street level bureaucrats, have a degree of discretion in policy implementation stating that in this way we can reconcile some of these tensions by finding 'a satisfactory balance between the realities of the job and personal fulfilment' (2010: xvi). Lipsky goes on to discuss how, in order to cope with the bureaucratic workload, discretion is used to achieve this by using mechanisms to streamline and simplify the workload in order to cope with these bureaucratic pressures. In this way, Lipsky suggests that the policy directives placed on public sector workers, such as teachers, can be managed with a certain degree of autonomy, in the form of discretion, in how they meet the performative demands of their work, but do not fully compromise their values and therefore their sense of responsibility for their learners' well-being. This is particularly pertinent in an era where excessive bureaucratic workloads mean teachers have less time for planning, and less time for their learners.

Despite the succession of policy to improve quality in FE, marketisation has done nothing to address the workforce concerns Foster reported on regarding retention, casualisation and lack of comparative parity in pay and conditions, which he claimed impoverished the professionalism of the sector in 2005, as these still persist today. Furthermore: 'free market policies in both education and the economy continue to have the effect of legitimizing continued inequality and the exclusion of weaker social groups' (Tomlinson, 2005: 213).

Activity 10.4

Consider an area of educational policy that has had an impact on curriculum and practice in your own area of specialism and explain ways in which the following factors have influenced your chosen policy:

- Social – this may include culture, employment status, social mobility, educational history and demographical area.
- Political – this may include regulation, legislation and political ideology.
- Economic – this will include funding and current economic policies.

Conclusion

This chapter has examined some of the significant policy changes within FE over the last few years, however there is not enough room to cover all the changes in this chapter, as there have been too many. A report published in 2015 by the Organisation for Economic Co-operation and Development (OECD) on education reform, found that, 'once new policies are adopted there is little follow-up. Only 10 per cent of the policies [examined had actually] been evaluated for their impact' (ibid.: 20). This highlights the short-termism of educational policy-making and its use as a political football rather than about addressing some of the fundamental issues and challenges facing young people, society and teachers currently. Whilst there have been attempts to professionalise the FE workforce, much reform has in fact restricted our professional room for manoeuvre, which limits the possibilities of us being able to develop our learners holistically. This is in part due to the prevalence of instrumental conceptions of learning as the acquisition of knowledge and skills. However, in FE in particular, we are working with many people who have not had a positive experience of education previously, and so we need to engage them, or rather re-engage them, in the process of learning.

> From this perspective, FE is about learning how to become a learner and how to develop an identity across education, training and perhaps also employment. It is about learners changing aspects of their lives and also the way they relate to the world (Teaching Learning and Research Programme, 2008: 29).

Nevertheless, with increasing pressures on teachers in FE which result from inspection, funding, targets, initiatives and the subsequent demands on their working practices to make these reforms work – because the stakes are high if they do not – the work of FE teachers can sometimes work against, rather than for, learners. This causes tensions in teachers' inner commitment to the learners with whom they work. In their investigation into the impact of policy in FE, Coffield et al. concluded that:

> those who struggle to make the reforms work and know most about how they impact on practice are excluded from their evaluation and redesign. In other words, the model is a closed system, which claims to have embedded

incentives for continuous improvement and innovation, but which instead treats 'the workforce' as another lever to be pulled rather than as creative and socially committed professionals who should be involved in the formation, enactment, evaluation and redesign of policy. (2007: 738)

There is a need for more democratic working practices in FE, where teachers and managers inform policy-making decisions, and contribute to their evaluation once implemented. I believe that one way in which to achieve this is for those of us who are working in FE to undertake practitioner-research and raise the profile of FE in the education sector. In this way, FE will be better understood, its triumphs and challenges heralded, so that it can better stand up for itself, its teachers and its learners, and make decisions that work in their interests, rather than those of politicians and policy-makers.

Action Research Link

- Consider an area of policy which impacts on your curriculum and/ or practice. Design and carry out an action research project that analyses its implementation on the front line and addresses some of the issues with its enactment in practice. These could be issues such as motivation, achievement, constraints of staffing, resources, timetabling, CPD, initial teacher education, funding, etc.

Suggested Further Reading

157 Group (2015) *Prevent Toolkit*. London: 157 Group Ltd.

Ball, S.J. (2004) *Education for Sale: The Commodification of Everything*. The Annual Education Lecture 2004. London: King's College London.

Coffield, F., Edward, S., Finlay, I., Hodgson, A., Spours, K., Steer, R. and Gregson, M. (2007) 'How policy impacts on practice and how practice does not impact on policy', *British Educational Research Journal*, 33 (5), pp. 723–42.

Hyland, T. and Johnson, S. (1998) 'Of cabbages and key skills: Exploding the mythology of core transferable skills in post-school education', *Journal of Further and Higher Education*, 22 (2), pp. 163–72.

Liberty (2010) *Liberty's Response to the Home Office Consultation on the Prevent Strand of the UK Counter-Terrorism Strategy*. London: Liberty.

Lupton, R., Unwin, L. and Thomson, S. (2015) *The Coalition's Record on Further and Higher Education and Skills: Policy, Spending and Outcomes 2010–2015*. Working Paper 14, January. London: London School of Economics.

Patrick, R. (2012) 'Work as the primary "duty" of the responsible citizen: A critique of this work-centric approach', *People, Place & Policy*, 6 (1), pp. 5–15.

CHAPTER 11

ACTION RESEARCH IN FURTHER EDUCATION

This chapter aims to give an introduction to action research, its purpose and its methodology of critical self-reflection (Lewin, 1943; 1946; 1948); Schön, 1983; Carr and Kemmis, 1986). The chapter will present examples of action research and invite readers to engage with these by reflecting on their own practice and potential areas for research. It is not intended to be a definitive account of action research, but more of an introduction to some of its origins, its theoretical perspectives and philosophical underpinnings, with some tools to help get you started on your action research project.

This chapter will cover the following:

- A brief background to action research
- The purpose of action research in education
- The action research process
- Methodology of action research and research methods in action research
- The role of action research in professional development
- Getting started on your action research project

The Origins of Action Research and its Aim

It is generally acknowledged that Kurt Lewin (1946) originally conceived the term 'action research'. Lewin was a German-American psychologist who is often credited as being the founder of social psychology. When Hitler came to power in 1933, he emigrated to America, becoming a refugee scholar. The work that Lewin undertook is founded on a commitment to resolving social conflict, with a particular emphasis on issues experienced by minority and disadvantaged groups in society most likely attributable to anti-Semitism he experienced as a German Jew with the rise of the Nazi Party prior to the second world war. Lewin's focus on social conflict was for two reasons, first he saw this approach as helping to develop and strengthen democratic values in society as whole, and second he believed that these values would protect society from discrimination and oppression from tyranny which overshadowed events in his own lifetime.

Lewin's work stemmed from his concern to find an effective approach to resolving social conflict, at either the group, institutional or societal level, through changing group behaviour. Lewin believed that the best approach to resolving social conflict was to facilitate learning which would enable individuals to understand the world around them, and their perceptions of it, and so to take action and make changes. In this way, his work was considerably influenced by the gestalt psychologists he worked with before leaving Germany. Lewin maintained that the learning, and the understanding, that occurred from this process was more valuable to individuals than the change itself.

Action research, and its use to solve conflict and bring about change, is characterised by three key principles:

- Change requires action
- Successful action needs careful analysis of the situation to ensure that the best possible solution is chosen
- A realisation that there is a need for change is vital, otherwise introducing change can be problematic

Underpinning Lewin's work was a fundamental ethical belief in democratic institutions and democratic values in society. His work is in some ways akin to Dewey's work, in that they share a belief in democratic education, and the generation of knowledge by all members of society through action and experimentation. Lewin was aware that 'nations need generations to learn the democratic way of living' (1999 [1943]: 321), and Dewey believed that 'democracy is more than a form of government; it is primarily a mode of associated living, a conjoint communicated experience' (1916: 87). In this way, the importance of democratic institutions, and in particular education, was advocated by both Lewin and Dewey as a fundamental prerequisite to creating a free and more equal society. The democratic principle of cooperation is a key element in the action research process as it involves teachers as researchers working with, and for, all those involved in the research.

Action research in education

Action research in education and the promotion of teacher as researcher in the UK was largely due to the work of Lawrence Stenhouse in the 1960s and 1970s, and later John Elliott, both of whom recognised the relationship between teacher enquiry, professional development and school improvement: 'it is teachers who, in the end, will change the world of the school by understanding it' (Stenhouse, 1981: 104).

Stenhouse was reacting against the Tyler model of curriculum that had been so enthusiastically adopted, both in the UK and in the USA. Tyler's model was a technical view of curriculum as a means to an end, which could be measured – an objectives-based approach which in turn promoted scientific educational research and so education became dominated by academics who designed curricula, not teachers. Action research became part of the political and social context at a time when decisions about education, and in particular curriculum development, were made externally which diminished teachers' professional autonomy.

> The teachers-as-researchers 'movement' to which Stenhouse (1975) contributed so great an impetus is perhaps more accurately seen as a response to political conditions. (Carr and Kemmis, 1986: 18)

Whilst the general approach to enquiry adopted by Stenhouse and other advocates of action research was a more qualitative method than previously used, there was debate regarding the primary aim of action research. Some emphasised its role in solving practice-based problems in learning environments (Nixon, 1981). Others have promoted educational action research as a means of social change (Carr and Kemmis 1986; Kemmis and McTaggart, 1988; 2000), or as instrumental in supporting personal professional development (Whitehead, 1989).

The Purpose of Action Research

Action research is 'carried out by practitioners who have themselves identified a need for change or improvement, sometimes with support from outside the institution; other times not' (Bell, 2005: 8). In short, it is the use of situated research to inform practice; the study of *praxis* or theory of action.

Praxis is the application, or use of, knowledge and/or skills informed by reflection on practice. The action research approach uses practice to develop theory about *praxis*, rather than our practice being subjected solely to academic research based entirely on theoretical knowledge (Figure 11.1).

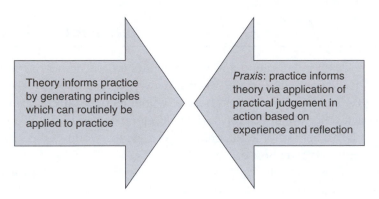

Theory informs practice by generating principles which can routinely be applied to practice

Praxis: practice informs theory via application of practical judgement in action based on experience and reflection

Figure 11.1   'Real' knowledge of theory versus practical knowledge of 'real-life' or *praxis*

Activity 11.1

1.   Think of an event in your own practice that has happened recently.
2.   What did you do in the moment the event occurred?
3a. Reflect on the event and the action you took in the moment if you haven't already. What can you learn from this experience?
     or:
3b. If you have already reflected on the event and your action, what did you learn from the experience?
4.   How will your reflection, and learning from the experience change your practice going forward?

A lot of educational research is unfortunately done on teachers rather than by teachers; as Carr and Kemmis put it: 'teachers became actors on the stage of education or, to use an unkinder image, operatives in its factories' (1986: 16). Generally, such research is either not practically applicable as it is often undertaken by researchers who are not teachers and in contexts which are not always relevant to individual teachers, or it is not readily accessible to teachers in their busy working lives. There is a traditional hierarchy of knowledge gained from theory, and knowledge gained from practice, with the former being given a higher status. Action research addresses this essential disparity between practice and theory by re-establishing the importance of teachers' knowledge and experience gained from practical situations on which they base their judgements: 'Theory building and critical reflection inform our practice and our action, and our practice and action inform our theory building and critical reflection' (Wink, 2000: 59).

Action research can be defined as:

> A form of collaborative self-reflective enquiry undertaken by participants in social situations in order to improve the rationality and justice of their own social or educational practices, as well as their understanding of these practices and the situations in which these practices are carried out. (Carr and Kemmis, 1986: 162)

This definition emphasises the dual role of action research in understanding practice and bringing about change as a result of systematic inquiry. As mentioned earlier, action research is a values-based approach to research which attempts to bring about positive change for research participants, and as a result has both political and emancipatory purposes. Paolo Freire (1921–97) is another figure recognised as being influential in the development of action research, in particular the branch of action research often referred to as Participatory Research. He developed adult literacy programmes, working with those most marginalised in society: illiterate rural peasants. In his seminal book *Pedagogy of the Oppressed* (1970; 2000), he developed a theory of oppression and introduced the idea of critical consciousness in the oppressed as the source of liberation. He writes that knowledge and action are both necessary to bring about change, and that everyone should have the right to be involved in the research process in order to ensure active participation in change, rather than change being imposed from external sources. Freire's work asserts that experience can be a basis of knowing and that experience can lead to a legitimate form of knowledge that influences practice. Action research is emancipatory in educational contexts because it equips teachers with the autonomy to make decisions about their own practice, about what works best for their learners in their own teaching contexts. This emancipatory component of action research, its potential to challenge the status quo, as well as the fact that it is undertaken by teachers, means that action research has in traditional academic circles been derided as being an inappropriate, and inferior, form of research which lacks rigour. This was the finding by Roulston et al in their study into teacher-research and the research of academics:

> it is not only that teachers are thought to be inadequate to the task of conducting quality research … also, some consider the kind of knowledge that teacher research produces to be inferior to and less valuable than other kinds of academic work. (2005: 182)

Action Research Methodology

Action research in education can be used for inquiry into more than just classroom practice and 'has been employed in school-based curriculum development, professional development, school improvement programmes, and systems planning and policy development' (Carr and Kemmis, 1986: 162).

According to Lewin, the course of action research 'proceeds in a spiral of steps, each of which is composed of a circle of planning, action and fact finding about the results of the action' (1948: 206; see Table 11.1).

Table 11.1   A summary of Lewin's spiral model of action research (1948)

1.   Identify a problem and area of interest within your own practice
2.   Explore existing data, literature and other sources of data
3.   Decide on the best option for action
4.   Design the action plan, implement and collect data
5.   Organise the data, analyse and evaluate the action(s)
6.   Revise the action plan in the light of findings and key priorities identified for further action(s)
7.   Implement the revised action plan, which then continues in another spiral of reflective enquiry

Smith (2001) has created a useful diagram which illustrates the action research process based on Lewin's original descriptions (1948). However, this does not capture the recurring nature of the action research spiral as represented by Kemmis and McTaggart (1988); I have therefore adapted the diagram, adding the final step which returns the teacher-researcher to the beginning of the spiral (see Figure 11.2).

Lewin particularly emphasised the importance of evaluation in action research. Without evaluation, those involved in the research process do not know to what extent the goals of the research are achieved. The evaluation activity may sometimes bring about changes in methods of intervention, suggest different approaches to solving the problem, and even change the whole course of the research. In this way, reflection informs the whole action research process, from identifying and planning action(s) to evaluating the impact of action.

Lewin's spiral model was simplified to a plan, act, observe and reflect staged process by Kemmis and McTaggart (1981). It is important to remember that reflection informs every stage of the process however. This 'spiral' of action research also influenced Kolb's reflective cycle model (1984). Action research does not have a fixed end point, it does not start with a hypothesis to be tested, rather it emerges from an idea that you develop, evaluate and revise as you go through each stage of the process. The 4 stages presented by Kemmis and McTaggart (1988), Plan/Re-plan-Act-Observe-Reflect, simplify the cyclical nature of the action research approach where each stage informs the next and the inquiry evolves during the research process. Action research involves

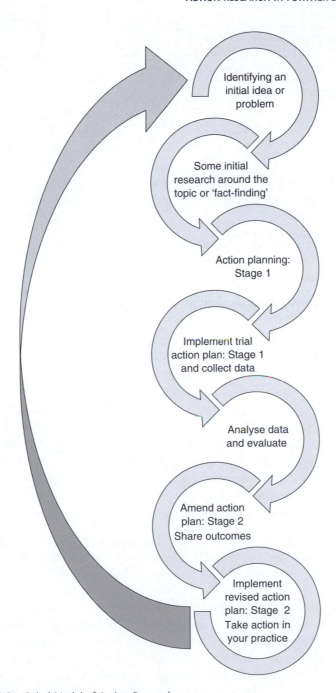

Figure 11.2 Spiral Model of Action Research

Source: Adapted from Kemmis and McTaggart (1988) and Smith (2001)

both learning and change; learning from the research process and change from the action brought about in the research process. The key elements of action research are summarised on the following page in Table 11.2.

Table 11.2   Key elements of action research

Summary of key elements of action research
It works on teachers' own problems
It seeks to improve practice
It is collaborative and participatory
It is problem-solving
It is undertaken *in situ*
It is an ongoing cycle of diagnosis, planning, implementation and evaluation
It is methodologically diverse
It requires reflection
It builds on professional development

Action Research and Professional Development

Action research is perceived as an understandable and workable approach to the improvement of practice through critical self-reflection (Carr and Kemmis, 1986). It thereby encapsulates important components of professionalism and professional development in its active promotion of self-reflective enquiry. It positions teachers as researchers in a methodology based on critical self-reflection. Action research is a practical way of improving our practice. It involves thinking about, and reflecting on, what we do as professionals in order to bring about change and it can therefore be called a form of self-reflective practice that is so integral to professional development. It is sometimes referred to as 'practitioner research' because the research is carried out by us, the teachers, or practitioners.

> The fundamental aim of action research is to improve practice rather than to produce knowledge. The production and utilisation of knowledge is subordinate to, and conditioned by, this fundamental aim. (Elliott, 1991: 49)

Each teacher's practice is unique, in so much as each learning environment has its own ecology with its own peculiarities and complexities due to variable learners and contexts, which Schön refers to a 'swampy lowland where situations are confusing "messes" incapable of technical solution' (1983: 42). One of the reasons why educationalists, policy-makers and politicians are unable to pinpoint what makes a good teacher is because so much of what we do as teachers is based on tacit knowledge. Schön (ibid.) uses the term 'knowing-in-action' as part of his work on the role of the reflective practitioner to define this aspect of professional knowledge, which he refers to as 'professional artistry'. It is that spontaneous and intuitive response to a given, and often unpredictable, situation, where a teacher's response is guided, more often than not, by experience. In Schön's own words, 'our knowing is ordinarily tacit, implicit in our patterns of action and in our feel for the stuff with which we are dealing. It seems right to say that our knowing is *in* our action' (ibid.: 49, italics in original). Figure 11.3 illustrates Schön's model of reflection and the contribution of practical knowledge to development of theory in action research.

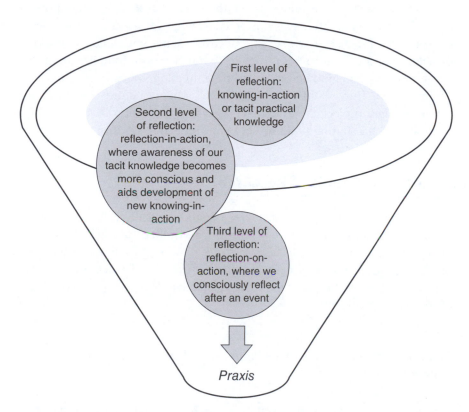

Figure 11.3   Reflective practice in action research: research in action

Source: Adapted from Schön's model of reflection (1983)

So, *praxis* is a process of reflection-in-action whereby the unconscious actions we take, our knowing-in-action, become more conscious as we interrogate assumptions in our knowing-in-action and become more aware of our implicit knowledge. Reflection-in-action, which includes reflection on our knowing-in-action, can be described as the relationship between practice and theory where as teachers we think, reflect and act on our feet in response to unexpected events, by drawing on our reserve of knowing-in-action, or creating a new solution in response to the event, which is then added to our repertoire of knowing-in-action, or practical knowledge.

In action research, reflection is used to move beyond the routine evalua-tive work that we as teachers carry out after a lesson albeit informally. It is more about raising questions and looking at our practice from different perspectives. From this point of view action research is as much about critically examining our general practice and the broader practices within our institution that affect our learners, as it is about resolving problems within our immediate situation.

As action research is a values-based approach to research, it is important to be aware of what influences our practice, what values and commitments underpin our practice. To be a self-reflective teacher you need to be aware of what motivates you to be a teacher. If you have not thought about this before, then you might need to spend time thinking about your values and commitments. This would be a good place to begin before you start your action research project. Go to Chapter 2; Activity 2.3 on professional values may be a useful starting point to help your reflection on this.

Action Research Methods of Research

As mentioned above, action research is methodologically eclectic, therefore employs a range of varying research methods to collect data, which includes interviews, questionnaires, tests, case studies and observation of your own practice, of participants, of peers' practice. It can also use a mixed method approach where both quantitative and qualitative data are collected as part of the research inquiry.

Reducing researcher bias to ensure reliability and accuracy in collected data

One of the main criticisms of action research is its lack of rigour, which is why you must consider carefully how you will ensure the data that is col-lected is reliable and accurate. Because we, the teachers, are the researchers usually of our own practice in action research, then the potential for bias, and subjectivity, is assumed to be greater. Some key points to bear in mind to help reduce researcher bias:

- Be honest with yourself about any preconceptions you may have regard-ing the issue being researched and what you expect to happen as a result of implementing your action plan
- Be open to, and prepared for, the unexpected – the results of your action research may not be what you had expected

- Be aware of your relationship with the learners involved in the research – is there a potential for subjectivity or thinking you know what they mean/why they do what they do without actually asking them?
- Making generalisations is an easy thing to do when first trying to write up a research project

Observation techniques

One of the most used methods in action research is the use of observation because it enables the researcher to investigate the events and behaviours in a specific context. Most common is the use of participant observation, where the teacher conducting the research is a participant in the activities being researched. However, there are issues with this approach if this is the sole method of collecting data. Primarily, being involved in the activities being researched means that it may be difficult, if not impossible, for the researcher to get an objective overall view of what is happening.

If you decide not to go down this route then there are other options available as to how to observe.

Structured observation uses a schedule with pre-specified criteria to be recorded. Very specific data is collected using this method. This is primarily used to collect concise quantitative data which can be statistically analysed because it is easier to manage, organise, record and analyse. It is said to reduce the potential for researcher bias, but there is also an argument that because you have preselected the criteria to be observed, there are assumptions being made about what you expect to happen, which is open to bias. Examples of an observation schedule include:

- Frequency or tally sampling
- Duration sampling
- Activity or event rating – measure of effect of action using a numerical scale
- Interval sampling – recording at set points, e.g. every three minutes

See Table 11.3 for an example of an observation schedule for a structured observation.

Another approach to observation is unstructured observation, where the observer watches and listens to record events, behaviours and interactions as they happen. It is used to collect qualitative data which can be analysed to generate a hypothesis but it can be harder to manage, organise, record and analyse the data. Examples include:

- Field notes
- Sociogram (diagram of interaction between individuals)

Table 11.3   An example of an observation schedule to collect data on behaviour management

Task							
Teacher preventative strategies							
Eye contact							
Proximity							
Used name(s)							
Directed question to learner(s)							
Other (add below)							
Teacher intervention							
Gave 1-1 support							
Moved learner(s) to another group/table							
Warning given							
Told to wait after lesson							
Other (add below)							

A sociogram is a visual representation of interaction between individuals, usually a diagram of circles connected with lines as in Figure 11.4. It can be useful if your enquiry is based on relationships within a learning environment – perhaps there are individuals who do not like to work together, or you want to investigate how individuals interact in activities, in which case a sociogram would be a useful tool to get a visual representation of what is happening in these instances. A word of caution: sociograms can get quite confusing if there are lots of individuals involved, so choose carefully.

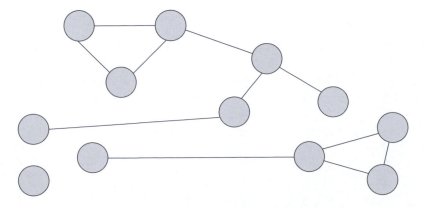

Figure 11.4   An example of a sociogram showing interaction between learners in a discussion

You may devise a key to indicate the nature of interaction, for example (and Table 11.4):

- Audio/video recording (this will require transcription for analysis)
- Taking photographs

Table 11.4   A sample key for a sociogram

A double headed arrow could indicate a two-way exchange between two individuals

A single arrow could indicate a one-way interaction with no response

Colours, or different shapes, could be used to indicate gender of individuals if appropriate to your enquiry

You could also annotate with notes on nature of interaction as appropriate to your research focus, e.g. you might record types of interaction such as interruptions or questions

---

Alternatively, you may decide that a semi-structured observation suits your action research project best. This is where you, as the observer set out with an adaptable agenda which could combine any of the data-collection methods mentioned in the structured and unstructured observation examples.

If you observe a peer's practice, be aware of the effect you have on the observation and its findings. This is known as the 'Hawthorne effect' or 'observer effect', and is widely recognised within research as a potential dilemma whereby the presence of the observer changes the behaviour of those being observed, so your findings may not be a true representation of what is really going on in your peer's practice.

Interview techniques

Interviews can be useful to probe into exploring the 'whys' of human behaviour, attitude and beliefs. The approach you use will depend on the data you are trying to collect.

Structured interviews collect specific data that has been decided before the interview takes place. This approach is used to collect quantitative data which can then be collated and analysed. It is believed to reduce researcher bias and is chosen if very specific information is being sought.

Semi-structured interviews will follow a set of questions that have been designed in advance, but the researcher will allow some space for the participants to add their own thoughts, and for the researcher to probe responses further if they are of interest or they need clarification from the participant.

Unstructured interviews would be used in qualitative research and can be more of a conversation than an interview. While there is no script as such, you may have a list of topics that will be covered in the interview. These interviews often uncover information that may not be uncovered in structured or even semi-structured interviews. The data collected from this type of interview will be voluminous and will need collating before analysis can take place, so you will need to take into account the time-consuming nature of the data collation and of transcribing the raw data when planning your research project.

In all types of interviews, the relationship between the researcher and participant needs to be taken into account. The participant needs to feel relaxed, and if asking questions about topics that are personal to the participants sensitivity and trust are both essential requisites. How questions are worded and phrased are really important, to make sure they are asking for the information you are looking for, that they are not leading questions which suggest particular answers and influence the responses from participants because the answer is suggested in the question itself.

For example, 'Do you prefer practical lessons?' is leading the respondent, whereas 'What lessons do you prefer?' is inviting the respondent to give their own answer.

A good way to avoid this is to run a pilot interview to test run your questions, and interview technique.

Other data collection methods may include, focus groups, learners' work and questionnaires (paper-based or online surveys).

Getting Started on an Action Research Project

Thinking of an area of your practice to investigate for an action research project is the difficult phase, as making the decision where to focus your inquiry to help you improve and build your repertoire of professional knowledge can seem daunting. The three case studies in this chapter have been provided as a tool to begin the reflection process on your own practice and context of teaching and learning. They cover aspects of policy, professional and institutional development to demonstrate the scope of potential enquiry available to you for your own action research project.

 Case study 11.1   Maths

Jasmine is an experienced maths teacher who has taught GSCE courses for most of her teaching career in further education. She has recently experienced issues with motivation and disengagement with a group of learners whose grades are on the C/D border-line. Almost half of this group did not achieve a grade D in maths before joining the college in September. She discussed this issue with her colleagues who reported that they were experiencing similar issues.

Jasmine brings this issue up at the next team meeting, which includes teachers who teach Functional Skills maths across the college. This issue seems to be widespread amongst the maths teachers at the meeting. Following the meeting, Jasmine and her manager decide that they would like to explore this issue further across the college: they set up an online survey which is sent out to all teachers who teach maths at the college, in this way everyone who teaches maths will have the opportunity to feedback on their experiences: both maths teachers and subject teachers who teach maths.

The survey reveals that the majority of teachers are struggling with behaviour and motivation. Jasmine decides that this would make a good topic for an action research project. She plans a series of peer observations to explore the problems that teachers are experiencing, and interviews some learners as well as teachers to get an overview of some of the issues. From this she is able to plan a series of CPD/training sessions to support maths teachers; she follows this up with another series of peer observations and interviews to analyse the impact of the CPD/training sessions. From her research, she is able to conclude that the CPD/training is having a positive impact for both teachers and learners, and she arranges a further session so the maths teachers can discuss and review the curriculum and explore different teaching and learning approaches. She recommends that they have regular CPD/training sessions where they can also share best practice, and that provision for individual support in maths should be implemented across the college.

Recent developments in the sector, such as the drive to get learners up to GCSE grade C in English and Maths, can be good topics for a research project. Here are some others which may be of interest to you for your own action research project:

- Education for Sustainable Development (ESD) (see Chapter 9)
- Employability
- E-learning
- English and maths

Case study 11.2   Inclusive teaching and learning

Yusef is a teacher educator and early on in the autumn term believes that one of his trainees may have dyslexia. The trainee is a 44-year-old woman and she has not disclosed any learning disability, either on her enrolment form or during interview. Yusef has a tutorial with her, and he asks about her previous learning and again she does not disclose anything to him. He has not had any previous experience of trainees with dyslexia in his two years of teaching.

He discusses this situation with his line manager and says that he would like to discuss this with the trainee further and perhaps suggest to her that she could possibly have dyslexia, and if she agrees, to help her arrange a dyslexia screening test, if she can afford to pay privately. However, by discussing this with his colleagues he becomes aware that across the college there are a number of staff with dyslexia who have gone through initial teacher education qualifications. He also discovers through discussion with his colleagues that in the current cohort of trainees going through the Level 5 Diploma programme some have significant literacy difficulties.

Yusef decides that teachers with dyslexia is an interesting area for action research. He gathers some background information about trainees on teacher education programmes at the college from learner information records, and discusses this with the other teacher educators at the college. By talking with trainees on teacher education programmes, he discovers that there are a considerable number who say they struggle with reading journal articles, referencing and/or academic writing, which matches what his colleagues have told him.

He negotiates with his line manager and the other teacher educators to add a more comprehensive element of study support in the first term. He reviews this intervention and finds that as a result of the study support his colleagues are reporting that trainees' work has benefitted greatly from the intervention and that it had has a positive impact on their first assignments. He decides to further investigate what aspects of trainees' job roles and teaching they find most affected by their dyslexia and what strategies they have developed to support their teaching.

Yusef decides that he will pursue getting a specialist qualification with the British Dyslexia Association so that he can better support trainees with dyslexia but also be able to potentially offer screening tests in the future. He would also be able to offer CPD/training sessions to managers, teachers and support staff across the college that would raise awareness of dyslexia generally, but also promote support for staff with dyslexia.

For your own action research project, you may like to identify an area where you feel either institutional or government policy is not compatible with inclusion in practice.

 Case study 11.3   Attitudes to learning

Dionne is a teacher with considerable experience who teaches on 16–19 programmes. After reading some literature on Dweck's theory of mindsets, she decides to explore attitudes to learning with a new group of learners in September. She devises some questions for an induction activity that focus on learning (see Appendix 3).

Using this information, Dionne decides to implement a range of 'hands-on' activities, short units of learning so that learners can see their progress, and a range of formative assessment activities in order to promote confidence and give learners opportunities to experience success. She encourages collaboration between learners to create a supportive learning environment, one where learners are willing to start taking responsibility for their learning, and to accept that making mistakes are a useful part of learning process.

At the end of the unit of learning where she has implemented this strategy, she sets them a challenging formative assessment task to establish whether a 'can-do' ethos has been achieved. She sees that some learners give up easily, whilst others really put in a lot of effort, and observes that the effort of others influences some learners to have another go. She concludes that progress has been made in challenging the fixed mindset, and promoting a 'can-do' ethos but still has work to do, so revises her initial action plan and implements it.

For your own action research project, you might like to consider the barriers to learning that a fixed mindset learner may encounter and devise and evaluate a strategy that promotes a can-do ethos (see Chapter 4 for more on Dweck's mindset theory).

Barrett and Whitehead (1985) devised six questions that should help you to get started with your action research project:

- What is your concern?
- Why are you concerned?

- What do you think you could do about it?
- What kind of evidence could you collect to help you make some judgement about what is happening?
- How would you collect such evidence?
- How would you check that your judgement about what has happened is reasonable, fair and accurate?

Activity 11.2

- Use the six questions devised by Barrett and Whitehead to start thinking about your own action research project.
- Once you have answered these questions, you could then complete a draft action research proposal (see Appendix 4).

Ethics

It is really important that you take into account ethical considerations as part of your planning. You need to make sure that any ethical issues your project might encounter are addressed before embarking on the research project, and that if dilemmas occur during the project that these are dealt with appropriately. The British Educational Research Association (BERA) Ethical Guidelines for Educational Research (2011) is a key guide to assist you with this aspect of your action research project.

Conclusion

Action research challenges the kind of knowledge that educational research traditionally privileges, namely theoretical knowledge over practical knowledge. By addressing the limitations of traditional research, action research attempts to bridge the gap between theory and practice in its direct relevance to the needs of teachers on the frontline. As well as often being seen in opposition to theoretical knowledge, the fact that action research supports a 'reflective practitioner' notion of professionalism, one where teachers are autonomous and able to make decision and judgements about their practice and what works best for their learners, has probably also contributed to its struggle for legitimacy within the research arena. Action research is a form of educational research which places control over processes of educational reform in the hands of those involved in the action and is 'seen by some as bringing about transformation with the aim of emancipation'

(Moon, 1999: 36). This potential for action research to bring about social change and empower teachers to take action is powerful, but is unfortunately constrained by narrow conceptions of professionalism within the sector. Action research is especially valuable at a time when the autonomy of teachers is being restricted by decisions about what to teach, and increasingly how to teach, decisions which are made externally, beyond learning environments and imposed on teachers.

Suggested Further Reading

British Educational Research Association (BERA) (2011) *Ethical Guidelines for Educational Research*. London: BERA.

Carr, W., and Kemmis, S. (1986) *Becoming Critical: Education Knowledge and Action Research*. London: RoutledgeFalmer.

Dewey, J. (1916) *Democracy and Education: An Introduction to the Philosophy of Education*. New York: Macmillan.

Freire, P. (2000) *Pedagogy of the Oppressed* (30th anniversary edn). London: Continuum International Publishing Group.

Kemmis, S. and McTaggart, R. (1988) *The Action Research Planner* (3rd edn). Geelong, Victoria: Deakin University Press.

Schön, D. (1983) *The Reflective Practitioner: How Professionals Think in Action*. London: Marcus Temple Smith.

CHAPTER 12

FUTURE CHALLENGES FOR FE

In the 2015 General Election in the UK, education noticeably featured very little. The Conservative manifesto was light on detail regarding further education and skills, the only publicly made promise was that 3 million apprenticeships would be set up. However, there is much that is currently evident about the future of FE; a future which will happen sooner rather than later.

This chapter will cover the following:

- Funding issues facing FE now and the potential future impact of funding
- The cost of competition
- The impact of the challenges on the FE workforce
- Skills and the economic agenda as state intervention in FE
- Future provision

Introduction

Funding is the biggest issue facing further education and skills. There will be a significant reduction in funding and the first wave of cuts will hit provision for adult education as this is not ring-fenced. Loans and increased course fees are likely to be used to offset the impact, with loans being extended to Level 2 courses, as well as possibly to under-24-year-olds. There is likely to be further growth of HE provision in FE, especially if university tuition fees increase further, which is highly probable. Digital learning is likely to become a more significant initiative to cut costs and staffing within institutions, and the Further Education Learning Technology Action Group (FELTAG) goal, which ran out of steam under the Coalition Government, may now come into force whereby one in ten lessons will be made available digitally. Life will be increasingly harder for the unemployed and low-skilled, and changes to funding means that gaining higher skills will undoubtedly become more expensive. The FE sector is likely to reduce in size, and perhaps, reading between the lines, become subsumed within the school system.

In the history and evolution of FE there has never been a more critical point; it has adeptly implemented numerous government policy initiatives imposed from on high, and its committed workforce have circumnavigated much of the potential fallout of this top-down policy drive which has been market-orientated and therefore often at the expense of the very learners it works with, and concomitantly to the detriment of teachers' professionalism. To maintain the three pillars at the heart of FE – dedication to learners, social inclusion and equality – has required innovative and creative navigation through a plethora of policy upon policy upon policy.

There is currently much that threatens the core of FE, which I have discussed throughout this book; here is a summary:

- 26 per cent cuts to adult funding
- Voluntarism in initial teacher education since deregulation in 2012
- The widespread appropriation of CPD for Ofsted-driven priorities rather than personal professional development of dual professionalism
- Increased bureaucratic workloads
- Constant policy top-down churn
- High-stakes, target-driven performativity
- Increased feelings of insecurity and disillusionment amongst teachers

This list goes on, but our creativity as a sector, and our professionalism which is founded on our inner commitment to our learners, means that we cannot allow the sector that we have worked in, championed and so strongly advocated in our professional lives to be decimated by government policy which brandishes austerity as its ideological shield.

The top ten issues identified by the Policy Consortium in *The Great FE & Skills Survey of 2015* as being of most concern are shown in Table 12.1.

Table 12.1   Top ten concerns in FE, 2015

Top ten concerns in FE, 2015
Levels/rates of institutional funding
Adequacy of learner funding
External bureaucracy
Workload
Pace and volume of change
English and maths assessment and capacity to deliver
Broad government 'direction of travel' for FE and skills
Complexity of the offer
Specialist teachers, e.g. of English, maths and/or vocational subjects
Capital funding

Source: Policy Consortium (2015)

This survey reveals the most important issues facing further education in the UK from the perspective of those who work in the sector, whilst almost half of the respondents were in management roles, the voice of teachers is also represented in the findings. There follows a discussion on some of the areas of major concern raised in this survey.

Funding

The FE sector has already had to pragmatically deal with the considerable changes in funding and make substantial savings, however the core funding for 16–19 years old and skills which was set for a £271 million reduction in the academic year 2015/16 has been protected, but this freezing of funding does mean a cut in real terms. The government, however, intend to make efficiency savings of £360 million from the adult skills budget by 2019–20 (HM Treasury, 2015). This is the most significant challenge facing FE. Much of the FE budget is not ring-fenced, therefore difficult decisions are going to have to be made by institutions, such as redundancies, increasing class sizes, reviewing adult learning provision, reducing the range of courses offered, as well as having to possibly review funds for discretionary learner support.

According to Keep, FE:

> faces a 'triple whammy' – governmental resources (central and local) are being substantially reduced, just at the moment at which the ability of employers and individuals to contribute more towards the costs of … [FE] … provision are also coming under sustained pressure. (2014: 6)

The savage 24 per cent cut to the adult skills budget means that this provision is under serious threat within the sector. Adult learning is a cornerstone of FE, it has always been a key part of its work within communities ever since I started working in the sector in the early 1990s. To think that this could be a feature of the past is not only unimaginable, but also nonsensical. Clearly institutions will have to make difficult decisions about whether to continue to offer courses for adults, but in order to survive these swingeing cuts it may be that they have to, albeit unwillingly, focus exclusively on pre-19 provision as this is the key to their survival within these harsh funding cuts. Adult learning has always provided an opportunity for people to return to education, to retrain, to upskill and in this unstable and fluctuating labour market, this opportunity for people of *all* ages is an absolute necessity for economic growth and sustainable employment. Therefore, to make it inaccessible and unaffordable seems inconceivable as a government policy. By disappearing altogether in some localities, adult learning will become inaccessible in many local communities, making adult provision a postcode lottery, and with the de-funding of 1500 adult qualifications, unaffordable due to the introduction of FE loans and the inevitable increasing costs of courses for adults. What is becoming clear is that we are living in an era of in-work poverty (MacInnes et al., 2014), therefore the opportunity to upskill and retrain is essential and suggesting that apprenticeships are the solution in and of themselves is both short-sighted and unrealistic. With more than 6 million working adults living in poverty, MacInnes et al. suggest that the rise in poverty within working households is the face of financial hardship in the UK and reveals the demands and challenges of modern living. It also undermines welfare reform, which has been an ardent centrepiece of the austerity measures undertaken by the Coalition Government, and now the Conservative Government. It reveals that the message 'work pays' is a falsehood, and therefore that welfare reform to reduce poverty and unemployment is not the solution: there are wider structural issues which need to be addressed.

Dangers of Competition

The intensification of the marketplace within education per se, with academies, free schools and the growth of 14–16 provision in FE, the expansion of HE in FE, Studio Schools and University Technical Colleges (UTCs), all under the rhetorical guise of choice, is quite a confusing landscape for learners, parents and employers. Furthermore, the raising of the participation age in education or training to 18, means that schools and colleges in local communities and regions are pitted against each other to retain and recruit learners respectively rather than affording opportunities for the education sector to work cohesively and collaboratively to ensure the learner is at the heart of provision, and not reduced to a commodity to be competed for. Unfortunately, the government's approach to generate competition in the rhetorical name of parental and learner choice, is actually damaging the potential for real partnership that can serve the needs of local communities under these unprecedented times of austerity.

In his report, *What does Skills Policy Look Like now the Money has Run Out* (2014), Keep explores the need for local funding coalitions, which can pool together resources and best serve their local communities through local coordination and planning. However, this requires a new way of thinking, a thinking that is cooperative and democratic. The danger, as Keep warns, is that in the current market-orientated educational landscape, where profits are key to survival, the most disadvantaged learners will slip through the consumer-net in FE provision. Competition sets up an ethos of division rather than collaboration between providers, and across the education sector, with the result being discriminating gaps in provision for those who are not prioritised by employers and government policy, and those who cannot afford to pay for their own education and training. With less government funding, alternative funding must be sourced, and this creates opportunities for more localism, but it requires a collective approach between educational providers, employers and other stakeholders to best meet the local needs of their communities.

Workforce Concerns

In my travels as an initial teacher educator, what I witness, and the most significant area of concern for the teachers I work with, is excessive workloads. These are having a negative impact on quality as it takes them away from their learners, from their planning and preparation during a period in which the stakes for improving quality are at their height. Whether teachers are working in a college, the prison service, the National Health Service (NHS), or the schools sector, the workloads obstruct their ability to spend time with their learners, to take up professional development opportunities, to have time and reflective space to develop their own teaching repertoire with new ideas and tools, and most importantly to be creative and innovative. With the cyclical rounds of redundancy over the last few years the workload pressures on the staff that remain have increased exponentially. However, the *Great FE & Skills Survey* acknowl-edged that: 'it is a testament to the sector that the spectre of redundancy takes second place in the comments to the damage to young people' (Policy Consortium, 2015: 11). As the work of teaching becomes more audit-driven and bureaucratic and increasingly conflicts with teachers' inner commitment to their learners, what we see is an exodus of good teachers leaving the profession, returning to industry or changing career. In FE, the conditions of low-pay, part-time/casual posts and job insecurity all contribute to the feelings of demoralisation which are currently preva-lent, however the passion and enthusiasm of teachers in FE – and their dedication to their learners – helps to sustain then in their teaching. But I do worry that we are nearing breaking point, and with redundancies, voluntary and forced, within the sector, the morale of those staff who remain will decline as their workloads intensify even further.

The deregulation of ITE in FE is also a significant issue going forward as it threatens to atomise us as professionals. The importance of FE remains despite the fact that the revised sector ITE qualifications which are now in force are ever more onerous and prescriptive in terms of content and assess-ment. Whilst this revision of the qualifications can be viewed as an attempt to deprofessionalise our profession, it has been suggested, however, that these attempts at intervention have served to reprofessionalise our profes-sion, whereby ITE becomes a key means to reprofessionalisation and teacher educators the key drivers behind this process (Furlong et al., 2000).

Future Provision

The intense policy focus for FE is the continuation of the skills agenda. For decades now, the skills policy has been seen as the cure all for social and economic issues within the UK. The Leitch Review of Skills (2005, 2006) lists the issues that skills have been conceived of addressing over the past few decades:

- Anti-social behaviour
- Welfare-dependency
- Low levels of intergenerational social mobility
- Poverty
- Widening income inequality
- Insufficient innovation by businesses
- Weak regional economic performance
- International competitiveness
- Improving productivity (Cited in Keep and Mayhew, 2010: 566)

Nevertheless, Keep and Mayhew (ibid.: 566) argue that skills policy is used to curtail other ways in which government addresses social and economic issues and inequalities, 'such as stronger social partnership, more active economic development and redistributive policies'.

From reading several articles and reports written by Keep on skills policy and the challenges and demands faced by FE in the current era of austerity, what is apparent is the misnomer of skills and economic prosperity and productivity which has been, and is, so prevalent in government rhetoric, but which in fact underpins an old way of thinking about the social and economic agenda and the current looming socioeconomic crisis:

> Skills policy makes sense as part of a broader sweep of business improvement, economic development and innovation policy, but rather less sense as a 'magic bullet' that on its own can produce transformative effects. (Keep, 2014: 14)

Skills, however, have been the key driver in policy-making in FE to address social and economic issues for successive governments in the UK. This lets the government off the hook, from having to confront wider structural issues which ensure that these policy ambitions are never truly realised, which in turn warrants an endless policy churn. Policy-making in FE is well represented by Keep's cycle of state intervention depicted in Figure 12.1.

This singular approach to policy-making ignores the scale and persistence of low-paid employment within the UK economy, and ignores the fact that there is a mounting crisis of unsustainable economic growth and unemployment in the UK.

Analysis of the UK labour market in 2010 concluded that the growth in supply of skills has outpaced the growth in demand and recent reports show that this growth in demand for skills is one of the lowest in the OECD (UKCES, 2010: 76). Another finding in the analysis is related to underemployment: being over-qualified, under-deployed and/or under-utilised. The research shows that there is an excess of jobs that require no qualifications, and that since 2001, two in every five workers are in jobs in which they are underemployed. The impact of this has been felt most acutely by graduates – the proportion of graduates underemployed has increased by 50 per cent over the last 20 years, but three-quarters of this average has occurred within the last 5 years. Whilst fluctuations and mismatches between supply and demand of skills occur in labour markets, the UKCES report warns that when they persist or increase they become 'more problematic, risking alienation and disillusionment for individual workers and, ultimately, deleterious consequences for firm performance and productivity' (ibid).

Gleeson and Keep (2004) suggest that skills provision that leads to an over-supply suits employers, because employers want a choice of recruits rather than a perfect match of supply to demand because an excess of skills

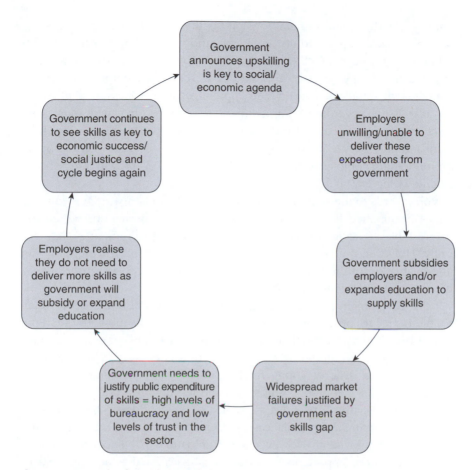

Figure 12.1   Cycle of state intervention

Source: Keep (2006: 52)

helps to depress wages. The authors go on to propose that the persistent employer dissatisfaction with the skills of young people and potential employees outmanoeuvres FE providers, and excuses employers in avoiding making any contribution to the initial training and upskilling of their employees:

> It also helps maintain the apparent need for an open UK labour market where migrant labour is always accessible and can be used as a means of lowering wages and avoiding training costs. (Keep, 2012: 374)

Traineeships are a key strategy for the government to reduce youth unemployment, and to engage young people in education, employment or training. It has been announced that the government's apprenticeship flagship has not fulfilled its original function of training young people and helping to reduce youth unemployment as the majority of apprenticeships have been taken up by adults aged 25+, and a report by the Institute for Public Policy Research (IPPR) and the Local Government Association (LGA) revealed that 67 per cent of apprentices were already employed by their company when they were given their apprenticeships (Raikes, 2015: 4). There are also issues regarding completion of apprenticeships, with significant numbers of apprentices not completing their programme of training. Data from a report by *FE Week* (Cooney, 2015) reveals a 5 per cent drop in apprenticeship completion between 2011–12 and 2013–14, with the national average being 68.9 per cent.

With regards to the skills agenda, the current obsession with performance data – exemplified by the OECD, which publishes international education league tables – seems to be a key driver behind government policy currently. However, much of this policy is recycling and borrowing and with little evaluation of the impact of these policies by successive governments, the policy churn seems inevitable.

If the government is serious in its view that skills and training for young people is vital to 'productivity growth', a term which fills me with dread the more I hear it in educational circles, then investment in further education is needed, not cuts to funding. Traineeships are a good way to help government tackle the issue of young people not in education, employment or training (NEETs), apprenticeships, vocational degrees and higher-level apprenticeships are all useful approaches to help address the skills gap, upskill the working age population and to help people find meaningful and sustainable employment. However, the trepidation that I feel with this is twofold. First, the important contribution of vocational education, and its workforce, to the education system needs to be recognised and its status raised within wider society. Post-16 participation in education and training in further education colleges exceeds participation in sixth form colleges. According to the AoC (2013), in the academic year 2013/14, nearly twice as many 16–18-year-olds chose to study in further education colleges rather than school sixth forms: 846,000 compared with 441,000, respectively.

Second, whilst it cannot be denied that employment has a significant impact on an individual, society and the economy, if the focus of education is solely on its input–output equation in terms of the labour market, then it loses its fundamental role in fostering creativity and harnessing passion for learning – learning for its own sake, rather than in exchange for financial return. Chris Hedges précises this powerfully in his book *Empire of Illusion*:

> We've bought into the notion that education is about training and "success", defined monetarily, rather than learning to think critically and to challenge. We should not forget that the true purpose of education is to make minds not careers. (2009: 95)

Conclusion

The low pay levels of teachers working in FE in comparison to industry, schools and HE, are a major concern, for both staff retention and recruitment. The public sector pay freeze which began in 2010 is ongoing and amounts approximately to a 15 per cent cut in salary in real terms. A number of other related concerns combine to result in a negative impact on staff morale and motivation. There is currently a great deal of uncertainty about future funding which will impact on provision and therefore on staffing. Redundancies lead to increased workloads for the remaining workforce, and the relentless pressures from Ofsted intensifies unnecessary bureaucracy and stress. Sadly, as a consequence of these concerns many of my colleagues are seeking to leave, and these are passionate and dedicated teachers.

The current obsession with OECD international education league tables, and the ramifications of the ranking within these league tables is having a devastating effect on education policy in the UK, and many other countries. The over-reliance on quantitative data advocated by the OECD to measure success is leading to increased promotion of standardised testing for both learner and teacher performance. This has a substantial influence on education policy-making. Furthermore, it is founded on old models of thinking about teaching and learning, and if we are to meet the demands of our rapidly changing world and the systemic challenges that we face in light of the threefold crisis as posited by Schumacher when he wrote about 'the crisis of resources, the ecological crisis, and the social crisis' (1997: 21), then we urgently need new ways of thinking about education, and new ways of educating. Essentially, we need to move away from market-based solutions to policy that serves the public good.

The impact of a high-stakes target-driven education system on the health and well-being of both learners and teachers and the perception that education is about qualifications and employment, rather than about learning, is uncertain, but there are warning signs beginning to emerge. The NUT commissioned research which was carried out by Professor Merryn Hutchings into the impact of accountability on learners and on teachers, and concluded that the consequences of the accountability agenda in education policy is threatening the self-esteem, confidence and mental health of children and young people, reducing the quality of teacher-learner relationships and undermining opportunities for creativity in teaching (Hutchings, 2015). In the UK, 11–16-year-olds feel more pressurised and stressed by standardised assessment regimes and exams than is the case in many other European countries (World Health Organization, 2012). ChildLine (2015) further reported that the pressure to perform in the current education system was related directly to young people developing mental health issues. Of course, these worrying trends continue into FE, with a significant increase in the number of young people with mental health conditions in the learner population (AoC, 2015).

The major funding challenges ahead suggests that to survive, colleges may have to become specialised Institutes of Technology as part of the government's plan to boost 'productivity growth' and seek sponsorship from employers which I see as a form of academisation within the further education sector. The other significant issues going forward, as I see it, are the need to maintain initial teacher education for all teachers working in FE, and the need to have teacher-initiated CPD which supports subject knowledge and personal professional development to improve teaching and learning rather than CPD which is focused on top-down policy implementation and Ofsted which is all too often the norm since deregulation in 2012.

The challenges are considerable and threaten the very foundations of FE, but I am not despondent. I believe in the creativity, resourcefulness and impressive dedication of FE professionals, and know that they will, we will, do whatever it takes to stand up and defend FE and its learners, and stand up against policy and practice that jeopardises its essence. But, we cannot do this individually, or we will burn out as a profession, we need to do this together – collectively, democratically and collaboratively, and have a voice that is heard and heeded by government, policy-makers, employers and regulators.

Case study 12.1   Tutor voices: National Network for Further, Adult, Community and Skills Educators

The National Network for Further, Adult, Community and Skills Educators democratic professional association arose in reaction to the on-going reduction of FE funding, with the associated erosion of professional agency under neoliberal managerialism. It was conceived as a way for FE professionals to collectively defend FE.

The association is not intended to replace any former or current FE professional bodies or government funded sector bodies, or to encroach on the vital work around pay and conditions of sector trade unions. Rather, it is hoped that the association will complement the work of these organisations. Tutor Voices intends to promote the values of democratic professionalism on issues of practice and policy by encouraging a network of practitioners and researchers committed to a culture of discussion, sharing, reflective inquiry and joint practice development. Ultimately, the aim is to influence policy by defending and promoting well-resourced vocational, academic and community-based education and comprehensive lifelong learning and education for democratic citizenship.

The founding principles of Tutor Voices include that it should be democratic so it can be a voice for FE professionals in order to mobilise the power of collective professional pressure to challenge government education policy, to defend FE and to promote participatory and empowering forms of teacher development.

Source: Kindly contributed by Joel Petrie, a founder member of Tutor Voices, and Lecturer at the City of Liverpool College

Tutor Voices embodies the determination to defend FE and respond to the policies and practices that are causing, and will continue to cause, so much harm to FE. However, as Coffield writes (2015: xxiv), the sector's ills are not the whole FE story; there is hope in the collective power of FE teachers to challenge and resist government policy and institutional governance and bring about positive change through principled dissent.

> A culture that does not grasp the vital interplay between morality and power, which mistakes management techniques for wisdom, which fails to understand that the measure of a civilization is its compassion, not its speed or ability to consume, condemns itself to death. (Hedges: 2009: 103)

To end then, in the face of the increasingly high-stakes educational climate which fundamentally reshapes the work of teaching, it is all the more imperative that we hold onto our core values which make FE what it is and transforms the lives of so many who work and study within it.

The emergence of democratic associations such as Tutor Voices shows how these unprecedented times of austerity and the concurrent conditions created by persistent neoliberal market-led policy and practices not only require alternative forms of professionalism, but foster opportunities for reprofessionalisation, as Furlong et al. (2000: 175) envisioned:

> we need to ask some fundamental questions about who does have a legitimate right to be involved in defining teaching professionalism. Are state control and market forces or professional self-governance really the only models of accountability available to us – or can we develop new approaches to teacher professionalism, based upon more participatory relationships with diverse communities?

Suggested Further Reading

Daley, M., Orr, K. and Petrie, J. (2015) *Further Education and the Twelve Dancing Princesses*. Stoke-on-Trent: Trentham Books.

Hedges, C. (2009) *Empire of Illusion: The End of Literacy and the Triumph of Spectacle*. New York: Nation Books.

Hutchings, M. (2015) *Exam Factories? The Impact of Accountability Measures on Children and Young People*. London: National Union of Teachers.

Keep, E. (2006) 'State control of the English education and training system: Playing with the biggest train set in the world', *Journal of Vocational Education & Training*, 58 (1), pp. 47–64.

Keep, E. (2012) 'Education and industry: Taking two steps back and reflecting', *Journal of Education and Work*, 25 (4), pp. 357–79.

Keep, E. (2014) *What Does Skills Policy Look Like now the Money has Run Out?* London: Association of Colleges.

Keep, E. and Mayhew, K. (2010) 'Moving beyond skills as a social and economic panacea', *Work, Employment and Society*, 24 (3), pp. 565–77.

APPENDIX 1

Coffield found the following questions most useful when starting a discussion on learning:

1. What was your best experience of learning? What made it so good? What can we learn from that experience? (Similar questions about 'your worst experience'.)
2. What do you enjoy learning? What do you not enjoy learning?
3. What helps you to learn? What prevents you?
4. How do tutors help you learn? How could they be more helpful?
5. What kind of things do you learn from your friends? How important is this informal learning to you?
6. How do you assess how well you are learning?
7. What kind of feedback or comments on your assignments do you learn best from?
8. How could you improve your learning? Do you set yourself targets? How do you assess if you have hit the targets?
9. Do you challenge yourself to learn something you find difficult? Are you prepared to move out of your 'comfort zone'?
10. Are you willing to try different ways of learning?

11. What gaps in knowledge and skills do you think you have? What are your plans for filling them?
12. What do you want to learn now?

Source: F. Coffield, *Just Suppose Teaching and Learning became the First Priority …* (London: Learning and Skills Network, 2008).

APPENDIX 2

Is yours a learning institution?

Rate your institution against each statement from 1 to 4 (1 is low and 4 is high)

Institutional area	Rating (1–4)
Institutional dynamics	
We are encouraged to manage our own learning and development	
A positive listening and feedback environment exists	
Training is available in how to learn	
Teams and individuals use reflection and act on their own learning	
Teachers are supported to take a strategic approach	

(Continued)

(Continued)

The institution's approach to change and development	
Senior managers accept the idea of a learning institution	
There is a climate which supports the idea of learning	
We learn from our weaknesses and our achievements	
Opportunities to learn are part of day-to-day business	
There is a flat, or horizontal, management structure which promotes communication and learning at all levels	
Empowerment of people	
The workforce is empowered to work and learn	
Authority is delegated and decentralised	
Managers have a facilitative, mentoring approach	
We share with other institutions to improve our and their service	
We participate in joint learning events with other relevant providers/stakeholders	
Managing knowledge	
We benchmark our best practices against others and seek to learn from them	
Training and support is available for staff in innovation and creative thinking	
Trialling and evaluating new areas of work is embedded in our practice	
We and others are able to make use of our accumulated knowledge in our field	
We share that knowledge systematically and on an ongoing basis with others	
Technological support	
Our uses of technology clearly benefit our key purpose	
Staff and students have ready access to the Internet and other learning technology	
Learning technology is embedded in our practice	
We make use of e-learning within our curriculum	
We make use of technology to support our evaluation and development systems	
Total score (out of 100)	

Interpreting the Scores

The maximum score here is 100. If you scored 40 or below, your institution is in trouble!

What does the score suggest about your institution?

Does this suggest anything about other institutions?

What steps could you take to help your institution improve as a learning institution?

Source: With thanks to Jim Crawley. Adapted with kind permission from J. Crawley, *In at the Deep End: A Survival Guide for Teachers in Post-Compulsory Education* (London: Routledge, 2010)

APPENDIX 3

Dweck's Mindset Questionnaire

1. Read each sentence below and decide whether you agree with it or not.
2. Be prepared to justify the reasons for your answer.

There are no right or wrong answers.

Question	Reason
1. You have a certain amount of intelligence, and you really can't do much to change it	
2. Your intelligence is something about you that you can't change very much	
3. You can learn new things, but you can't really change your basic intelligence	

Source: Adapted from C.S. Dweck, *Self-Theories: Their Role in Motivation, Personality, and Development* (Hove: Psychology Press, Taylor and Francis Group, 2000)

APPENDIX 4

Action research proposal		
Topic/area of research with justification for this choice		
Proposed research question/aim		
Selected literature relating to research topic/area		
Outline and justification of planned intervention strategy *with timescales*		
Justification for proposed methodology quantitative/ qualitative, and research methods questionnaires, observations, interviews, etc.		
Brief outline of how data will be analysed		
Potential ethical considerations		

APPENDIX 5

QUALIFICATIONS FRAMEWORK

Level	Qualification
Level 8	Doctorate
Level 7	Master's degree
Level 6	Bachelor's degree
Level 5	Bachelor's degree, Foundation degree, Higher National Diploma
Level 4	Bachelor's degree, Foundation degree, Higher National Certificate
Level 3	A-level, BTEC Extended Diploma, BTEC National Certificate
Level 2	GCSE (grades A*–C), BTEC First Diploma
Level 1	GCSE (grades D–G), BTEC First Diploma, Foundation Diploma
Entry Level 3	Key Stage 3, E3 Diploma

Regulated Qualifications Framework (RQF) in England, Wales and Northern Ireland 2015 (adapted from Ofqual, 2015)

REFERENCES

157 Group (2014) *A New Conversation: Employer and College Engagement*. London: UK Commission for Employment and Skills (UKCES), 157 Group.

157 Group (2015) *The Economic Impact of Further Education Colleges*. London: 157 Group.

Armitage, A., Bryant, R., Dunnill, R. and Hayes, D. (2012) *Teaching and Training in Lifelong Learning* (4th edn). Maidenhead: Open University Press.

Arnstein, S. (1969) 'A ladder of citizen participation in the USA', *Journal of the American Institute of Planners*, 35 (4), pp. 216–24.

Association of Colleges (AoC) (2013) *College Key Facts 2013–2014*. London: Association of Colleges.

Association of Colleges (AoC) (2015) *Survey on Students with Mental Health Conditions in Further Education Summary Report, June 2015*. London: Association of Colleges.

Association for Experiential Education (2007–13) *What is Experiential Learning?* (www.aee.org).

Avis, J. (2002) 'Imaginary friends: Managerialism, globalisation and post-compulsory education and training in England', *Discourse: Studies in the Cultural Politics of Education*, 23 (1), pp. 75–90.

Babad, E. (1980) 'Expectancy bias in scoring as a function of ability and ethnic labels', *Psychology Reports*, 46, pp. 625–6.

Baird, J. and Bridle, N. (2000) *A Feasibility Study on Anonymised Marking in Large-Scale Public Examinations*, AQA Research Report, RC/91. Manchester: AQA Centre for Education Research and Policy.

Ball, S. (2003) 'The teacher's soul and the terrors of performativity', *Journal of Education Policy*, 18 (2), pp. 215–28.

Ball, S.J. (2004) *Education for Sale: The Commodification of Everything*. Annual Education Lecture 2004. London: King's College London.

Ball, S.J. (2008) *The Education Debate*. Bristol: Policy Press.

Ball, S.J. and Olmedo, A. (2013) 'Care of the self, resistance and subjectivity under neoliberal governmentalities', *Critical Studies in Education*, 54 (1), pp. 85–96.

Barrett, J. and Whitehead, J. (1985) *Supporting Teachers in their Classroom Research*. Bath: School of Education, University of Bath.

Beck, J. and Young, M. (2005) 'The assault on the professions and the restructuring of academic and professional identities: A Bernsteinian analysis', *British Journal of Sociology of Education*, 26 (2), pp. 183–97.

Bell, J. (2005) *Doing your Research Project* (4th edn). Maidenhead: Open University Press.

Belsey, C. (1988) 'Marking by numbers', *AUT Woman*, 15, pp. 1–2.

Biesta, G. (2005) 'The role of educational ideals in teachers' professional work', University of Exeter, England, and Örebro University, Sweden. Invited presentation at the seminar on Identity, Agency and Policy in Teachers' Professional Lives, as part of the ESRC seminar series on Changing Teacher Roles, Identities and Professionalism. King's College London, 20 January.

Binet, A. (1905) 'New Methods for the Diangnosis of the Intellectual Level of Subnormals', First published in *L'Année Psychologique*, 12, pp.191–244.

Blumenbach, J.F. (1940 [1795]) *De generis humani varietate nativa* (3rd edn), trans. T. Bendyshe (1865). Quoted, e.g., in A. Keith, '"Blumenbach's Centenary"', *Man: Journal of the Royal Anthropological Institute of Great Britain and Ireland*, 40, pp. 82–5.

Bobbit, F. (1918) *The Curriculum*. Boston:Houghton Mifflin.

Bonnell, J., Copestake, P., Kerr, D., Passy, R., Reed, C., Salter, R., Sarwar, S. and Sheikh, S. (2011) *Teaching Approaches that Help to Build Resilience to Extremism among Young People*. Department for Education (DfE) Research Report No. 119. London: DfE.

Bourdieu, P. (1974) 'The school as a conservative force: Scholastic and cultural inequalities', in L. Eggleston (ed.), *Contemporary Research in the Sociology of Education*. London: Metheun.

Brinkley, I. (2006) *Defining the Knowledge Economy: Knowledge Economy Programme Report*. London: Work Foundation.

Broecke, S. and Nicholls, T. (2007) *Ethnicity & Degree Attainment*. Research Report No. RW92. London: Department for Education and Skills (DfES).

Brooks, R. (1991) *Contemporary Debates in Education: An Historical Perspective*. London: Longman.

Brophy, J. and Good, L.E. (1984) *Teacher Behavior and Student Achievement*. Occasional Paper No. 73.Ann Arbor, MI: Institute for Research on Teaching, Michigan State University.

Buddery, P., Kippin, H. and Lucas, B. (2010) *The Further Education and Skills Sector in 2020: A Social Productivity Approach*. Coventry: Learning and Skills Improvement Service (LSIS).

Burr, V. (2015) *Social Constructionism* (3rd edn). London: Routledge.

Business, Innovation and Skills, Department for (BIS) (2011a) *Prior Qualifications of Learners in Adult Learner Responsive Provision 2009/2010*. London: BIS.

Business, Innovation and Skills, Department for (BIS) (2011b) *Making Prisons Work: Skills for Rehabilitation: Review of Offender Learning*. London: BIS.

Business, Innovation and Skills, Department for (BIS) (2012) *Evaluation of FE Teachers Qualifications (England) Regulations 2007, March 2012*. Research Paper No. 66. London:BIS.

Business, Innovation and Skills, Department for (BIS) (2014) *The Future of Apprenticeships in England Funding Reform Technical Consultation March 2014*. London: BIS.

Callanan, M., Griggs, J., Lloyd, C., Kitchen, S. and Wollny, I. (2014) *Evaluation of the 16–19 Bursary Fund: Year 1 Report*. – Department for Education Research Report 265. London: Department for Education (DfE) and National Foundation for Educational Research (NFER).

Cantle, T. (2011) *The August Riots 2011: Comment by Ted Cantle September 2011*. Nottingham: Institute of Community Cohesion.

Carr, W. and Kemmis, S. (1986) *Becoming Critical: Education Knowledge and Action Research*. London: RoutledgeFalmer.

Chartered Quality Institute (CBI) (2013) *Changing the Pace: CBI/Pearson Education and Skills Survey*. London: CBI.

Chartered Quality Institute (CBI) (2015) *Total Quality Management (TQM)*. (www.thecqi.org/Knowledge-Hub/Resources/Factsheets/Total-quality-management/).

ChildLine (2015) *Under Pressure: ChildLine Annual Review 2013–2014*. (http://www.nspcc.org.uk/globalassets/documents/annual-reports/childline-review-under-pressure.pdf).

Clarke, D. (1991) 'The negotiated syllabus: What is it and how is it likely to work?', *Applied Linguistics*, 12 (1), pp. 13–28.

Coe, R. (2014) *Lesson Observation: It's Harder than you Think*. TeachFirst TDT Meeting, 13 January.

Coffield, F. (2005) 'Looking back in amazement'. Paper presented at Learning Styles: Help or hindrance? National School Improvement Network (NSIN) *Research Matters*, No. 26. London: Institute of Education, University of London.

Coffield, F. (2008) *Just Suppose Teaching and Learning Became the First Priority* … London: Learning and Skills Network.

Coffield, F. (2015) 'Preface', in M. Daley, K. Orr and J. Petrie (eds), *Further Education and the Twelve Dancing Princesses*. Stoke-on-Trent: Trentham Books.

Coffield, F., Moseley, D., Hall, E. and Ecclestone, K. (2004) *Learning Styles and Pedagogy in Post-16 Learning: A Systematic and Critical Review*. London: Learning and Skills Research Centre, Learning and Skills Development Agency.

Coffield, F., Edward, S., Finlay, I., Hodgson, A., Spours, K., Steer, R. and Gregson, M. (2007) 'How policy impacts on practice and how practice does not impact on policy', *British Educational Research Journal*, 33 (5), pp. 723–42.

Cole, J. and Cole, B. (2009) *Martyrdom: Radicalisation and Terrorist Violence among British Muslims*. London: Pennant Books Ltd.

Cooney, R. (2015) 'Apprenticeship success rates fall nearly 5pc points', *FE Week*, 20 April. London: Learning and Skills Events Consultancy and Training.

Crawley, J. (2010) *In at the Deep End: A Survival Guide for Teachers in Post-Compulsory Education*. London: Routledge.

Crown Prosecution Service (CPS) (2008) *Hate Crime Report 2007–2008*. Bolton: Blackburns.

Curzon, L.B. and Tummons, J. (2013) *Teaching in Further Education: An Outline of Principles and Practice* (7th edn). London: Bloomsbury Publishing Inc.

Daley, M., Orr, K. and Petrie, J. (eds) (2015) *Further Education and the Twelve Dancing Princesses*. Stoke-on-Trent: Trentham Books.

Day, C. and Kington, A. (2008) 'Identity, well-being and effectiveness: The emotional contexts of teaching', *Pedagogy, Culture and Society*, 16 (1), pp. 7–23.

Department for Education (DfE) (1986) *The Education Act (No 2) 1986*. London: Department for Education,The Stationery Office (TSO).

Department for Education (DfE) (2006) *Raising Skills, Improving Life Chances*. London: DfE.

Department for Education (DfE) (2013a) Education and Training Statistics for the United Kingdom: 2013. London: DfE.

Department for Education (2013b) Reform of the National Curriculum in England: Report of the consultation conducted February – April 2013. London: DfE.

Department for Education (DfE) (2014a) *Statistical First Release: Provisional GCSE and Equivalent Results in England, 2013 to 2014*. London: DfE.

Department for Education (DfE) (2014b) *Stakeholder Briefing: The Latest Developments in Maths and English in Post-16 Education 2 July 2014 Maths and English GCSEs*. London: DfE.

Department for Education (DfE) (2014c) *First Statistical Release: Provisional GCSE and Equivalent Results in England, 2013–2014, Issued 23rd October 2014*. London: DfE.

Department of Education and Science (DES) (1978) *Special Educational Needs: Report of the Committee of Enquiry into the Education of Handicapped Children and Young People (The Warnock Report)*. London: HMSO.

Department for Education and Skills (DfES) (2004) *Equipping our Teachers for the Future*. London: DfES.

Department for Environment, Food and Rural Affairs (Defra) (2005) *Securing the Future: Delivery UK Sustainable Development Strategy*. Norwich: The Stationery Office (TSO) Ltd.

Dewey, J. (1916) *Democracy and Education: An Introduction to the Philosophy of Education*. New York: Macmillan.

Dewey, J. (1938) *Experience and Education*. New York: Macmillan.

Dusek, J.B. and Joseph, G. (1983) 'The bases of teacher expectancies: A meta-analysis', *Journal of Educational Psychology*, 75(3), pp. 327–46.

Dweck, C. (2000) *Self-Theories: Their Role in Motivation, Personality, and Development*. Philadelphia, PA: Psychology Press.

Dweck, C. (2006) *Mindset: The New Psychology of Success*. New York: Random House.

Dweck, C.S. and Mueller, C.M. (1998) 'Intelligence praise can undermine motivation and performance', *Journal of Personality and Social Psychology*, 75, pp. 33–52.

Edge Foundation (2014) *Children Labelled 'Too Clever' for Vocational Education*, 5 February. (http://www.edge.co.uk/news/2014/february/children-labelled-too-clever-for-vocational-education).

Edwards, R. (2007) 'Education: An impossible practice', *Scottish Educational Review*, 40, pp. 4–11.

Education and Training Foundation (ETF) (2014) *Professional Standards for Teachers and Trainers in Education and Training*. (www.et-foundation.co.uk/wp-content/uploads/2014/05/4991-Prof-standards-A4_4-2.pdf).

Eisner, E. (1967) 'Educational objectives: help or hindrance?', *The School Review*, 75, pp. 250–60.

Electoral Commission (2010) *The Completeness and Accuracy of Electoral Registers in Great Britain*, March. London. Electoral Commission.

Elliott, J. (1991) *Action Research for Educational Change*. Milton Keynes: Open University Press.

Engestrom, Y. (2001) 'Expansive learning at work: Toward an activity theoretical reconceptualization', *Journal of Education and Work*, 14 (1), pp. 133–56.

Equality Challenge Unit (2011) *Equality in Higher Education: Statistical Report 2011*. London: Equality Challenge Unit.

Ferguson, R.F. (2003) 'Teachers' perceptions and expectations and the black–white test Score gap', *Urban Education*, 38 (4), pp. 460–507.

Fielding, M. (2001a) 'Students as radical agents of change', *Journal of Educational Change*, 2, pp. 123–41.

Fielding, M. (ed.) (2001b) 'Special issue on student voice', *Forum*, 43 (2), pp. 123–41.

Fielding, M. (2004) 'Student voice and personalised learning'. Presentation to the Specialist Schools Trust and Secondary Heads Association Personalising Learning Conference, January.

Florian, L. (2009) 'Towards an inclusive pedagogy', in P. Hick, R. Kershner and P.T. Farrell (eds), *Psychology for Inclusive Education*. New York: Routledge.

Foster, A. (2005) *Realising the Potential: A Review of the Future Role of Further Education Colleges*, The Foster Review. London: Department for Education and Skills (DfES).

Freire P. (1970) *Pedagogy of the Oppressed*. London: Continuum International Publishing Group Ltd.

Freire, P. (2000) *Pedagogy of the Oppressed* (30th anniversary edn). London: Continuum International Publishing Group Ltd.

Furlong, J., Barton, L., Miles, S. and Whitty, G. (2000) *Teacher Education in Transition*. Buckingham: Open University Press.

Giroux, H.A. (2014) *Barbarians at the Gate: Authoritarianism and the Assault on Public Education*. (www.truth-out.org/news/item/28272-barbarians-at-the-gates-authoritarianism-and-the-assault-on-public-education).

Gleeson, D. and James, D. (2007) 'The paradox of professionalism in English further education: A TLC project perspective', *Educational Review*, 59 (4), pp. 451–67.

Gleeson, D. and Keep, E. (2004) 'Voice without accountability: The changing relationship between employers, the state and education in England', *Oxford Review of Education*, 30 (1), pp. 37–63.

Gleeson, D., Davies, J. and Wheeler, E. (2007) 'On the making and taking of professionalism in the further education workplace', *British Journal of Sociology and Education*, 26 (4), pp. 445–60.

Goddard-Spear, M. (1984) 'The biasing influence of pupil sex in a science-marking exercise', *Research in Science and Technological Education*, 2 (1), pp. 55–60.

Gould, J., and Roffey-Barentsen, J. (2014) *Achieving your Diploma in Education and Training*. London: Sage.

Graves, J.L. (2001) *The Emperor's New Clothes: Biological Theories of Race at the Millennium: Biological Theories of Race at the Millenium*. New Brunswick, NJ: Rutgers University Press.

Green, K. (2013) *Curriculum Redesign in Further Education Colleges: Exploring Current Challenges and Opportunities*. London: 157 Group Ltd.

The Guardian (2013) 'GCSE students face new English and maths hurdle', 2 September.

Hammersley, M. (2004) 'Some questions about evidence-based practice in education', in G. Thomas and R. Pring (eds), *Evidence-Based Practice in Education*. Maidenhead: Open University Press.

Harari, H. and McDavid, J. (1973) 'Name stereotypes and teachers' expectations', *Journal of Educational Psychology*, 65, pp. 222–5.

Hargreaves, D. (2004) *Personalising Learning 2: Student Voice and Assessment for Learning*. November. London: Specialist Schools Trust, Secondary Heads Association.

Hattie, J. (2003) 'Distinguishing expert teachers from novice and experienced teachers: Teachers make a difference, what is the research evidence?', Australian Council for Educational Research,, University of Auckland, October 2003.

Hattie, J. (2008) *Visible Learning: A Synthesis of over 800 Meta-Analyses Relating to Achievement*. Abingdon: Routledge.

Hay McBer Report (2000) *Research into Teacher Effectiveness: A Model of Teacher Effectiveness*. London: Department for Education and Employment (DfEE), HMSO.

Hedges, C. (2009) *Empire of Illusion: The End of Literacy and the Triumph of Spectacle*. New York: Nation Books.

Heider, F. (1958) *The Psychology of Interpersonal Relations*. New York: Wiley.

Hildyard, N., Hegde, P., Wolvekamp, P. and Reddy, S. (2001) 'Pluralism, participation and power: Joint forest management', in B. Cooke and U. Kothari (eds), *Participation: The New Tyranny?* London: Zed Books.

Hirst, P.H. (1974) *Knowledge and the Curriculum*. London. Routledge.

HM Government (2011) *Prevent Strategy*. London: The Stationery Office (TSO).

HM Government (2015) *Revised Prevent Duty Guidance*. London: The Stationery Office (TSO).

HM Treasury (2015) *Spending Review and Autumn Statement 2015*. London: The Stationery Office (TSO).

Horgan, J. (2005) 'The social and psychological characteristics of terrorism and terrorists', in T. Bjorgo (ed.), *Root Causes of Terrorism: Myths, Realities and Ways Forward*. London: Routledge.

Horgan, J. (2008) 'From profiles to pathways and roots to routes: Perspectives from psychology on radicalization into terrorism', *Annals of the American Academy of Political and Social Science*, 618 (1), pp. 80–94.

Horgan, J. (2009) *Walking away from Terrorism: Accounts of Disengagement from Radical and Extremist Movements*. New York: Routledge.

Hough, D. (2014) *Youth Unemployment Statistics 17th December 2014*. London: House of Commons Library.

House of Commons (2007) *Explanatory Memorandum to the Further Education Teachers' Qualification (England) Regulations 2007*. London: The Stationery Office.

House of Commons (2013) *Draft Deregulation Bill*. London: The Stationery Office.

House of Commons Library (2015) *Apprenticeships Policy, England 2015,* Briefing Paper Number 03052, 1 December 2015. London: House of Commons Library.

Hutchings, M. (2015) *Exam Factories: The Impact of Accountability Measures on Children and Young People*. Research commissioned by the National Union of Teachers. Chelmsford: Ruskin Press.

Hyland, T. and Johnson, S. (1998) 'Of cabbages and key skills: Exploding the mythology of core transferable skills in post-school education', *Journal of Further and Higher Education*, 22 (2), pp. 163–72.

Illeris, K. (2007) *How we Learn: Learning and Non-Learning in School and Beyond*. London: Routledge.

Illeris, K. (ed.) (2009) *Contemporary Theories of Learning; Learning Theorists in their own Words*. London: Routledge.

Illeris, K. (2014) *Transformative Learning and Identity*. Abingdon, Oxon: Routledge.

Institute for Learning (IfL) (2012) *Professionalism: Education and Training Practitioners Across Further Education and Skills*. London: IfL.

James, D. and Biesta, G. (2007) *Improving Learning Cultures in Further Education*. Abingdon: Routledge.

Jarvis, P. (1987) *Adult Learning in the Social Context*. London: Croom Helm.

Jarvis, P. (2006) *Towards a Comprehensive Theory of Human Learning*. Abingdon: Routledge.

Jarvis, P. (2009) *Learning to Be a Person in Society*. London: RoutledgeFalmer.

Jephcote, M. and Salisbury, J. (2009) 'Further education teachers' accounts of their professional identities', *Teaching and Teacher Education*, 25 (7), pp. 966–72.

Joseph Rowntree Foundation (2011) *The Influence of Parents, Places and Poverty on Educational Attitudes and Aspirations*. York: Joseph Rowntree Foundation.

Jussim, L. and Harber, K.D. (2005) 'Teacher expectations and self-fulfilling prophecies: knowns and unknowns, resolved and unresolved controversies', *Personality and Social Psychology Review*, 9 (2), pp. 131–55.

Keep, E. (2006) 'State control of the English education and training system: Playing with the biggest train set in the world', *Journal of Vocational Education & Training*, 58 (1), pp. 47–64.

Keep, E. (2012) 'Education and industry: Taking two steps back and reflecting', *Journal of Education and Work*, 25 (4), pp. 357–79.

Keep, E. (2014) *What does Skills Policy Look Like now the Money has Run Out?* ESRC Centre on Skills, Knowledge and Organisational Performance and Association of Colleges, Oxford and London.

Keep, E. and Mayhew, K. (2010) 'Moving beyond skills as a social and economic panacea', *Work, Employment and Society*, 24 (3), pp. 565–77.

Keep, E., Mayhew, K. and Payne, J. (2006) 'From skills revolution to productivity miracle: Not as easy as it sounds?', *Oxford Review of Economic Policy*, 22 (4), pp. 539–59.

Keltchermans, G. (2005) 'Teachers' emotions in educational reforms: Self-understanding, vulnerable commitment and micropolitical literacy', *Teaching and Teacher Education*, 21, pp. 995–1006.

Kemmis, S., and McTaggart, R. (1981) *The Action Research Planner*. Geelong, Victoria: Deakin University Press.

Kemmis, S. and McTaggart, R. (1988) *The Action Research Planner* (3rd edn). Geelong, Victoria: Deakin University Press.

Kemmis, S. and McTaggart, R. (2000) 'Participatory action research', in N.K. Denzin and Y.S. Lincoln (eds), *Handbook of Qualitative Research* (2nd edn). London: Sage.

Kennedy, H. (1997) *Learning Works: Widening Participation in Further Education*, Kennedy Report. Coventry: Further Education Funding Council.

Kettlewell, K., Southcott, C., Stevens, E. and McCrone, T. (2012) *Engaging the Disengaged*. Slough: National Foundation for Educational Research (NfER).

Kolb, D. (1984) *Experiential Learning as the Science of Learning and Development*. New Jersey: Prentice Hall Inc.

Knight, P.T., and Yorke, M. (2006) *Learning and Employability Series One: Embedding Employability into the Curriculum*. Heslington, York:HEA.

Lave, J. and Wenger, E. (1991) *Situated Learning: Legitimate Peripheral Participation*. Cambridge: Cambridge University Press.

Lawton, D. (1983) *Curriculum Studies and Educational Planning*. London: Hodder and Stoughton.

Learning and Skills Improvement Service (LSIS) (2012) *Talking Learner Voice: Listening more Carefully to Learners' Voices Guidance Notes*. Coventry: LSIS.

Learning and Skills Improvement Service (LSIS) (2013) *Further Education College Workforce Data for England: An Analysis of the Staff Individualised Record Data 2011–2012*. London: LSIS.

Leitch, S. (2005) *Skills in the UK: The Long Term Challenge*, Interim Report December 2005. Norwich: Her Majesty's Stationery Office (HMSO).

Leitch, S. (2006) *Prosperity For All in The Global Economy – World Class Skills*, Final Report December 2006. Norwich: Her Majesty's Stationery Office (HMSO).

Lentini, P. (2009) 'The transference of neojihadism: Towards a process theory of transnational radicalisation', in S. Khatab, M. Bakashmar and E. Ogru (eds), *Radicalisation Crossing Borders: New Directions in Islamist and Jiuhadist Political, Intellectual and Theological Thought and Practice: Conference Proceedings*. Melbourne: Global Terrorism Research Centre, Monash University.

Lewin, K. (1999 [1943]) 'Psychology and the process of group living', in M. Gold (ed.), *The Complete Social Scientist: A Kurt Lewin Reader*. Washington, DC: American Psychological Association.

Lewin, K. (1946) 'Action research and minority problems', *Journal of Social Issues*, 2, pp.34–46.

Lewin, K. (1948) *Resolving Social Conflicts*. New York: Harper and Row Publishers.

Liberty (2010) *Liberty's Response to the Home Office Consultation on the Prevent Strand of the UK Counter-Terrorism Strategy*. London: Liberty.

Lingfield, R. (2012) *Professionalism in Further Education: Final Report*, The Lingfield Report. London: Department for Business, Innovation and Skills (BIS).

Lipsky, M. (2010) *Street-Level Bureaucracy: Dilemmas of the Individual in Public Services* (30th anniversary expanded edn). New York: Russell Sage Foundation.

Lucas, N. (2004) *Teaching in Further Education: New Perspectives for a Changing Context*. London: Institute of Education, University of London.

Lucas, N. and Nasta, T. (2010) 'State regulation and the professionalization of further education: A comparison with schools and HE?', *Journal of Vocational Education & Training*, 62 (4), pp. 441–54.

Lucas, N., Nasta, T. and Rogers, L. (2011) 'From fragmentation to chaos? The regulation of initial teacher training in further education', *British Educational Research Journal*, 38 (4), pp. 677–95.

Lupton, R., Unwin, L. and Thomson, S. (2015) *The Coalition's Record on Further and Higher Education and Skills: Policy, Spending and Outcomes 2010–2015*. Working Paper 14, January. London: London School of Economics.

Lyotard, J.F. (1997) *The Postmodern Condition: A Report on Knowledge*. Manchester: Manchester University Press.

MacInnes, T., Aldridge, H., Bushe, S., Tinson, A. and Born, T.B. (2014) *Monitoring Poverty and Social Exclusion 2014*. York: Joseph Rowntree Foundation.

Marzano, R.J., Pickering, D.J. and Pollock, J.E. (2001) *Classroom Instruction that Works*. Alexandria, VA: Association for Supervision and Curriculum Development (ASCD).

Mason, G. and Bishop, K. (2010) *Adult Training, Skills Updating and Recession in the UK: The Implications for Competitiveness and Social Inclusion*. LLAKES Research Paper No. 19. London: Centre for Learning and Life Chances in Knowledge Economics and Societies (LLAKES), UCL Institute of Education, University College London.

McKown, C. and Weinstein, R.S. (2008) 'Teacher expectations, classroom context, and the achievement gap', *Journal of School Psychology*, 46, pp. 235–61.

Mezirow, J. (1978) *Education for Perspective Transformation: Women's Re-entry Programs in Community College*. New York: New York Teachers College, Columbia University.

Mezirow, J. (2000) *Learning as Transformation: Critical Perspectives on a Theory in Progress*. San Francisco, CA: Jossey-Bass.

Millerson, G. (1964) *The Qualifying Associations*. London: Routledge Kegan Paul.

Moghaddam, F. M. (2005) 'The Staircase to Terrorism: A Psychological Exploration', *American Psychologist*, 60(2), pp.161–9.

Moon, J.A. (1999) *Reflection in Learning and Professional Development: Theory and Practice*. London: Kogan Page Ltd.

Moore, A. (2004) *The Good Teacher: Dominant Discourses in Teaching and Teacher Education*. London: RoutledgeFalmer.

Morrell, A. and O'Connor, M. (2002) 'Introduction', in E. O'Sullivan, A. Morrell and M. O' Connor (eds), *Expanding the Boundaries of Transformative Learning: Essays on Theory and Praxis*. New York: Palgrave Macmillan.

Morrison, A. (2010) '"I want an education": Two case studies of working-class ambition and ambivalence in further and higher education', *Research in Post-Compulsory Education*, 15 (1), pp. 67–80.

Moser, C. (1999) *A Fresh Start: Improving Literacy and Numeracy, The Moser Report*. London: Department for Education and Employment (DfEE).

National Careers Council (2013) *An Aspirational Nation: Creating a Culture Change in Careers Provision*. London: National Careers Council.

National Council of Further Education (NCFE) (2013) *The Study Programme: A New Approach to Lead 16–19-Year-Olds into Further Education and Employment*. (www.ncfe.org.uk/news/2013/2/25/16-19-study-programmes).

National Foundation for Educational Research (NfER) (2012) *Engaging the Disengaged*. Slough: NfER.

National Human Genome Research Institute (2006) *2006 Release: About Whole Genome Association Studies*. (www.genome.gov/17516714).

National Institute of Adult Continuing Education (NIACE) (2009) *FE Colleges in a New Culture of Adult and Lifelong Learning*. Leicester: NIACE.

National Literacy Trust (2014) *How many Illiterate Adults are there in England?* (www.literacytrust.org.uk/adult_literacy/illiterate_adults_in_england).

National Numeracy (2012) *Facts and Figures: The Headlines for Numeracy in the UK*. (www.nationalnumeracy.org.uk/news/16/index.html).

Nixon, J. (ed.) (1981) *A Teacher's Guide to Action Research: Evaluation, Enquiry and Development in the Classroom*. London: Grant McIntyre.

Noel, P. and Waugh, G. (2014) 'Confronting the difference: Ethnicity and patterns of achievement in initial teacher education for the further education and skills sector', *Teaching in Lifelong Learning: A Journal to Inform and Improve Practice*, 6 (1), pp. 20–31.

Office for National Statistics (ONS) (2011) *Earnings by Qualification, 2011*. (www.ons.gov.uk/ons/dcp171776_229888.pdf).

Office for National Statistics (ONS) (2014) *Young People not in Education, Employment or Training (NEET), August 2014*. London: ONS.

Office for Standards in Education, Children's Services and Skills (Ofsted) (2003) *The Initial Training of Further Education Teachers November 2003*. London: Ofsted.

Ofsted (2008) *A Handbook for Inspecting Colleges*. London: Ofsted.

Ofsted (2010) *Progress in Implementing Reforms in the Accreditation Band Continuing Professional Development of Teachers in Further Education*. London: Ofsted.

Ofsted (2012) *Handbook for the Inspection of Further Education and Skills*. London: Ofsted.

Ofsted (2013a) *Unseen children: access and achievement 20 years on*, Evidence report. London:Ofsted.

Ofsted (2013b) *Local Accountability and Autonomy in Colleges*. London: Ofsted.

Ofsted (2015) *Common Inspection Framework: Education, Skills and Early Years from September 2015*. London: Ofsted.

Ofqual (2015) *After the QCF: A new Qualifications Framework*. Coventry: Office of Qualifications and Examinations Regulation.

Okihiro, G.Y. (2001) *Common Ground: Reimagining American History*. Princeton, NJ: Princeton University Press.

O'Leary, M. (2006) 'Can inspectors really improve the quality of teaching in the PCE sector? Classroom observations under the microscope', *Research in Post-Compulsory Education*, 11 (2), pp. 191–8.

Organisation for Economic Co-operation and Development (OECD) (2015) *Education Policy Outlook 2015: Making Reforms Happen*. Paris: OECD Publishing.

Orr, K. and Simmons, R. (2010) 'Dual identities: The in-service teacher trainee experience in the English Further Education Sector', *Journal of Vocational Education & Training*, 62 (1), pp. 75–88.

Osberg, D. and Biesta, G. (2010) 'The end/s of education: Complexity and the conundrum of the inclusive educational curriculum', *International Journal of Inclusive Education*, 14 (6), pp. 593–607.

Oxford Dictionaries (2014) Oxford: Oxford University Press. (www.oxforddictionaries.com/definition/english/intelligence).

Ozga, J. (1995) 'Deskilling a profession: Professionalism, deprofessionalisation and the new managerialism', in H. Busher and R. Saran (eds), *Managing Teachers as Professionals in Schools*. London: Kogan Page.

Paik, S.J. and Wahlberg, H.J. (2007) *Narrowing the Achievement Gap: Strategies for Educating Latino, Black, and Asian Students*. New York: Springer Publishing.

Patrick, R. (2012) 'Work as the primary 'duty' of the responsible citizen: A critique of this work-centric approach', *People, Place & Policy*, 6 (1), pp. 5–15.

Peters, M. (2001) 'Education, enterprise culture and the entrepreneurial self: A Foucauldian perspective', *Journal of Educational Enquiry*, 2 (2), pp. 58–7.

Pinar, W.F. (2012) *What is Curiculum Theory?* (2nd edn). Abingdon, Oxon: Routledge.

Policy Consortium (2015) *Take 2: The Pulse of Further Education: The Great FE & Skills Survey of 2015*. (www.policyconsortium.co.uk/wp/wp-content/uploads/2015/03/150511-PC-survey-2015-final2.pdf).

Powell, S. and Tummons, J. (2011) *Inclusive Practice in the lifelong Learning Sector*. Exeter: Learning Matters.

Pring, R. (1976) *Knowledge and Schooling*. Wells: Open Books.

Pring, R. (1999) *Closing the Gap: Liberal Education and Vocational* Preparation. London: Hodder and Stoughton.

Punter, A. and Burchell, H. (1996) 'Gender issues in GCSE English assessment', *British Journal of Curriculum and Assessment*, 6 (2), pp. 20–3.

Raikes, L. (2015) *Learner Drivers: Local Authorities and Apprenticeships*. London: Institute for Public Policy Research.

Randle, K. and Brady, N. (1997) 'Managerialism and professionalism in the Cinderella Service', *Journal of Vocational Education & Training*, 49 (1), pp. 121–39.

Reed, J. and Stoltz, P.G. (2013) *Put your Mindset to Work: The One Asset you Really need to Win and Keep the Job you Love*. London: Penguin Books.

Richards, A. (2012) 'Characterising the UK terrorist threat: The problem with non-violent ideology as a focus for counter-terrorism and terrorism as the product of "vulnerability"', *Journal of Terrorism Research*, 3 (1). (www.ojs.standrews.ac.uk/index.php/jtr/issue/view/46).

Robinson, K. (2009) *The Element: How Finding your Passion Changes Everything*. London: Penguin Books.

Robinson, K. and Aronica, L. (2015) *Creative Schools: Revolutionizing Education from the Ground Up*. London: Penguin Books.

Rogers, A. (1986) *Teaching Adults*. Milton Keynes: Open University Press.

Rogers, C. (1959) 'A theory of therapy, personality, and interpersonal relationships: As developed in the client-centered framework', in S. Koch (ed.), *Psychology: A Study of a Science*, Vol. 3. New York: McGraw-Hill.

Rogers, C (1969) *Freedom to Learn: A View of What Education Might Become.* Columbus, OH: Merrill.

Rosenthal, R. and Jacobson, L. (2003 [1968]) *Pygmalion in the Classroom: Teacher Expectation and Pupils' Intellectual Development.* Carmarthen: Crown House Publishing.

Roulston, K., Legette, R., Deloach, M. and Buchalter Pitman, C. (2005) 'What is "research" for teacher-researchers?', *Educational Action Research*, 13 (2), pp. 169–89.

Rouse, M. (2007) *Enhancing Effective Inclusive Practice: Knowing, Doing and Believing.* Kairaranga: New Zealand Ministry of Education.

Rubie-Davies, C. (2008) 'Teacher expectations', in T. Good (ed.), *21st Century Education: A Reference Handbook.* Thousand Oaks, CA: Sage.

Ruddock, J. (1988) ' Teacher research and research based teacher education', *Journal of Education for Training*, 11 (3), pp. 281–9.

Sachs, J. (2000) 'Activist professional', *Journal of Educational Change*, 1 (1), pp. 77–94.

Sachs, J. (2001) 'Teacher professional identity: Competing discourses, competing outcomes', *Journal of Educational Policy*, 16 (2), pp. 149–61.

Sachs, J. (2003) 'Teacher activism: Mobilising the profession'. Plenary Address presented to the British Educational Research Association Conference, Heriot Watt University, Edinburgh, 11–13 September.

Sallis, E. (2005) *Total Quality Management in Education* (3rd edn). London: Kogan Page.

Schiro, M. (1978) *Curriculum for Better Schools: The Great Ideological Debate.* Englewood Cliffs, NJ: Educational Technology Publications.

Schön, D. (1983) *The Reflective Practitioner: How Professionals Think in Action.* London: Marcus Temple Smith.

Schön, D. (1987) *Educating the Reflective Practitioner.* San Francisco: Jossey-Bass Inc.

Schumacher, E.F. (1997) *This I Believe and Other Essays.* Totnes: Resurgence Book.

Shain, F. and Gleeson, D. (1999) 'Under new management: Changing conceptions of teacher professionalism and policy in the further education sector', *Journal of Education Policy*, 14 (4), pp. 445–62.

Sharp, B. (2011) *A Dynamic Nucleus: Colleges at the Heart of Local Communities.* Leicester: National Institute of Adult Continuing Education.

Sheffield University Research (2010) *The Levels of Attainment in Literacy and Numeracy of 13- to 19-Year-Olds in England, 1948–2009.* London: National Research and Development Centre.

Shulman, L.S (2004) *The Wisdom of Practice: Essays on Teaching, Learning, and Learning to Teach.* San Francisco, CA: Jossey-Bass.

Siddique, H. (2015) 'Majority of UK's most influential had independent school education: Survey', *The Guardian*, 25 January.

Silber, M.D. and Bhatt, A. (2007) *Radicalization in the West: The Home-Grown Threat.* New York: New York City Police Department.

Skilbeck, M. (1984) *School-Based Curriculum Development*. London: Harper Row.

Skills Funding Agency (SFA) (2012) *Equality and Diversity Data Report 2008/09–2010/11*. Coventry: SFA.

Skills Funding Agency (SFA) (2014a) *Statistical First Release: Further Education & Skills: Learner Participation, Outcomes and Level of Highest Qualification Held 26th November 2014*. London: Department for Business, Innovation and Skills (BIS).

Skills Funding Agency (SFA) (2014b) *Key Facts about Apprenticeships*. London: Department for Business, Innovation and Skills (BIS).

Slee, R. (2001) 'Social justice and the changing directions in educational research: The case of inclusive education', *International Journal of Inclusive Education*, 5 (2/3), pp. 167–77.

Smith, D. and Smith, B. (2008) 'Urban educators voices: Understanding culture in the classroom', *Urban Review*, 41, pp. 334–51.

Smith, J. (2002) 'Learning styles: Fashion fad or lever for change? The application of learning style theory to inclusive curriculum delivery', *Innovations in Education and Teaching International*, 39, (1), pp. 63–70.

Smith, M.K. (2001) *Kurt Lewin: Groups, Experiential Learning and Action Research*. (www.infed.org/mobi/kurt-lewin-groups-experiential-learning-and-action-research/).

Social Exclusion Unit (2002) *Reducing Re-offending by Ex-Offenders*. London: Social Exclusion Unit.

Spielhofer, T., Benton, T., Evans, K., Featherstone, G., Golden, S., Nelson, J. and Smith P. (2009) *Increasing Participation: Understanding Young People who do not Participate in Education or Training at 16 and 17*. London: Department for Children, Schools and Families (DCSF).

St Clair, R., Kintrea,K., and Houston.M. (2011) *The Influence of Parents, Places and Poverty on Educational Attitudes and Aspirations*. York: Joseph Rowntree Foundation.

Stamou, E., Edwards, A., Daniels. H., and Ferguson, L. (2014) *Young People At-risk of Drop-out from Education: Recognising and Responding to their Needs*. Oxford: Oxford University.

Stenhouse, L. (1975) *An Introduction to Curriculum Research and Development*. London: Heinemann.

Stenhouse, L. (1981) 'What counts as research?', *British Journal of Educational Studies*, 29, pp. 103–14.

Sterling, S. (2009) *Sustainable Education: Revisioning Learning and Change*. Dartington: Green Books.

Strand, S. (2008) *Minority Ethnic Pupils in the Longitudinal Study of Young People in England: Extension Report on Performance in Public Examinations at Age 16*. Department For Children, Schools and Families (DCSF) Research Report. London: DCSF.

Strike, K. (2004) *The Ethics of Teaching* (4th edn). New York: Teachers College Press.

Strong, M., Gargani, J. and Hacifazlioglu, O. (2011) 'Do we know a successful teacher when we see one? Experiments in the identification of effective teachers', *Journal of Teacher Education*, 62 (4), pp. 367–82.

Swann, J. and Pratt, J. (eds) (2003) *Educational Research in Practice: Making Sense of Methodology*. London: Continuum.

Teaching Learning and Research Programme (TLRP) (2008) *Challenge and Change in Further Education: Commentary by the Teaching Learning and Research Programme*. London: TLRP.

Tenenbaum, H.R. and Ruck, M.D. (2007) 'Are teachers' expectations different for racial minority than for European American students? A meta-analysis', *Journal of Educational Psychology*, 99, pp. 253–73.

Tennant, M. (1988) *Psychology and Adult Learning*. London: Routledge.

Tennant, M. (2006) *Psychology and Adult Learning* (3rd edn). Abingdon: Routledge.

Thompson, S. (2013) *States of Uncertainty: Youth Unemployment in Europe*. London: Institute for Public Policy Research.

Tomlinson, J. (1996a) *Report of the Further Education Funding Council Learning Difficulties and/or Difficulties Committee*. Coventry: Further Education Funding Council (FEFC).

Tomlinson, J. (1996b) *Inclusive Learning: Principles and Recommendations*. London: Further Education Funding Council (FEFC).

Tomlinson, S. (2005) *Education in a Post-Welfare State* (2nd edn). Maidenhead: Open University Press.

Trade Union Congress (TUC) (2014) *Labour Market and Economic Reports: Only One in Every Forty Nets Jobs since Recession is for a Full-Time* (www.tuc.org.uk/ economic-issues/labour-market-and-ecoomic-reports/only-one-every-forty-net-jobs-recession-full-time).

Travis, A. (2008) *MI5 Report Challenges Views on Terrorism in Britain*. London: Guardian.

Tyler, R.W. (1949) *Basic Principles of Curriculum and Instruction*. Chicago, IL: University of Chicago Press.

UK Commission for Employment and Skills (UKCES) (2010) *Ambition 2020: World Class Skills and Jobs for the UK*. London: UKCES.

United Nations Children's Fund (UNICEF) Office of Research (2013) *Child Well-being in Rich Countries: A Comparative Overview*. Innocenti Report Card 11. Florence: UNICEF Office of Research.

Usher, R., Bryant, I. and Johnston, R. (1997) *Adult Education and the Postmodern Challenge: Learning Beyond the Limits*. London: Routledge.

van den Bergh, L., Denessen, E., Holland, R., Voeten, M. and Hornstra, L. (2010) 'Implicit prejudiced attitudes of teachers: Relations to teacher expectations and the ethnic achievement gap', *American Educational Research Journal*, 47 (2), pp. 497–527.

Waldegrave, H. and Simons, J. (2014) *Watching the Watchmen: The Future of School Inspections in England*. London: Policy Exchange.

Weber, E. (2007) 'Globalization, "glocal" development and teachers' work: A research agenda', *Review of Educational Research*, 77 (3), pp. 279–309.

Weiner, B. (1974) *Achievement, Motivation and Attribution Theory*. Morristown, NJ: General Learning Press.

Wenger, E. (1998) *Communities of Practice: Learning, Meaning and Identity*. Cambridge: Cambridge University Press.

Whitehead, J. (1989) 'Creating a living educational theory from questions of the kind, 'How do I improve my practice?', *Cambridge Journal of Education*, 19 (1), pp. 41–52.

Whitty, G. (2006) 'Teacher professionalism in a new era'. Institute of Education, University of London. Paper presented at the first General Teaching Council for Northern Ireland Annual Lecture, Belfast, March.

Whitty, G., Matthews, P. and Sammons, P. (2004) *Improvement through Inspection: An Evaluation of the Impact of Ofsted's Work*, July. London: Ofsted.

Wink, J. (2000) *Critical Pedagogy: Notes from the Real World* (2nd edn). New York: Longman.

Wolf, A. (1991) 'Assessing core skills: Wisdom or wild goose chase?', *Cambridge Journal of Education*, 21 (2), pp. 89–201.

Wolf, A. (2011) *Review of Vocational Education: The Wolf Report*. London: Department for Education.

World Health Organization (WHO) (2012) *Social Determinants of Health and Well-Being among Young People: Health Behaviour in School-Aged Children Study: International Report from the 2009/2010 Survey*. (www.euro.who.int/__data/assets/pdf_file/0003/163857/Social-determinants-of-health-and-well-being-among-young-people.pdf).

Yorke, M. (2006) *Employability in Higher Education: What it is – What it is not. Learning & Employability Series One*. Heslington, York: Higher Education Academy.

Zeichner, K. (2010) 'Competition, economic rationalization, increased surveillance, and attacks on diversity: Neo-Liberalism and the transformation of teacher education in the U.S', *Teaching and Teacher Education: An International Journal of Research and Studies*, 26 (8), pp. 1544–52.

INDEX